# Maritime Insurance and the Law

This book provides a comprehensive examination of direct-action rights within Protection and Indemnity (P&I) Clubs, a cornerstone of the maritime industry, providing robust insights into the interplay of legal frameworks and maritime insurance in an increasingly globalized industry.

P&I Clubs provide shipowners with extensive liability coverage under rules largely governed by English law due to its global maritime influence. Through a comparative analysis of English and Turkish legal approaches, the book examines how these differing frameworks affect the development and functioning of P&I insurance. It highlights critical disparities in the legal treatment of direct action against P&I Clubs, shedding light on their implications for maritime insurance policy, practice, and industry growth. It also covers the unique principles that distinguish P&I Clubs from other types of liability insurance. Additionally, the book offers recommendations for harmonizing national legal systems with P&I Club rules, highlighting strategies to promote the growth and effectiveness of the maritime insurance sector. Drawing on extensive primary legal texts, case law, and comparative legal methodologies, the book suggests regulatory reforms for Türkiye and other jurisdictions worldwide.

The book will be of interest to researchers in the field of maritime law, maritime insurance, and insurance law.

**Feray Firinciogullari** graduated with high honours from Istanbul University Faculty of Law and completed her master's degree in private law at Marmara University. She earned her Ph.D. from the University of Exeter, specializing in maritime and insurance law. Dr Firinciogullari has distinguished herself through her academic research and publications, with a particular focus on marine insurance and direct actions. She is currently teaching Maritime and Insurance Law at Yalova University and continues her academic work at an international level.

# Maritime Insurance and the Law

## Legal Action Against Protection and Indemnity Club

**Feray Firinciogullari**

Routledge
Taylor & Francis Group
LONDON AND NEW YORK

First published 2026
by Routledge
4 Park Square, Milton Park, Abingdon, Oxon OX14 4RN

and by Routledge
605 Third Avenue, New York, NY 10158

*Routledge is an imprint of the Taylor & Francis Group, an informa business*



*British Library Cataloguing-in-Publication Data*
A catalogue record for this book is available from the British Library

ISBN: 978-1-041-03596-1 (hbk)
ISBN: 978-1-041-04570-0 (pbk)
ISBN: 978-1-003-62889-7 (ebk)

DOI: 10.4324/9781003628897

Typeset in Times New Roman
by Apex CoVantage, LLC

**Dedicated to the eternal memory of my dearest brother, Ali Emre Firinciogullari**

# Contents

# Preface

Embarking on my Ph.D. journey in the United Kingdom on 20 July 2019 was a significant turning point in my life. It was a decision marked by a whirlwind of emotions – excitement for the opportunities ahead, apprehension about the challenges, fear of the unknown, loneliness from leaving loved ones behind, and joy at taking a bold step toward realizing my aspirations. Stepping into a new country with unfamiliar systems, cultures, and people was both daunting and transformative. Reflecting on this journey, I feel immense gratitude for the courage it took to begin and for the enriching experiences that followed.

This Ph.D. was made possible through the generous scholarship provided by the Republic of Türkiye. I am deeply thankful to my homeland for offering me such a meaningful opportunity to pursue advanced education and personal growth.

Throughout this process, I was fortunate to receive the guidance of exceptional mentors. I owe special thanks to my first supervisor, Kyriaki Noussia, for her invaluable support and encouragement during the initial stages of my research. I am also profoundly grateful to Robert Merkin, Andrea Lista, Matthew Channon, James Griffin, Mimi Zou, Severine Saintier, and Mihail Danov for their critical insights and thoughtful contributions to my work. Their expertise and guidance greatly shaped the direction of this book.

This journey was not without its challenges. On 20 February 2020, while in Exeter, I received the devastating news of the passing of my younger brother, Lieutenant Ali Emre Fırıncıoğulları, who lost his life in the line of duty. His loss remains one of the most profound moments of my life. However, his memory became a source of strength and resilience for me. His enduring smile and unwavering spirit continue to inspire me, and I dedicate this work to his cherished memory. May he rest in eternal peace.

My family has been my pillar of strength throughout this journey. To my beloved mother, Munteha, and father, Remzi Firinciogullari, your unwavering love and support have been my anchor through every challenge. To my dear siblings, Esra, Ferda, Koray, and Ali Emre, my beloved nephews, Birce and Ali, as well as my family members Burcu, Ozgur, and Seckin, you have all been my unwavering source of strength and joy. Thank you for your belief in me and for encouraging me to keep going.

I am also deeply grateful for the friendships that sustained me during my time in Exeter. My heartfelt thanks go to Aslı Bacak, Mustafa Biber, and Ilayda Ozdemir for their unwavering support and the joy they brought to my life. Your friendship has been my greatest gift. I also wish to thank Birsen and Ahmet Aydın, who became my second family in Exeter, for their kindness and care during my time away from home.

Furthermore, I extend my sincere gratitude to the Routledge publishing team and editors for their belief in my work and their commitment to excellence. Your professionalism and dedication have played a pivotal role in bringing this research to a wider audience, and I am truly thankful for your collaboration.

To all who have walked alongside me during this transformative chapter of my life, thank you. This book is a testament to the collective support, encouragement, and inspiration I have received along the way.

Feray Firinciogullari
Exeter, UK

# Table of Cases

AES Ust-Kamenogorsk Hydropower Plant LLP v Ust-Kamenogorsk Hydropower Plant JSC [2013] UKSC 35.

Africa Finance Corporation & others v Aiteo Eastern E & P Company Limited [2022] EWHC 768 (Comm).

Aggeliki Charis Compania Maritima SA v Pagnan SpA (The Angelic Grace) [1995] 1 Lloyd's Rep 87.

Allianz SpA (formerly Riunione Adriatica di Sicurtà SpA) v West Tankers Inc, (The Front Comor) (2009) CJEU Case C-185/07, [2009] ECR I–00673.

American International Specialty Lines Insurance Co v. Abbott Laboratories [2004] 1 Lloyd's 815.

Aspen Insurance UK Ltd v Pectel Ltd [2008] EWHC 2804 (Comm).

Axa Insurance UK plc v Financial Claims Solutions Ltd (CA) [2018] EWCA Civ 1330.

Bank of Nova Scotia v Hellenic Mutual War Risk Association (Bermuda) Ltd (The Good Luck) [1992] AC 233 (HL).

BAI (Run Off) Ltd v Durham [2012] UKSC 14.

Bradley v Eagle Star Insurance Co Ltd [1989] AC 957.

Burnard v Rodocanachi (1882) 7 App Cas 333 (HL).

Carter v Boehm (1766) 3 Burr 1905.

Case C-159/02 Turner v Grovit and Others [2004] ECR I–03565.

Case C-26/91 Jakob Handte & Co GmbH v Traitements Mécano-chimiques des Surfaces SA [1992] ECR I-3967 [16].

Catherine v. Anna (1801) 4 C Rob 39.

Centre Reinsurance International Co v Freakley (CA) [2005] EWCA Civ 115.

Continental Illinois National Bank & Trust Co of Chicago v Bathurst (The Captain Panagos DP) [1988] EWCA Civ J0729–10.

Cooperative Retail Services Ltd v Taylor Young Partnership Ltd [2002] UKHL 17.

Court of Justice of the European Union (CJEU), Case C-700/20 (London Steam-Shipowners' Mutual Insurance Association Limited v. Kingdom of Spain).

Crowley v Cohen (1832) 3 B & Ad 478.

Cumberland Bone Co v Andes Insurance Co 64 Me 466 (1874).

De Costa v Scandret (1723) 2 P. Wms. 170.

De Vaux v Salvador (1836) 4 Ad. & E. 420.
Delanoy v Robson (1814) 5 Taunt 605.
Dennehy v Bellamy [1938] 2 All ER. 262.
Dunlop Pneumatic Tyre Co Ltd v Selfridge & Co Ltd [1915] A.C. 847.
Enka Insaat ve Sanayi AS v OOO "Insurance Company Chubb" [2020] EWCA Civ 574.
Feasey v Sun Life Assurance Co [2003] EWCA Civ 885.
Fenton Insurance Co Ltd v Gothaer Versicherungsbank VVAG [1991] 1 Lloyd's Rep 172.
Field Steamship Company v Burr [1899] 1 QB 579.
First National Tricity Finance Ltd v OT Computers Ltd (In Administration) [2004] EWCA Civ 653.
Freshwater v Western Australia Insurance Co Ltd [1933] 1 KB 515.
Gard Marine & Energy Ltd v China National Chartering Co Ltd (The Ocean Victory) [2017] UKSC 35.
Global Process Systems Inc. v Syarikat Takaful Malaysia Berhad (The Cendor MOPU) [2011] UKSC 5.
Groom v Crocker [1939] 1 KB 194.
Haberdashers' Aske's Federation Trust Ltd. v Lakehouse Contracts Ltd (QBD (TCC)) [2018] EWHC 558 (TCC).
Harcourt v FEF Griffin [2007] EWHC 1500 (QB).
Hay v Le Neve (1824) 2 Shaw's Scot App Cases 395 (HL).
HIH Casualty & General Insurance Ltd v Axa Corporate Solutions (formerly Axa Reassurance SA) [2002] EWCA Civ 1253.
J. J. Lloyd Instruments Ltd v Northern Star Insurance Co. Ltd. (Miss Jay Jay) [1985] 1 Lloyd's Rep 264 (QBD (Comm Ct)).
Kairos Shipping Ltd v Enka & Co LLC (The Atlantic Confidence) [2014] EWCA Civ 217.
Lucena v Craufurd (1806) 2 B & P (NR) 269.
Macaura v Northern Assurance Co Ltd [1925] AC 619.
Montgomerie v United Kingdom Mutual Steamship Association [1891] 1 QB 370.
Mountain v Whittle [1921] AC 615.
National Oilwell (UK) Ltd. v Davy Offshore Ltd [1993] 2 Lloyd's Rep 582.
Nori Holdings Ltd & Ors v Public Joint-Stock Company Bank Otkritie Financial Corporation [2018] EWHC 1343 (Comm).
OT Africa Line Ltd v Magic Sportswear Corporation [2005] EWCA Civ 710.
Pacific & General Insurance Co. Ltd v. Hazell & Ors [1997] LRLR 65 (QB Com Ct).
Pan Atlantic Insurance Co Ltd v Pine Top Insurance Co Ltd. [1995] 1 A.C. 501.
Petrofina (UK) Ltd v Magnaload Ltd 1984 QB 127.
Pioneer Concrete v National Employers Mutual Insurance [1985] 1 Lloyd's Rep 274.
Post Office v Norwich Union Fire Insurance Society Ltd [1967] 2 QB 363.
QBE Europe SA/NV and QBE (UK) Ltd v Generali Espaa de Seguros y Reaseguros [2022] EWHC 2062 (Comm).

Quadra Commodities SA v XL Insurance Company SE and Others [2023] EWCA Civ 432.
Re London County Commercial Reinsurance Office Ltd. [1922] 2 Ch 67.
Schiffahrtsgesellschaft Detlef Von Appen GmbH v Wiener Allianz Versichrungs AG & Voest Alpine Intertrading GmbH [1997] EWCA Civ 1420.
Scott v Avery (1843–1860) All E.R. Rep 1 (HL).
Shipowners' Mutual Protection and Indemnity Association (Luxembourg) v Containerships Denizcilik Nakliyat Ve Ticaret AS [2015] EWHC 258 (Comm).
Shipowners' Mutual Protection and Indemnity Association (Luxembourg) v Containerships Denizcilik Nakliyat ve Ticaret AS (The Yusuf Cepnioglu) [2016] EWCA Civ 386.
T. M. Noten BV v Paul Charles Harding [1990] EWCA Civ J0621–4.
The Fanti and the Padre Island [1991] 2 AC 1.
The Allobrogia [1979] 1 Lloyd's Rep. 190.
The London Steam Shipowners Mutual Insurance Association Ltd v The Kingdom of Spain (The Prestige (No. 2)) [2013] EWHC 3188 (Comm).
The London Steam Shipowners Mutual Insurance Association Ltd v The Kingdom of Spain (The Prestige (Nos. 3 & 4)) [2021] EWCA Civ 1589.
The London Steam Shipowners Mutual Insurance Association Ltd v The Kingdom Spain [2023] EWHC 2473.
The London Steamship Owners' Mutual Insurance Association Limited v. The French Republic (M/T Prestige) (II) [2023] EWHC 2474.
The Padre Island [1987] 2 Lloyd's Rep 529.
The Rugby Football Union v Clark Smith Partnership Limited and FM Conway Limited [2022] EWHC 956 (TCC).
The United Kingdom Mutual Steamship Ass'n Association v Nevill [1887] 19 QBD 110 (CA).
The UK P&I Club & Anor v Republica Bolivariana de Venezuela [2023] EWCA Civ 1497.
The Vainqueur Jose [1979] 1 Lloyd's Rep. 557.
The Yasin [1979] 2 Lloyd's Rep 45.
Thomas v Thomas (1842) 2 QB 851.
Thomas Wilson Sons & Co v Owners of Cargo of the Xantho (The Xantho) (1887) LR 12 App Cas 503 (HL).
Thornton Springer v NEM Insurance Co Ltd and others [2000] 2 All ER 489.
Through Transport Mutual Insurance Association (Eurasia) Ltd v New India Insurance Co (The Hari Bhum) [2005] EWHC 455 (Comm).
Times Trading Corporation v National Bank of Fujairah (Dubai Branch) (The Archagelos Gabriel) [2020] EWHC 1983 (Comm).
Turkish Supreme Court Law General Assembly No. K. 1996/18 dated 31.01.1996.
Turkish Supreme Court of Commerce Department No. E. 1971/1376, K. 1971/5339 dated 13/07/1971.
Turkish Supreme Court, 2nd Law Department, Decision No. E. 2012/616, K. 2012/26084, dated November 5, 2012.
Turkish Supreme Court, Judgement No. 5101/2606, April 25, 1989.

Tweddle v Atkinson [1861] EWHC J57 (QB).
Tyco Fire & Integrated Solutions (UK) Ltd v Rolls-Royce Motor Cars Ltd [2007] EWHC 3159 (TCC).
Ulusoy Denizcilik AS v. COFCO Global Harvest (Zhangjiagang) Trading Co Ltd [2020] EWHC 3645 (Comm).
Volkswagenwerk A.G. and Wolfsburger Transport Gesellschaft M.B.H. v International Mutual Strike Assurance Co. (Bermuda) Ltd [1977] 2 Lloyd's Rep. 503.
Young v Royal and Sun Alliance Insurance Plc [2020] CSIH 25.

# Abbreviations

| | |
|---|---|
| **1930 Act** | Third Parties (Rights against Insurers) Act 1930 |
| **1992 CLC** | 1992 International Convention on Civil Liability for Oil Pollution Damage |
| **1999 Act** | Contracts (Rights of Third Parties) Act 1999 |
| **2001 Bunker Convention** | 2001 International Convention on Civil Liability for Bunker Oil Pollution Damage |
| **2007 Nairobi International Convention** | 2007 Nairobi International Convention on the Removal of Wrecks |
| **2010 Act** | Third Parties (Rights against Insurance) Act 2010 |
| **2015 Act** | Insurance Act 2015 |
| **All ER** | All England Law Reports |
| **Art.** | Article |
| **BATIDER** | Journal of Bank and Commercial Law |
| **BIMCO** | Baltic and International Maritime Council |
| **BMLA** | British Maritime Law Association |
| **CA** | Court of Appeal (England) |
| **Ch.** | Chancery Division (England) |
| **Chap.** | Chapter |
| **Cl.** | Clause |
| **CLC** | International Convention on Civil Liability for Oil Pollution Damage |
| **CMI** | Comity Maritime International |
| **COM** | Commission (EC) |
| **CONF** | Conference (IMO) |
| **Comm.** | Commentary |
| **Comp.A** | Companies Act (England) |
| **CJEU** | Court of Justice of the European Union |
| **CTPA** | Contracts (Rights of Third Parties) Act, 1999 (England) |

| | |
|---|---|
| **Doc.** | Docket |
| **EC** | European Communities |
| **EWHC** | England and Wales High Court |
| **EU** | European Union |
| **FC** | International Convention on the Establishment of an International Fund for Compensation for Oil Pollution Damage |
| **GT** | Gross tonnage |
| **HL** | House of Lords (England) |
| **HNS** | International Convention on Liability and Compensation for Damage in Connection with the Carriage of Hazardous and Noxious Substances by Sea, 1996 |
| **IA** | Insurance Act 2015 |
| **IGP&I** | International Group of Protection and Indemnity Clubs |
| **ILO** | International Labour Organization |
| **IMO** | International Maritime Organization |
| **IOPC (Funds)** | International Oil Pollution Compensation Funds |
| **JR** | Joint Report |
| **KB** | King's Bench (England) |
| **LEG** | Legal Committee (IMO) |
| **LLMC** | Convention on Limitation of Liability for Maritime Claims |
| **Llyod's Rep.** | Llyod's Law Reports |
| **Ll.L.Rep.** | Llyod's List Law Reports |
| **LOG** | Letter of Guarantee |
| **LOI** | Letter of Indemnity |
| **LOU** | Letter of Undertaking |
| **MARPOL** | International Convention for the Prevention of Pollution from Ships |
| **MIA** | Marine Insurance Act, 1906 (England) |
| **MLA** | Maritime Law Association (America) |
| **MSA** | Merchant Shipping Act (England) |
| **OJ** | Official Journal (EC) |
| **OPA 90** | Oil Pollution Act, 1990 |
| **P&I** | Protection and Indemnity |
| **RDC** | Running Down Clause |
| **Rep.** | Report |
| **RG** | Resmi Gazete (Official Gazette) |
| **SDR** | Special Drawing Right |
| **Scot.** | Scottish |
| **Sec.** | Section |
| **STOPIA** | Small Tanker Oil Pollution Indemnification Agreement |

| | |
|---|---|
| **QB** | Queen's Bench (England) |
| **TOPIA** | Tanker Oil Pollution Indemnification Agreement |
| **TPA** | Third Parties (Rights Against Insurers) Act, 1930 (England) |
| **TCC** | Turkish Commercial Code No. 6102 |
| **UNCITRAL** | United Nations Commission on International Trade Law |
| **USD** | United States Dollar |
| **v.** | Versus |
| **Vol.** | Volume |
| **WTO** | World Trade Organization |
| **YA** | York Antwerp Rules |

# 1 The P&I Club Insurance's Definition, Historical Development, Basic Features, Parties, and Entry Procedures

## I. Introduction

Club insurance plays a pivotal role in maritime trade and insurance, providing extensive coverage to shipowners through mutual insurance structures. Despite its critical importance, Türkiye's club insurance industry remains in a developmental stage, significantly lagging behind the well-established English system. Given that P&I insurance originated and evolved within the English legal framework, understanding its historical and structural foundations is essential for evaluating Türkiye's regulatory approach.

This chapter provides an in-depth examination of P&I Clubs, tracing their historical evolution within the English legal system. Establishing a foundational understanding of their structure, operational dynamics, and the motivation behind their emergence is necessary for subsequent discussions on club insurance development. Additionally, the chapter identifies distinctions and commonalities between English and Turkish P&I Clubs, offering a critical evaluation of potential pathways to advance Türkiye's club insurance sector.

The English model, built on principles of mutuality and strict enforcement of Club rules, has contributed to a stable and effective insurance system. In contrast, Türkiye's legal approach treats P&I Clubs similarly to conventional insurers, creating regulatory inconsistencies that may hinder their growth. One of the critical issues in Türkiye is the unrestricted direct action right granted to third parties, which differs significantly from the English legal framework. This chapter explores whether adopting English legal principles, particularly in enforcing Club rules, would enhance the stability and legal certainty of Turkish P&I insurance.

The chapter concludes by analyzing the impact of legal disparities on Türkiye's ability to restructure its club insurance system. The discussion aims to provide a well-reasoned argument for the necessity of legal reform while identifying challenges in adopting the English model and proposing viable solutions to align Türkiye's legal framework with international standards.

DOI: 10.4324/9781003628897-1

## II. Definition and Historical Development of P&I Clubs

### *A. Definition*

When navigating at sea, a ship faces many risks and dangers.[1] Therefore, shipowners must insure their vessels against potential risks or dangers at sea. To compensate for potential damages, shipowners or charterers must insure several risks for which they could be liable, leading to the emergence of P&I insurance.[2] The term P&I insurance stands for protection and indemnity. Operating a ship without insurance is considered imprudent. Similarly, cargo owners cannot afford the significant risks of shipping goods without insurance.

P&I insurance is a type of marine insurance that provides coverage against third-party liability for shipowners who are Club members.[3] This insurance covers a wide range of liabilities, such as injury and death of passengers or seafarers and collision liability.[4] Additionally, P&I insurance covers a member's liability for various risks, including cargo, pollution, damage to fixed or floating objects, and debts arising from a collision with another ship.[5] Due to its comprehensive protection, P&I insurance is essential in maritime law.

P&I insurance is mostly called club insurance in the marine insurance industry. The P&I Club, or simply the Club, is the insurer that provides this insurance. Unlike in other states, in America, Clubs are called "insurers" by the Courts. The term "member," on the other hand, refers to both the insured and Club partners and is specific to mutual Clubs.[6]

P&I Clubs are associations formed by commercial shipowners and charterers to provide protection services to their members against the dangers that ships may encounter during their industrial activities. Unlike P&I insurance, hull and machinery insurance aims to protect the insured's ship.[7] However, the P&I insurance offered by P&I Clubs provides protection and indemnity services to its members for damage caused by the shipowner or operator to third

1 George B Freehill, "Mutually Excepted Perils" (1974–1975) 49 *Tulane Law Review* 899; Simon Baughen, *Shipping Law* (6th edn, Routledge 2015) 81; John D Kimball, "The Central Role of P&I Insurance in Maritime Law" (2013) 87 *Tulane Law Review* 1147, 1148; Ayca Ucar, *Perils of the Seas and Inherent Vice in Marine Insurance Law* (Routledge 2023) 34.

2 Steven J Hazelwood and David Semark, *P&I Clubs: Law and Practice* (4th edn, LLP 2010) 1; Ozlem Gurses, *Marine Insurance Law* (3rd edn, Routledge 2023) 8.

3 Yvonne Baatz, *Maritime Law* (4th edn, Routledge 2017) 458; Michael Bundock, *Shipping Law Handbook* (5th edn, Informa 2011) 323; Hazelwood and Semark, 3; Gillian Musgrave and David Heaselden, "Understanding P&I Club" (Presentation, Standard Asia and Shipowners' Mutual 2014) https://www.gia.org.sg/files/8th_19_12_2014_Understanding_P_I_Club.pdf accessed 20 December 2022.

4 Philip Anderson, *The Mariner's Guide to Marine Insurance* (The Nautical Institute 1999) 33.

5 Howard Bennett, *The Law of Marine Insurance* (Clarendon Press 1996) 484; Baatz, 458.

6 Robert Merkin and Jenny Steele, *Insurance and the Law of Obligations* (Oxford University Press 2013) 66; Kimball, 1148.

7 *De Vaux v Salvador* (1836) 4 Ad & E. 420; *Field Steamship Company v Burr* [1899] 1 QB 579.

parties during the ship's operation.[8] In other words, P&I insurance covers the obligations of shipowners to third parties not covered by hull insurance. Even when the hull insurer covers collision liability, P&I insurance remains necessary. The primary and most significant reason for this is that the hull insurer's collision liability coverage is limited in terms of the nature of the liabilities it addresses. Therefore, a distinction must be drawn between collision liabilities covered under hull insurance and those fully addressed by P&I insurance. Liability exceeding the insured amount under hull insurance, and possibly hull interest insurance, is covered by P&I insurance, where coverage is subject to the shipowners' right to limit their liability.[9]

The first purpose of the emergence of P&I insurance was to protect shipowners from liability in the event of personal injuries and deaths of third parties, a danger not covered by other types of insurance.[10] Today, the scope of risks and dangers covered by P&I insurance has been significantly expanded to include comprehensive protection and indemnity insurance covering all shipowners' liabilities regarding cargo damages, marine pollution, deaths and injuries, damage to the crew, passengers, fixed or floating objects, and debts arising from collisions with other ships.[11]

The principle of "mutuality" is the basis of P&I insurance. Each member contributes to the losses of other members under this principle.[12] Shipowners register as Club members who share risks against potential risks and dangers at sea. These Clubs have various rules, including the Club's functioning, membership procedures, and dispute resolution procedures between members and the Club. Clubs do not intend to make a profit; their primary purpose is to spread the risks that may occur at sea among their members. Thirteen Clubs[13] formed the International Group of P&I Clubs to serve this purpose better. Today, these Clubs insure over 90% of the world's ocean tonnage.[14]

8 Hazelwood and Semark, 1.

9 Nordic Marine Insurance Plan 2013 Version 2023 – Commentary (2023) Ch 13, p 76.

10 W. R. A. Birch Reynardson, "History and Development of P&I Insurance: The British Scene" (1968–1969) 43 *Tulane Law Review* 457, 465.

11 Mya Thida Lin, "A Selective Appraisal of the P&I Insurance System with Special Reference to Claims for Personal Injury, Illness and Loss of Life" (World Maritime University Dissertations 413, 2009) 9.

12 Gurses, 8.

13 American Steamshipowners Mutual Protection and Indemnity Association, Inc., Assuranceforeningen Gard, Assuranceforeningen Skuld, The Britannia Steam Ship Insurance Association Limited, The Japan Shipowners' Mutual Protection & Indemnity Association, The London Steam-Shipowners' Mutual Insurance Association Limited, North of England P&I, Standard Limited, The Shipowners' Mutual Protection & Indemnity Association (Luxembourg), The Steamship Mutual Underwriting Association (Bermuda) Limited, The Swedish Club, United Kingdom Mutual Steam Ship Assurance Association (Bermuda) Limited, and The West of England Shipowners Mutual Insurance Association (Luxembourg).

14 International Group of P&I Clubs, "P&I Clubs" https://www.igpandi.org/about accessed 24 April 2023.

## *B. Historical Development of P&I Clubs*

### *1. In England*

#### A. GENERAL FRAMEWORK AND LEGAL REFORMS

Examining the general framework and legal processes through which club insurance has evolved in England is essential to understanding the development of this industry. One of the book's arguments is that club insurance's progress is intricately linked to the legal developments in the respective country. It is necessary to examine the legal development of club insurance in England to demonstrate the effectiveness of legal reforms in enhancing club insurance.

The birthplace and the epicentre of the development of club insurance is England. England's leading position in the club insurance industry is attributed to its historical background, experience, and accumulated knowledge. For countries aiming to enhance club insurance, it is crucial to closely examine England's historical development to gain insights and knowledge.

In London during the 16th and 17th centuries, marine insurance policies were underwritten by individual merchants known as "underwriters." Despite the presence of these individual merchants, there were no chartered marine insurers until 1720. The inability of underwriters to meet high-value insurance claims occasionally led to the bankruptcy of many of them.

In the early 1720s, with the increasing number of potential marine insurance companies seeking to benefit from royal charters, a committee of the House of Commons was established to oversee companies with unpaid shares. Subsequently, the Bubble Act 1720, also known as the Royal Exchange and London Assurance Corporation Act 1720, was an English law passed during the reign of King George I.[15] The Bubble Act required payments to the royal treasury to benefit from charters for establishing marine insurance companies. This measure aimed to prevent the misuse and inappropriate use of charters. As a result, the Royal Exchange Assurance Corporation and the London Assurance Corporation were established with royal charters to operate as monopolies in the marine insurance sector.[16] The Act aimed not only to guarantee the solvency of chartered companies but also to control insurable risks and facilitate the payment of claims. After it was recognized that the Act effectively hindered the establishment of any insurance company, the section related to the marine insurance monopoly was repealed in 1824, followed by the complete repeal of the Act in 1825.[17]

15 For more information about historical background, see Ron Harris, "The Bubble Act: Its Passage and Its Effects on Business Organization" (1994) 54(3) *The Journal of Economic History* 610, 627.

16 The market share of the Royal Exchange and London Assurance, the two chartered companies, was minor. For more information, see Robert Merkin, *Marine Insurance: A Legal History* (Edward Elgar Publishing 2021) para 9–0001.

17 Merkin, *Legal History*, para. 2–014; Reynardson, 464.

However, despite the Bubble Act effectively prohibiting non-chartered joint-stock companies with transferable shares, it did not prevent individuals from issuing marine insurance policies. Claims unmet by chartered companies were covered by mutual funds established by shipowners based on the principle of mutuality.

While the privileges granted to the two companies by the Bubble Act eliminated corporate competition, it increased the demand for individual insurers. For instance, Edward Lloyd's coffeehouse in London, where individual marine insurance policies began to be issued, played a crucial role in the emergence of Lloyd's. Lloyd's coffeehouse evolved into an informal insurance marketplace, which served as the precursor to the contemporary Lloyd's insurance market. The individuals who assumed insurance risks within the coffeehouse were known as "underwriters," a term derived from their practice of inscribing their names and signatures at the bottom of the policy documents, positioned "under" the stated terms and conditions. Lloyd's reputation for issuing marine insurance policies spread over time and began to be preferred by ships coming from Europe.

The P&I Clubs are the successors of small hull insurance clubs that English shipowners established during the 18th century. These shipowners were discontented with the limited coverage and high boat insurance cost, so they formed hull clubs. These clubs were cooperative or association-like entities without legal personalities, and each shipowner shared the hull risks.[18]

The dawn of the 19th century coincided with significant economic and technological changes and developments as ships' cargo, size, and value increased. The growth and development of the industry resulted in increased responsibilities for shipowners. Marine insurance policies, which had previously provided adequate protection to shipowners, could not cover the new responsibilities that emerged during this period. Subsequently, some shipowners who had previously operated as boat insurers began to transform their businesses to insure new responsibilities and to counteract the monopoly of insurers working under Lloyd's.[19]

The marine insurance sector saw an influx of new insurance companies alongside Lloyd's underwriters, intensifying competition, particularly for higher-quality risks. As a result, mutual insurance Clubs increasingly faced the challenge of insuring older and deteriorating vessels, leading to a strain on their resources due to the rising claims. This financial strain caused several Clubs to cease operations.

It is conceivable that mutual insurance Clubs might have vanished entirely in England were it not for certain developments in the early 19th century. Specifically, shipowners' significant liabilities increased demand for enhanced and expanded insurance coverage.

A significant factor influencing the evolution of marine insurance was the collision risk. Although this risk was relatively minor during the 18th century, it gained prominence by the early 19th century, leading to increased collision cases reported

18 Serdar Acar, *Club Insurance (P&I)* (Vedat 2008) 9.

19 Charles B Anderson and Colin de la Rue, "The Role of the P&I Clubs in Marine Pollution Incidents" (2011) 85 *Tulane Law Review* 1257.

in legal literature. The House of Lords established several critical principles in the landmark case of *Hay v. Le Neve*[20] in 1824: A ship that caused a collision due to its fault was held liable for the damages sustained by the other vessel, and when a collision resulted from the fault of both ships involved, liability was to be shared equally between them.

In another landmark case, the *de Vaux v Salvador* (1836), which significantly influenced the development of P&I Club insurance, the ship de Vaux collided with the Salvador and was found liable for the damage caused to the latter. This ruling established that a shipowner's liability due to a collision cannot be considered a peril of the seas,[21] which significantly influenced the development of P&I Club insurance. The ship de Vaux collided with the Salvador and was found liable for the damage caused to the latter. This ruling established that a shipowner's liability due to a collision cannot be considered a peril of the seas.[22] However, this situation gave rise to a dispute, as marine insurance policies were designed to cover only damages that occurred on the shipowner's vessel. After this case, when it was decided that the shipowner should cover the damages caused to the other ship due to the collision, it became apparent that the coverage provided by the existing marine insurance policies was inadequate.[23] As a result, hull insurers and shipowners collaborated to introduce the Running Down Clause (RDC) to cover damages arising from collisions.[24] The RDC covered 3/4 of the damage, and the remaining 1/4 was to be covered by the shipowners. The aim was to encourage shipowners to exercise greater caution while navigating.[25]

The formation of the P&I Clubs was not primarily driven by shipowners' exposure to the one-fourth collision liability stipulated in the standard hull policy. Instead, the impetus for establishing the Clubs stemmed from the need for collision coverage exceeding the insured value of the ship. Furthermore, shipowners had to assume other responsibilities to third parties. For instance, the Fatal Accidents Act (Lord Campbell's Act) 1846 enabled the personal representatives of a deceased individual to seek damages from any person whose wrongful act, negligence, or default had led to death. Prior to this legislation, common law held that the right to pursue damages for a wrongful death ceased with the deceased, leaving their dependents without legal recourse. This legislation was particularly significant for the owners of passenger ships transporting tens of thousands of emigrants across the Atlantic to North America between 1845 and 1848.

20 *Hay v Le Neve* (1824) 2 Shaw's Scot App Cases 395 (HL).

21 *De Vaux v Salvador* (1836) 4 Ad. & E. 420.

22 Robert Merkin and Sarah Derrington, "Marine Insurance Act 1906: Magnificent Achievement or Monstrous Aberration" in Rhidian Thomas (ed), *The Modern Law of Marine Insurance: Volume Four* (Informa Law 2015) 33.

23 Kyriaki Noussia, *The Principle of Indemnity in Marine Insurance Contracts: A Comparative Approach* (Springer 2007) 66.

24 Reynardson, 466.

25 Reynardson, 466.

Additionally, the Harbour, Docks, and Piers Clauses Act of 1846,[26] which came into effect in 1847, imposed a duty on shipowners to compensate port authorities for any damage that may occur in the port caused by ships under their ownership.[27] Implementing these legal reforms has engendered a notable escalation in the liability for compensation borne by shipowners and charterers, consequently augmenting the imperative for P&I Club insurance.

### B. DEVELOPMENTS INFLUENCING THE EMERGENCE OF THE FIRST P&I CLUBS

The first P&I Clubs emerged in England. The influence of these Clubs' emergence in England cannot be overlooked in contributing to the country's legal and commercial expertise regarding club insurance. It is essential to examine the purposes behind the establishment of these Clubs and the processes they underwent to understand the development of the club insurance industry.

To alleviate the pressures faced by shipowners, Mr Peter Tindall Riley, an insurance broker, established the Shipowners Mutual Protection Society, the first of its kind, in Topsham, Devon, on 1 May 1855.[28] The Club, which later became known as the Britannia P&I Club,[29] was founded after implementing the Merchant Shipping Act in 1854, which allowed insurers to offer coverage for crew members seeking compensation from shipowners for death or injury.[30] This Club operated on the principle of mutuality, like boat insurance, but also covered personal injury, death, third-party property damage, and collision-related damage to other ships.

In the latter half of the 19th century, the liability of shipowners for cargo damage began to come to the forefront. In 1870, the ship Westenhope, transporting cargo to Cape Town, took on additional cargo and deviated to Port Elizabeth before disappearing off South Africa's coast while returning to Cape Town.[31] The cargo owners sought compensation from the shipowner for their losses, alleging that the shipowner had breached the contract of carriage by deviating from the agreed route and, therefore, bore responsibility for the loss of the cargo. The Court accepted these claims and ruled that the shipowner was liable for the total cost of the cargo. The shipowner subsequently applied to the Protection Club for compensation, but their request was denied since liability for the cargo was not covered by insurance.[32] Consequently, the shipowner had to bear the cost of the damages themselves.[33]

Shortly after, another ship, the Emily, ran aground due to negligent navigation and suffered cargo damage. The cargo owners claimed the total cost of the damages from the shipowner, arguing that the loss was not due to "perils of the sea" but

26 Harbour, Docks, and Piers Clauses Act 1846, ss 56, 74.
27 Anderson and Rue, 1260.
28 Hazelwood and Semark, 7; Reynardson, 467; Noussia, *The Principle*, 5.
29 Noussia, *The Principle*, 5; Anderson, 23.
30 Anderson and Rue, 23.
31 Reynardson, 468.
32 Hazelwood and Semark, 7.
33 Hazelwood and Semark, 7.

rather to the shipowner's negligence. Following these events in 1874, shipowners proposed to the Protection Club that a new coverage class be established, including compensation for risks such as cargo damage.[34] As a result, a new coverage category was created, and the word "indemnity" was added to the Club's name.[35] The first indemnity Club, "The Steamshipowners Mutual Indemnity Association," was established.[36] The North of England Protection and Indemnity Club, the first protection and indemnity Club, was established in 1886.

### C. SOLVING INCREASED CLAIMS: THE POOLING AGREEMENT

Following 1873, the number of members joining P&I Clubs increased significantly, causing challenges in collecting contributions from the expanding membership base. P&I Clubs transitioned to operating as companies possessing legal personalities to manage their operations more efficiently.[37]

As risks grew in the P&I market, Clubs sought to mitigate their exposure by seeking reinsurance.[38] In 1899, six P&I Clubs – UK Club, Britannia, Standard Club, London Club, Newcastle Club, and Sunderland Club – entered the first-ever Pooling Agreement.[39] The International Group Agreement guarantees collaborative efforts between member Clubs[40] in administrating the Pooling Agreement, "an annually renewed agreement between the Clubs to mutually reinsure each other by sharing claims between themselves."[41]

Most P&I Clubs were initially established in various towns and cities in the United Kingdom. However, similar Clubs were established in other countries, such as Scandinavia, the United States, and Japan. While originating from the United Kingdom, many P&I Clubs are administered in Bermuda due to legal considerations and other favourable factors.[42]

In summary, club insurance emerged in England due to other marine insurance coverage inadequacies as maritime trade activities developed. Factors such as increasing risks faced by shipowners during commercial activities, the inability of existing insurance to cover these risks, and rising insurance costs influenced the emergence of club insurance. Countries aiming to strengthen club insurance

34 Noussia, *The Principle*, 5.
35 Noussia, *The Principle*, 6.
36 Anderson, 15.
37 Acar, *Club Insurance*, 11.
38 Elizabeth Germano, "A Law and Economics Analysis of the Duty of Utmost Good Faith (Uberrimae Fidei) in Marine Insurance Law for Protection and Indemnity Clubs" (2016) 47 *St Mary's Law Journal* 727, 802.
39 See International Group of P&I Clubs, "Group Agreements" https://www.igpandi.org/about accessed 28 April 2023.
40 Today, the 12 clubs that are party to the agreement. See "The International Group of P&I Clubs" igpandi.org accessed 28 April 2023.
41 Germano, 810.
42 For example, Gard P&I (Bermuda) Limited; The Steamship Mutual Underwriting Association (Bermuda) Limited.

today need to analyze these processes. Examining the historical processes in the country where the industry first emerged contributes to the legislative process when legal reforms are made. Therefore, examining the historical background of club insurance in England is essential for understanding its impact on legal policies regarding Clubs and for serving as a model for other countries in terms of legal policies.

### 2. *A Different Example from the English Model: Club Insurance in Türkiye*

As stated in the book argument, supporting appropriate legal policies is essential to contribute to the country's economy by developing the club insurance industry. The reason for preferring to explain this argument through two countries is to demonstrate the current framework more concretely through country models with different legal policies. In this context, Türkiye will be examined as a model country aiming to develop the maritime sector[43] and club insurance but adopting an interventionist legal approach towards club insurance. Other countries with a similar legal approach to club insurance as Türkiye can also benefit from these analyses and results.

Türkiye is a country surrounded by sea on three sides and thus has heavy maritime trade traffic. Legal policies are being implemented to develop the country's maritime trade and marine insurance industries to leverage this geographical advantage. The development of club insurance is part of these policies. The goal of developing the club insurance industry in Türkiye emerged initially with the idea of establishing a domestic Club.[44]

The necessity of a Turkish P&I Club sparked debate among lawyers, scholars, and industry experts in Türkiye.[45] Some scholars argued that establishing a domestic Club was difficult and that the need for club insurance should continue to be met through foreign Clubs.[46] They claimed that establishing a P&I Club or company in Türkiye would require a solid legal background and economic support.[47] However, in line with Türkiye's strategic maritime trade and insurance policy, excluding club insurance from this framework was impractical. Club insurance is pivotal in fostering the advancement of maritime endeavours and effectively addressing the insurance requisites of shipowners. Disregarding this necessity within the context

43 Deniz Servantie, "Comparative Analysis of EU and Türkiye's Maritime Transport Policy" (IKV-European Union and Economic Relations Research Centre, July 2015) https://www.ikv.org.tr/icerik/get/4263/215/ accessed 19 September 2022.

44 Nurullah Hakan Peksen, "Türk P&I Kulübünün Kurulmasının Avantaj ve Dezavantajlarının Analizi" (Master thesis, Istanbul University 2012) 2.

45 Peksen, 2; Didem Alganturk, "Kulüp Sigortası" (PhD thesis, Marmara University 2000) 213; Muhammet Alper Keceli, "Establishing a New Protection and Indemnity (P&I) Insurance Institution in Türkiye" (Master thesis, World Maritime University 2012) 93; Acar, *Club Insurance*, 614.

46 Alganturk, 213; Keceli, 93; Acar, *Club Insurance*, 614; Peksen, 106.

47 Acar, *Club Insurance*, 614.

of Türkiye would have hindered the progress of maritime activities and the club insurance industry. Therefore, this viewpoint was not supported in Türkiye.

Understanding the fundamental legal framework of club insurance entails discussions of lawsuits and legal issues according to national laws. Supporting the activities of the club insurance industry in Türkiye requires a closer examination of this area and facilitates the resolution of legal disputes. As these activities increase, more disputes will arise, leading to a diversification of legal analyses and discussions regarding their resolution. Enhancing this legal knowledge base also influences the approach to club insurance. Therefore, establishing and increasing P&I Clubs that provide club insurance in Türkiye should be supported.[48]

Before establishing a domestic club insurance entity in Türkiye, the requisites for club insurance coverage for vessels primarily relied on foreign counterparts. However, given the foreign domicile of these Clubs and the ensuing necessity to pursue legal recourse in foreign courts and arbitration forums, substantial impediments have surfaced in satisfying compensation claims, precipitating multifaceted legal and financial challenges. Consequently, an imperative demand for domestic P&I insurance offerings emerged. Furthermore, in congruence with the state's strategic agenda for advancing maritime trade and insurance in Türkiye, particular emphasis has been placed on the development and promotion of club insurance. To address this need, the first Turkish P&I insurance company was established in 2014 with the support of the Ministry of Transport, Maritime Affairs, and Communications. With 50% government support, the company's establishment ensured a robust economic infrastructure. The Turkish P&I Club was registered in the Commercial Register on 31 December 2013 as a public limited company operating in non-life insurance branches under Insurance Law No. 5684. In 2014, it officially commenced its commercial activities.[49] The Turkish P&I Club is the first and only company established in Türkiye in club insurance, with its headquarters in Istanbul.

In conclusion, with the establishment of Turkish P&I, the first step towards developing the club insurance industry has been taken. However, establishing a domestic Club alone is insufficient to achieve this goal. Countries like Türkiye, taking their first steps in the club insurance industry, need an appropriate legal policy. Attempting to develop club insurance with an interventionist legal approach slows this goal. Therefore, Türkiye's current legal policy should prioritize contract freedom in club insurance and provide legal validity to Club rules.

## III. Analysis of the Legal Classification of Club Insurance in English Law

One of the arguments advocated in the book is that one of the main reasons behind the leadership position of England in the club insurance industry is attributed to its legal policy. Each section in this chapter will examine several aspects of

48 Alganturk, 213; Peksen, 106; Keceli, 93.
49 Türk P&I, "About TPI" https://turkpandi.com/ accessed 28 April 2023.

how club insurance is positioned legally in England. Examining the fundamental characteristics of club insurance and how it is classified in English law will guide countries aiming to develop club insurance in determining what kind of changes they need to make in their legal systems.

### *A. The Distinctive Characteristics of Club Insurance Compared to Other Marine Insurance Types*

This title will explore club insurance's varying features and aspects compared to other marine insurance. Marine insurance is a type of insurance that provides coverage against damages and risks occurring at sea.[50] P&I Club insurance, on the other hand, is a distinct form of insurance within the scope of marine insurance, characterized by its unique set of rules. The MIA 1906[51] defines marine insurance contracts as agreements committing to indemnify losses suffered by the insured to the extent and manner stipulated in the contract due to maritime risks and perils.[52]

The extant provisions of the MIA 1906 also clarify the concepts of maritime adventure and maritime perils. In the context of the MIA 1906, a maritime adventure pertains to situations where a ship, goods, or other movable property is exposed to maritime perils. Accordingly, a maritime adventure occurs when the insured subject matter is exposed to maritime perils.[53] The subject matter of any marine insurance contract is one of the three maritime adventures detailed by Section 3(2) of the MIA 1906.

The first instance of a maritime adventure, as specified by the MIA 1906, involves the exposure of any ship, goods, or other movable property to maritime perils. Such property is referred to as "insurable property." The MIA 1906 further encompasses scenarios where the earning or obtaining of freight, passage money, commission, profit, or other pecuniary benefits, or securing any advances, credits, or payments is jeopardized due to the exposure of insurable property to maritime perils.[54] Furthermore, MIA 1906 considers any liability incurred by the owner of the insurable property or by any person concerned or responsible for them, arising from maritime perils, as constituting a maritime adventure.[55]

50 Gurses, 12; Bennett, *Marine Insurance*, 22.

51 Marine Insurance Act 1906, s 1.

52 According to Marine Insurance Act 1906, Section 1: "A contract of marine insurance is a contract whereby the insurer undertakes to indemnify the assured, in manner and to the extent thereby agreed, against marine losses, that is to say, the losses incident to marine adventure."

53 Gurses, 13.

54 See Marine Insurance Act 1906, s 3/2: "(a) Any ship goods or other moveables are exposed to maritime perils. Such property is in this Act referred to as 'insurable property'; (b) The earning or acquisition of any freight, passage money, commission, profit, or other pecuniary benefit, or the security for any advances, loan, or disbursements, is endangered by the exposure of insurable property to maritime perils; (c) Any liability to a third party may be incurred by the owner of, or other person interested in or responsible for, insurable property, by reason of maritime perils."

55 Gurses, 13.

To briefly discuss the doctrine of insurable interest, this principle aims to serve two functions. Its primary function is to play an influential role in enforcing public policy that prohibits the use of marine insurance contracts through gambling or betting. The second function is to establish a prerequisite for the insured's right to compensation in the event of any accident, which is the existence of the insured's insurable interest.

However, according to Bennett, this doctrine does not provide a beneficial contribution to insurance contract law in both respects.[56] While Bennett acknowledges the appropriateness of the Act's prohibition of betting on the outcomes of maritime adventures to prevent an increase in specific risks, he finds it unnecessary for this policy to be considered within the framework of the insurable interest doctrine.[57] The policy against betting on the outcomes of maritime adventures reduces the risk of fraud against insurance companies, contributing to protecting the lives of the crew, the environment, and the goods of cargo owners.[58] However, determining whether an insurance contract violates this policy can be done without using the insurable interest doctrine.[59]

We must note our agreement with Bennett's criticisms on this matter. The stringent interpretation and application of the insurable interest doctrine within the framework of the MIA 1906, particularly from the perspective of insured parties, may lead to unjust outcomes. Therefore, we advocate for a more lenient evaluation of the doctrine, considering that such a rigid application could result in unfair consequences for insured parties. We will revisit this topic later, delving into the Law Commission's views, the doctrine's debates, and our general assessments of the "insurable interest."[60]

The concept of "maritime perils" encompasses any damage suffered by goods transported on a ship due to seawater, storms, collisions, grounding, or other hazards specific to maritime vessels. These perils are unanticipated as necessary or incidents of a contemplated adventure by the shipowner or the crew onboard. The definition of "maritime peril" was scrutinized by the English Court in *Xantho*,[61] where a vessel carrying goods sank because of a collision. During this examination, emphasis was placed on whether the vessel carrying the goods was at fault. In cases where the shipowner is at fault, relying on the "perils of the sea and accidents" exception is not a means to escape liability. Likewise, engaging in negligent behaviour eliminates the shipowner's chance of relying on maritime perils. When examining the point of fault in the case, Lord Herschell stated, "A loss by foundering, owing to a vessel coming into collision

56 Howard Bennett, "The Marine Insurance Act 1906: Reflections on a Century" (2006) 18 *Singapore Academy of Law Journal* 669.

57 Bennett, "Reflections".

58 Bennett, "Reflections".

59 Bennett, "Reflections".

60 See Chapter 1, "Members" title.

61 *Thomas Wilson Sons & Co v Owners of Cargo of the Xantho (The Xantho)* [1887] LR 12 App Cas 503 (HL) per Lord Herschell at 509.

with another vessel, even when the collision results from the negligence of that other vessel, falls within the 'perils of the sea' category."[62] Therefore, as a result of this case, a collision or any risk, even if caused by the negligence of the crew, may still be considered a "maritime peril" by the Court unless it was previously foreseeable.

Maritime peril denotes consequences arising from the unique dangers of navigation at sea, occurring fortuitously.[63] Some restrictions have been imposed in insurance policies and court judgements regarding the scope of maritime perils. For instance, within these limitations, the effects of wind and waves, whether ordinary or inevitable, and situations such as water ingress due to the opening of hatches do not fall within the scope of maritime perils. Maritime perils include grounding, sinking, fire, vessel loss, piracy, capture, war risks, jettisoning cargo into the sea, seizure, barratry, and other unforeseeable dangers.[64]

The MIA 1906 intentionally broadened the limits of obligations that could be considered within the scope of maritime adventure.[65] This implies that any material or physical damage for which shipowners or other relevant parties are responsible during the operation of the ship is encompassed by marine insurance contracts. Therefore, these individuals have insurable interests, and marine insurance contracts maintain legal validity in such cases. Maritime insurance is a significant component of the maritime industry, and the concepts of maritime adventure and maritime perils, as defined in the MIA 1906, continue to impact the scope of coverage within insurance contracts significantly. However, it should be noted that the parties to the contract have the freedom to agree on the limits of liability, and careful examination of the policy is necessary to identify the covered risks and perils.[66]

Nevertheless, the definitions of "maritime perils" and "maritime adventure" in the MIA 1906 have faced criticism due to their outdated language and ambiguity. According to Section 3(2) of the MIA 1906,

> "Maritime perils" means the perils consequent on, or incidental to, the navigation of the sea, that is to say, perils of the seas, fire, war perils, pirates, rovers, thieves, captures, seisures, restraints, and detainments of princes and peoples, jettisons, barratry, and *any other perils*, either of the like kind *or which may be designated by the policy.*
>
> (emphasis in original)

62 *Thomas Wilson Sons & Co v Owners of Cargo of the Xantho (The Xantho)* [1887] LR 12 App Cas 503 (HL) per Lord Herschell at 509.

63 Giulia Argano, "Pirates: A Charterers' Peril of the Sea" (2011) 1 *Southampton Student Law Review* 169.

64 Argano, "Pirates".

65 Zehra Seker, *Insurance Coverage in The Transport of Cargo by Sea* (Beta Basım Yayın, Istanbul 2001) 46.

66 Gurses, 227.

Merkin states that the phrases "or which may be designated by the policy" and "any other perils" mentioned in the concluding sentences of the definition of maritime perils have been interpreted to encompass risks similar in nature to those specified in the Lloyd's SG policy, indicating the need for explicit statements to broaden the scope further.[67] However, these phrases in the law do not permit the designation of non-marine risks as the subject matter of a marine insurance policy.[68]

Seker states that MIA 1906 deliberately avoids defining the concept of maritime adventure not to limit the scope of liability that could be considered within maritime adventure and maritime perils.[69] This implies that the boundaries of maritime perils and maritime adventure can be freely determined by the parties to the contract.

Bennett criticizes this definition in the MIA 1906 for encompassing situations that may not apply to contemporary conditions and for ambiguously expanding the scope of maritime perils. According to him, elements such as "rovers" and "restraints and detainments of princes and peoples" are no longer relevant to modern maritime policies.[70] Additionally, the phrase "either of the like-kind or which may be designated by the policy" creates uncertainty that could lead to the interpretation that non-maritime dangers fall within the scope of "maritime perils." While court judgements attempt to clarify the limits of "maritime perils," MIA 1906 requires reconsideration to reflect contemporary conditions better.[71] For instance, expanding the scope of maritime perils to include any risk specified in the policy poses challenges in determining the existence of such risks. When interpreted, this phrase carries the risk of considering a peril as a maritime peril even without any maritime connection. However, while expressing concerns that the definitions in the MIA 1906 may not be adaptable to present-day conditions and may lead to an uncertain expansion of the scope of maritime perils, the English Courts adopted a cautious approach.[72] In cases where it is necessary to define maritime perils to determine the existence of a maritime adventure, courts refer to the definitions without adhering strictly to them, opting instead to establish the limits of these risks through court judgements based on the specifics of each case.[73] For example, in *Re London County Commercial Reinsurance*,[74] the Court determined that a risk specified in the policy was not specific to maritime adventure, concluding that the

67 Merkin, *Legal History*, para. 17–022.

68 Merkin, *Legal History*.

69 Seker, 46.

70 Bennett, *Marine Insurance*, 24.

71 For example, *Global Process Systems Inc v Syarikat Takaful Malaysia Berhad (The Cendor MOPU)* [2011] UKSC 5; *T. M. Noten BV v Paul Charles Harding* [1990] EWCA Civ J0621–4; *J J Lloyd Instruments Ltd v Northern Star Insurance Co Ltd (The Miss Jay Jay)* [1985] 1 Lloyd's Rep 264 (QBD (Comm Ct)); *Mountain v Whittle* [1921] AC 615.

72 *Continental Illinois National Bank & Trust Co of Chicago v Bathurst (The Captain Panagos DP)* [1988] EWCA Civ J0729–10.

73 Bennett, *Marine Insurance*, 24.

74 *Re London County Commercial Reinsurance Office Ltd* [1922] 2 Ch.

contract was not a marine insurance contract.[75] Therefore, while concerns about the adaptability of the definitions in the MIA 1906 to present-day conditions and the ambiguous expansion of the scope of maritime perils are valid, the approach of English courts to determine the existence of maritime perils and maritime adventure based on the requirements of each concrete case, without strictly adhering to these definitions, effectively mitigates these concerns.

Nevertheless, considering the continuously evolving and changing nature of maritime adventures, a need arises to update definitions and regulations to effectively address the increasing variety of risks that may be encountered.[76] The absence of definite boundaries in the law makes it challenging to determine whether specific perils are related to maritime matters, complicating determining coverage within marine insurance contracts.[77] Therefore, a more explicit definition of the connection between hazards that may occur at sea and the maritime industry is required to ensure the coverage of risks within marine insurance contracts.[78] While it is acknowledged that English court judgements serve as a crucial tool in establishing these boundaries, it is essential to recognize that not every specific case is brought before the court, and the relevant regulations of the MIA 1906, as advocated by Bennett[79] and Merkin,[80] should be reviewed.

It should be noted that the term "maritime adventure" is specifically used in cases where ships or cargoes are exposed to hazards at sea. Marine insurance contracts are subject to the same principles of contract law as other insurance contracts.[81] However, the technical, commercial, and geographical terms commonly used in maritime trade and found in marine insurance policies require a comprehensive understanding of these contracts to be effectively interpreted.[82] P&I insurance, which falls under liability insurance covering legal responsibilities towards third parties related to or arising from the navigation, is one type of marine insurance contract.[83] Unlike other types of marine insurance, P&I insurance is not regulated by law in any legal system, including English law.[84] However, P&I Clubs in England often refer to the MIA 1906 and the IA 2015 in their insurance policies.

75 Bennett, *Marine Insurance*, 24.
76 Ucar, 33.
77 Ucar, 33.
78 Bennet emphasizes that the rules codified by the MIA 1906 are rooted in incredibly old foundations and underscores the necessity for reform. He provides examples to illustrate that many provisions of this Act do not serve a useful purpose. For instance, he argues that limiting the policy to a paper document impedes the development of electronic commerce, and he advocates the need for reform by pointing out that most definitions in the Act are no longer aligned with modern commercial practices. See Bennett, "Reflections", 678.
79 Bennett, "Reflections".
80 Merkin, *Legal History*, para. 17–022.
81 Lin, 26.
82 Lin, 26.
83 Terence Coghlin, "Protection & Indemnity Clubs" (1984) *Lloyd's Maritime and Commercial Law Quarterly* 403.
84 Acar, *Club Insurance*, 14.

The MIA 1906, established during the 18th and 19th centuries in the UK based on common law principles, initially focused on regulating marine insurance but gradually extended its application to various commercial insurance sectors. Over time, it became apparent that the legislation, designed to protect insurers from exploitation, inadvertently created disparities in rights and obligations between insurers and policyholders. Recognizing these shortcomings, the Law Commission proposed reforms to modernize non-consumer insurance law, leading to the enactment of the IA 2015. This Act, which took effect on 12 August 2016, introduced significant changes relevant to P&I Clubs in the UK, affecting the Clubs more than a century after the enactment of the MIA 1906.

The IA 2015 amended specific provisions of the MIA 1906 to address issues such as inflexibility and inadequate remedies for breach of disclosure duties, aiming to restore balance and effectiveness in the insurance industry.

The primary purpose of the IA 2015 is to establish a fairer balance between the insurance company and the insured. However, the IA 2015 only provides a default regime, and contract parties can waive a massive portion of this law through contractual agreements. The Law Commission explicitly stated in its 2014 report that this flexibility is expected, noting,

> In some sophisticated markets, including the marine insurance market, we expect contracting out will be more widespread. The enormous value of the UK insurance market depends on the existence of a flexible legal regime which allows non-standard risks to be written. Given the range of risks which may be covered by the non-consumer regime, parties may need the freedom to agree on bespoke arrangements in their contracts.[85]

Accordingly, insurance companies can enter contracts specifying terms that exclude the provisions of the IA 2015.

Similarly, there is significant contractual freedom[86] in insurance contracts between P&I Clubs and their members.[87] Each P&I Club has its own "rules" governing the relationships between the Club and its members and among the members

85 Law Commission and Scottish Law Commission, Insurance Contract Law: Business Disclosure; Warranties; Insurers' Remedies for Fraudulent Claims; And Late Payment (Law Com No 353, Scot Law Com No 238, 2014) para. 29.25.

86 The principle of freedom of contract is based on the belief in laissez-faire, which holds that the courts should minimize their interference in the affairs of individuals. See further: Scott Salisbury, "The Principle of Freedom of Contract: Are the Courts Too Interventionist?" (2016) 5 *Manchester Review of Law, Crime and Ethics* 58; Paul Richards, *Law of Contract* (11th edn, Pearson 2013) 151.

87 e.g., North of England P&I Club Rule 6: "These Rules and all contracts of insurance made by North UK or North EU shall be subject to and incorporate the provisions of the Marine Insurance Act 1906 and the Insurance Act 2015 and any statutory modifications thereof except insofar as such Acts or modifications may have been expressly excluded by these Rules or by any term of such contract."; Steamship Mutual P&I Club Rule 2(x): "To the extent that these Rules and any Certificate of Entry or other policy document issued hereunder are subject to the English Insurance Act 2015, from its entry into force."

themselves.[88] Therefore, most English P&I Clubs specify in their Club rules that certain sections of the law will not apply to insurance contracts between the member and the Club, and the Club's own rules will prevail.[89]

However, insurance companies and Clubs cannot enter contracts contrary to the IA 2015 in two areas. Firstly, according to section 9(2) of the IA 2015, a statement made by an insured before the contract cannot be considered as a warranty through a contract provision such as the "basis of the contract" clause. This means that insurance companies can no longer rely on such a provision to avoid liability arising from it. Instead, they must prove that a statement pertains to a specific warranty, the breach of which would result in a proportionate remedy. Secondly, Section 13A of the IA 2015 implies a condition for reimbursing claims for non-consumer insurance contracts within a reasonable time. Due to this implied condition, the IA 2015 does not allow a waiver to prevent liability for intentionally or maliciously not paying a claim within a reasonable time.

English P&I Clubs are affected by the IA 2015 because their Club rules are subject to English law. A consensus between English P&I Clubs and the International Group of Protection and Indemnity Clubs (IG) is to waive certain aspects of the IA 2015 while adopting specific provisions of the IA 2015 that clarify ambiguities present in the MIA 1906. For example, Clubs have accepted the "fair presentation of risk and the duty of disclosure" regimes in Sections 3–7 of the IA 2015. This is because of the fair presentation and the professional evaluation of risk-benefit both Club members and the Club mutually. However, Clubs have regulated the consequences of their members violating the "proper disclosure" obligation more rigorously in their Club rules than in the IA 2015. Therefore, the weakened provisions in Section 8 of the IA 2015 are excluded from contractual agreements. This choice aims to prevent circumvention of the policy against unfair presentation of the risk.

P&I insurance distinguishes itself from other types of marine insurance in several significant ways.[90] For a shipowner who enters their ship into a Club, a premium (referred to as a "call" in the Club's rules) must be paid within the framework of mutual insurance to contribute to covering the damages claimed by the members. Primarily, the Clubs do not operate to make a profit from these premiums collected while providing insurance services to their members. The principle

88 For example, UK P&I Club Rule 5/L(i): "The following provisions of the Insurance Act 2015 ('the Act') are excluded from the Rules and any contract of insurance as follows: a) Section 8 of the Act is excluded. As a result, any breach of the duty of fair presentation shall entitle the Association to avoid the policy, regardless of whether the breach of the duty of fair presentation is innocent, deliberate or reckless." Britannia Class 3 Rule 3/C; Steamship Mutual Club Class 1 Rule 7(iv); North of England P&I Club Rule 6(2) (b), (c); London Class 5 Rule 43 etc.

89 Baris Soyer, *Warranties in Marine Insurance* (Cavendish Publishing 2006) 116.

90 For a comprehensive analysis arguing for the classification of Club insurance as insurance despite these differences, see Rhidian Thomas, "Protection and Indemnity Insurance: Is It Truly Insurance?" in Ozlem Gurses (ed), *Research Handbook on Marine Insurance Law* (Edward Elgar Publishing 2024) Ch 2, 39.

of "mutuality"[91] forms the foundation of P&I insurance, and members commit to financially supporting each other against incidents for which they are legally liable to compensate.[92] Despite not aiming for profit, P&I Clubs must balance gains and losses to prevent losses and meet their members' claims.[93] Therefore, the premiums collected from members are closely monitored. In the event of a claim against the Club by a member, if the case is successful, the claim is paid from the contributions of all members, including the claimant. Thus, each member occupies the roles of both insurer and insured.[94]

Another distinctive feature of club insurance is the scope of the liability insurance it provides to its members. Concerning P&I insurance, coverage encompasses the decrease in assets resulting from a member's payment of damages to a third party. In this regard, Clubs offer their members a broad range of liabilities. Within this scope, various liabilities include loss of life and personal injury to the crew, passengers, and other persons on board, loss and damage to cargo, pollution caused by oil and other hazardous substances, wreck removal, collision, and property damage. "Protection" refers to the insurance coverage related to members' liabilities to personnel and property, while "indemnity" encompasses a member's liabilities towards cargo owners under the carriage contract.[95] Unlike traditional liability insurance, P&I insurance makes payments directly to the member responsible for compensating the third party, not to the third party who has suffered direct damage. This distinction is crucial because it implies that the member must compensate for the damage before claiming a decrease in their assets from the Club according to the insurance policy terms. The "pay to be paid"[96] rule sets P&I insurance apart from traditional liability insurance, where the insurer guarantees and compensates for the damage caused by the insured to third parties under the coverage. This topic will be further elaborated in subsequent sections.

### B. *Classification of Club Insurance as Liability Insurance and Its Impact on Third Parties' Direct Action Rights*

This section will examine the legal debates in English law regarding the classification of club insurance as liability insurance. It will explain why the discussions surrounding the classification of club insurance as liability insurance lost their significance after English courts accepted the "pay to be paid" rule.

Before delving into the debate over whether P&I insurance is a liability or indemnity insurance, it is necessary to examine liability insurance's legality and

91 According to the Marine Insurance Act of 1906, s 85, mutuality: "Where two or more persons mutually agree to insure each other against marine losses there is said to be a mutual insurance."

92 Didem Alganturk Light, *Club Insurance in Marine Insurance Law* (Arikan 2006) 25.

93 Lin, 27.

94 Thomas, "Protection and Indemnity", 34.

95 Gurses, 8.

96 For detailed information about "pay to be paid" rule, see Chapter 3.

morality dimensions. In England, liability policies outside of marine insurance only emerged in the second half of the 19th century. The argument against their legality stemmed from judicial decisions initially prioritizing responsibility over compensation, thereby viewing liability insurance with suspicion due to concerns about "moral hazard."[97] The underlying premise was that liability insurance rewarded individuals for their unlawful actions.[98] Concerns that an insured individual might become careless by relying on this insurance, making it easier for them to engage in threatening actions against others' property or lives, fuelled prejudice and concerns against this type of insurance.[99]

In England, the earliest case that can be linked to liability insurance is *Catherine v Anna*.[100] The policy in question insured the liability of the captors in the event of the loss or damage to the ship or cargo. The court accepted that the insurance was taken out for the captors' own security. In this ruling, there was no challenge to the policy's validity. However, in *Delanoy v Robson*,[101] the defendant argued that it would be illegal to insure against the consequences of wrongful acts.[102] Doubts regarding the legality of liability insurance were dispelled in the 1832 case of *Crowley v Cohen*,[103] where the court upheld the validity of a policy covering the carrier's liability to third-party cargo owners.

Similarly, in the 1836 case of *De Vaux v Salvador*,[104] the issue of the validity of a policy insuring the shipowner's liability for collision was not contested. The Merchant Shipping Act Amendment Act 1862, section 55, further solidified the legality of insuring risks that occur without the insured's actual fault or knowledge. The Merchant Shipping Act of 1854[105] was significant in England's evolution of civil liability insurance. Section 506 of the Act[106] stipulated that shipowners' civil liability for death, bodily damage, and other developments could be insured.[107]

97 Merkin and Steele, 64.

98 Christopher Parsons, "Moral Hazard in Liability Insurance" (2003) 28(3) *The Geneva Papers on Risk and Insurance: Issues and Practice* 448, 455.

99 Parsons, "Moral Hazard in Liability Insurance", 454.

100 *Catherine v Anna* (1801) 4 C Rob 39.

101 *Delanoy v Robson* (1814) 5 Taunt 605: "It would be an illegal insurance to insure against what might be the consequences of the wrongful acts of the assured."

102 Merkin and Steele, 65; Merkin, *Legal History*, para. 9–142.

103 *Crowley v Cohen* (1832) 3 B & Ad 478.

104 *De Vaux v Salvador* (1836) 4 Ad. & E. 420.

105 Merchant Shipping Act 1854, s 506.

106 According to s 506 of the Act: "An insurance effected against the happening, without the owner's actual fault or privity, of any or all of the events in respect of which the liability of owners is limited under this Part of this Act shall not be invalid by reason of the nature of the risk."

107 Listed circumstances in s 503 of the Act: "The owners of a ship, British or foreign, shall not, where all or any of the following occurrences take place without their actual fault or privity; (that is to say,) (a)Where any loss of life or personal injury is caused to any person being carried in the ship;(b)Where any damage or loss is caused to any goods, merchandise, or other things whatsoever on board the ship;(c)Where any loss of life or personal injury is caused to any person carried in any other vessel by reason of the improper navigation of the ship;(d)Where any loss or damage is caused to any other vessel, or to any goods, merchandise, or other things whatsoever on board any

The MIA 1906[108] recognized the insurable interest of the shipowner's civil liability to third parties. The Act granted the parties to the contract broad freedom of contract concerning insurable responsibilities, which allowed for the coverage of many risks by P&I insurance. This freedom of contract was particularly crucial for developing and strengthening P&I Clubs in England, where they insured more comprehensive responsibilities and risks.

This debate continued in the United States, where the legal and moral aspects of insuring legal liability were questioned.[109] Holding someone accountable for causing harm to another was considered morally reprehensible and legally unenforceable.[110] Parsons described liability insurance as "insurance against carelessness" today.[111] The author argued that this insurance threatens to maintain public order, potentially encouraging individuals to act negligently.[112] Simultaneously, the author pointed out a contradictory situation between the nature of liability insurance as "insurance against carelessness" and the insurers' behaviour of encouraging clients to be cautious.[113] However, implementing Parsons' ideas in contemporary conditions seems unlikely. Criticisms that liability insurance encourages negligence are based on assumptions that lack concrete and objective data. The contribution of liability insurance to the development of economic activities should not be disregarded.[114] Today, liability insurance and other types of insurance cover personal and commercial risks, making them an integral part of the economic atmosphere.[115]

The recognition that underwriting civil liability serves the public interest and has a social function began to emerge globally in the latter half of the 20th century. Today, no debate exists about liability insurance's legal and moral validity. Even criminal liability can be insured within certain limits.

While trivial in contemporary times, the discussion of whether P&I insurance should be categorized as liability or indemnity insurance holds significance in understanding the historical context of P&I Clubs and their desire to limit their responsibilities towards third parties concerning direct action claims. There is no consistent view on whether the primary purpose of liability insurance is to protect the policyholder from ruinous claims or to compensate third-party victims in the event of insolvency. This ambiguity arises from the complexity of interpreting the

---

other vessel, by reason of the improper navigation of the ship; be liable to damages beyond the following amounts; (that is to say,)."

108 Marine Insurance Act 1906, s 3(2) (c).

109 For detailed information, see Kenneth S. Abraham, *The Liability Century: Insurance and Tort Law from the Progressive Era to 9/11* (Harvard University Press 2009) 245.

110 Willard Phillips, *Treatise on the Law of Insurance* (New York 1823) 158.

111 Parsons, 454.

112 Parsons, 454.

113 Parsons, 455.

114 Competition and Consumer Protection Commission, "Public Liability Insurance Market Study" (2020) https://www.ccpc.ie/business/wp-content/uploads/sites/3/2020/12/2020.12.22-CCPC-Public-Liability-Insurance-Market-Study accessed 3 December 2023.

115 Competition and Consumer Protection Commission, "Public Liability Insurance Market Study".

purpose of liabilities and the courts' uncertainty regarding the extent to which they can stretch policy terms to reflect the nature and purpose of the insurance.[116]

There are three main reasons for this situation: Firstly, the tension between the two objectives becomes crucial only when the claimant's sole means of obtaining compensation is the defendant's insurance. When the defendant has their own resources, policy recovery is seen as compensating a first-party loss, and the broader social function of liability is not considered.[117] Adjusting judgements based on perceptions of the defendant's financial position would be inappropriate. Secondly, every judicial ruling sets a precedent regarding the terms' meaning. Adopting a strained interpretation to fit the facts of a particular case would be wrong, as it could have implications for other policyholders, the market, and reinsurers.[118] Thirdly, coverage terms in some policies might express exclusions in others, necessitating consistent interpretation. For instance, policies may limit coverage by setting deductibles and specifying the maximum recoverable amount for each event, occurrence, cause, or claim.[119]

Some judgements can be explained by the desire to protect third-party claims and by interpreting policy terms to compensate victims.[120] However, courts often decide similar cases on traditional grounds without focusing on third-party claims. In such situations, courts have acknowledged the consequences of their decisions, mainly when the insured is insolvent, expressing concerns about whether the third party will receive compensation.[121] Thus, although many court rulings indicate that liability insurance primarily protects the policyholder rather than third parties,[122] in the past, the clubs have preferred to define themselves as indemnity insurers to mitigate their liabilities toward third parties fully. Hazelwood also supported this view, arguing that the Clubs are indemnity insurers.[123] However, this debate has lost its relevance in England, primarily due to the "pay to be paid" rule. This rule, considered valid by English Courts, allows Clubs to eliminate direct action claims by third parties. Thus, irrespective of whether Clubs are classified as liability or indemnity insurers, they can avoid direct action claims by third parties.

In a liability insurance policy, the insured pays a premium, and the insurer must meet the insured's claims without any additional contributions from the insured.[124] However, in P&I insurance, the insured must fulfil their obligations, and the Club pays the member only if they meet the specified conditions in the Club rules.[125]

116 Merkin and Steele, 74.
117 Merkin and Steele, 74.
118 Merkin and Steele, 74.
119 Merkin and Steele, 74.
120 *BAI (Run Off) Ltd v Durham* [2012] UKSC 14.
121 *Pioneer Concrete v National Employers Mutual Insurance* [1985] 1 Lloyd's Rep 274.
122 *Pioneer Concrete v National Employers Mutual* Insurance [1985] 1 Lloyd's Rep 274; *Aspen Insurance UK Ltd v Pectel Ltd* [2008] EWHC 2804 (Comm).
123 Hazelwood and Semark, 335.
124 Alganturk, 81; Acar, *Club Insurance*, 26.
125 For detailed information, see Chapter 3.

Therefore, while P&I insurance shares similarities with liability insurance, it also has unique features that differentiate it from classic liability insurance. Nevertheless, according to English law, these differences do not preclude P&I insurance from being classified as liability insurance.

### C. Classification of Club Insurance as Voluntary and Its Impact on Third Parties' Direct Action Rights

#### 1. In English Law

This analysis will examine club insurance, categorized as voluntary insurance, and its implications for the direct action rights of third parties. Examining and determining the compulsory/voluntary nature of P&I insurance in English law, particularly regarding the direct action rights of third parties, holds significance.[126] Before delving into this examination within the framework of P&I insurance, it is beneficial to discuss the scope of compulsory insurance in England and the preferred legal regime.

Compulsory insurance is an effective mechanism for ensuring the efficient compensation of damages to third parties.[127] In a legal system, the prescription of compulsory insurance implies a legal preference.[128] The underlying rationale for this preference is to facilitate the prompt and complete compensation of the third party.[129] In England, compulsory insurance within the realm of private insurance is regulated explicitly by law only concerning liabilities.[130] For instance, since 1930, routine liabilities arising from road traffic have been encompassed by compulsory liability insurance enacted by the legislative body.[131] This compulsory insurance is envisaged to be undertaken consciously to facilitate the compensation of third parties arising from traffic accidents. In legislating this compulsory insurance, the legislative body in England has also defined the scope and conditions of its applicable requirements.

Another area in England where compulsory liability insurance is legislatively regulated pertains to liabilities arising from workplace accidents.[132] In addition to compulsory insurance regulations, England has embraced a "strict" liability regime for injuries resulting from workplace accidents since 1897.[133]

One of the significant functions of compulsory insurance is to effectively protect third parties who suffer damage from the insured's tort.[134] In this context,

126 Rhidian Thomas (ed), *The Modern Law of Marine Insurance: Volume Five* (Informa Law 2023) 69.

127 Yueyun Chen and Dongmei Chen, "The Review and Analysis of Compulsory Insurance" (2013) 4(1) *Insurance Markets and Companies: Analyses and Actuarial Computations* 11.

128 Merkin and Steele, 256.

129 Erik Røsæg, "Compulsory Maritime Insurance" (2000) 25(2) *Scandinavian Institute of Maritime Law Yearbook* 3; Chen and Chen, 11.

130 Merkin and Steele, 256.

131 Merkin and Steele, 260.

132 Employers' Liability (Compulsory Insurance) Act 1969 (the 1969 Act).

133 Merkin and Steele, 253.

134 Norman A Martinez Gutierrez and Raymon van Anrooy, "Compulsory Insurance (Third-Party Liability) Requirements for Fishing Vessels: A Case for the Introduction of Compulsory Fishing

compulsory liability insurance is a crucial instrument in remedying damages resulting from tort liability.[135] Third parties can benefit from compulsory insurance to compensate for damages arising from tort liability.[136]

The legislative prescription of compulsory liability insurance as a legal obligation for the adequate protection of third parties is insufficient. In addition to the legislative regulation of compulsory insurance, other conditions necessary for third parties to claim this compensation from insurers must also be stipulated and established by law.[137] For instance, the legal regime must specify whether insurers can raise defences arising from the policy against third parties, whether the legal regulation alters policy rights, and whether direct action rights against the insurer are granted to third parties.[138] It is crucial to emphasize that the legal system must explicitly recognize the right of third parties to claim compensation from the insurer directly.[139] The achievement of the high-level protection goal of the compulsory insurance system for third parties depends on the explicit legal recognition of the direct action right of the third parties against insurers. Through this right, the third party who has suffered damage due to the insured's tort can file a lawsuit directly against the insurer without approaching the insured. In this regard, there is a tight relationship between the direct action right and compulsory insurance.[140] This right is granted to third parties by law when liability is within the scope of compulsory insurance.[141]

Another crucial point is the ability of the insurer to raise defences arising from the policy against the third party. Under general insurance contract law in England, insurers have various defences against compensation claims. These defences include the violation of the utmost good faith, deficiencies in coverage, or non-compliance with the policy terms by the insured.[142] Even in areas where compulsory insurance is regulated in law, advancing these defences by insurers can significantly complicate compensating third parties.[143]

In summary, examining and determining the compulsory/voluntary nature of P&I insurance in English law involves evaluating the legislative framework

---

Vessel Insurance in the Caribbean" (2020) *FAO Fisheries and Aquaculture Circular* 6.

135 Aysegul Bugra, "Room for Compulsory Product Liability Insurance in the European Union for Smart Robots? Reflections on the Compelling Challenges" in P. Marano and K. Noussia (eds), *InsurTech: A Legal and Regulatory View, AIDA Europe Research Series on Insurance Law and Regulation: Volume 1* (Springer, Cham 2020) https://doi.org/10.1007/978-3-030-27386-6_8 accessed 1 December 2023.

136 Bugra, "Room for Compulsory Product Liability Insurance in the European Union for Smart Robots? Reflections on the Compelling Challenges".

137 Merkin and Steele, 256.

138 Merkin and Steele, 256.

139 The Law Commission Consultation Paper No 121, Privity of Contract: Contracts for the Benefit of Third Parties, Appendix.

140 Thomas, *Volume Five*, 69.

141 Thomas, *Volume Five*, 69.

142 Bulent Sozer, *Unmanned Ships and the Law* (Informa Law from Routledge 2023) 153.

143 Sozer, *Unmanned Ships and the Law*.

governing compulsory insurance and the conditions under which third parties can directly claim compensation from insurers. The interaction between the legal regulation of compulsory insurance, the direct action right of third parties, and the ability of insurers to raise policy-based defences plays a critical role in protecting third parties from damages resulting from the insured's tort.

After discussing the compulsory insurance regime and the adopted legal approach in English law, it is necessary to determine how P&I insurance is positioned within the framework of English law, especially concerning the direct action rights of third parties. One of the reasons for this analysis is to determine that English law has a legal approach that emphasizes the development of P&I Club insurance, which is one of the main arguments of the book. This book argues that a country's legal policies significantly impact the development of P&I Club insurance. In this context, the compulsory insurance practice that expands the direct action rights of third parties is among the legal policies that most hinder the growth of the P&I Club insurance industry and Clubs. English law adopts an approach that acknowledges that compulsory insurance creates economic pressure on Clubs. If P&I Club insurance were to fall under compulsory insurance, Clubs could not rely on defences arising from Club rules against direct claims by third parties. They would have to meet these claims. To prevent this risk, England has adopted a legal policy that preserves the voluntary nature of P&I Club insurance.

P&I insurance is a type of voluntary insurance under English law. This insurance is not regulated as compulsory insurance under any law in England. However, as a general rule, it is challenging for a shipowner to use their ship for commercial activities without obtaining P&I insurance. For example, those leasing a ship request proof of a valid P&I entry certificate from the shipowner before entering into a lease agreement. Similarly, financial banks require P&I insurance to provide a loan secured by a mortgage on a ship. While P&I insurance is not legally mandated, practical indicators suggest its quasi-mandatory nature for the shipowner to continue their commercial activities.

In summary, the designation of P&I Club insurance as compulsory insurance in a legal system is linked to the ability of third parties to exercise direct action against the Club.[144] However, the designation of insurance as compulsory does not automatically grant third parties the right to sue the insurer directly. To effectively protect third parties through compulsory insurance, the law must also expressly grant third parties the right to bring a direct legal claim within the scope of this insurance. In England, since P&I insurance is not regulated as compulsory insurance, third parties do not have a general right to bring a direct claim against the Club.[145] Instead, third parties must fulfil certain conditions, such as the insured's

144 Thomas, *Volume Five*, 69.

145 Peter MacDonald Eggers, "Direct Action Against Insurers and P&I Clubs" in Baris Soyer and Andrew Tettenborn (eds), *Maritime Liabilities in a Global and Regional Context* (Informa Law from Routledge 2019) 168.

insolvency, before exercising such a right.[146] This topic will be detailed in the fifth section of the book. Thus, this heading will clarify the relationship between compulsory insurance and the direct action right of third parties.

In contrast to English law, efforts have been made in international maritime liability contracts to establish the relationship between club insurance and compulsory insurance explicitly.[147] The latter half of the 20th century witnessed a global movement toward recognizing the mandatory nature of marine insurance. This movement was motivated by the high-risk nature of maritime transportation activities, necessitating insurance coverage to prevent environmental disasters resulting from accidents involving ships and expedited compensation. To achieve these goals, the International Maritime Organization (IMO) regulates international agreements to ensure the safe conduct of international maritime trade.[148] Some types of marine insurance are mandated under IMO agreements as compulsory insurance.[149] For instance, after the "Torrey Canyon" incident in the UK waters in 1967, one of the most significant oil spills in terms of size and impact, the necessity and importance of compulsory insurance were emphasized.[150] Subsequently, various international agreements were enacted worldwide to prevent and minimize damage caused by oil pollution.[151]

The International Convention on Civil Liability for Oil Pollution Damage (CLC 1969)[152] is the first international agreement that mandates marine insurance concerning oil pollution. This convention aims to compensate and minimize environmental damage caused by tanker oil pollution. Unlike other international liability agreements, CLC 1969[153] adopts a strict liability regime rather than a fault-based liability.[154] This faultless liability regime has been adopted in later international legislation and contracts related to liability for environmental damage in maritime law. For example, the International Convention on Liability and Compensation for Damage in Connection with the Carriage of Hazardous and Noxious Substances by Sea (HNS) 1996,[155] modelled on CLC 1992, mandated marine insurance against marine pollution caused by dangerous and harmful substances. International

146 Eggers, "Direct Action Against Insurers and P&I Clubs".

147 Thomas, *Volume Five*, 69.

148 Sozer, 153.

149 Sozer, 153.

150 The enormously important oil-tanker spill that took place in European waters was the Torrey Canyon disaster of Cornwall, England, in 1967 (119,000 metric tons of crude oil were spilt). For detailed information, see Britannica, "Oil Spill". https://www.britannica.com/science/oil-spill#ref1085819 accessed 29 November 2020.

151 For example, International Convention on Civil Liability for Bunker Oil Pollution Damage 2001 (Bunkers Convention); The Nairobi International Convention on the Removal of Wrecks 2007 (Wreck Removal Convention).

152 International Convention on Civil Liability for Oil Pollution Damage 1969.

153 International Convention on Civil Liability for Oil Pollution Damage 1969 (as renewed in 1992).

154 Martinez and Anrooy, 6.

155 International Convention on Liability and Compensation for Damage in Connection with the Carriage of Hazardous and Noxious Substances by Sea (HNS) 1996.

conventions like the Bunkers Convention,[156] Athens Convention 2002,[157] and Wreck Removal Convention[158] have been envisioned based on CLC 92.[159]

While these contracts guide determining whether specific marine insurances are under the scope of compulsory insurance, they do not constitute sufficient grounds for categorizing P&I insurance as compulsory insurance in England. The fact that P&I Clubs have agreed to cover certain marine pollution damages under international agreements[160] does not serve as a convincing argument. As mentioned earlier, national legislation must expressly state this requirement as compulsory insurance. Since there is no such regulation in English law, P&I insurance cannot be considered compulsory insurance in the legal context. Restricting contractual freedom in P&I insurance through compulsory insurance practices is not a method favoured by English law.[161] For instance, after the implementation of the IA 2015, which provides the option to deviate from legal provisions through contracts, P&I Clubs have predominantly not engaged in the recent defaults reform in English insurance law.[162] Instead, they have adhered to their Club rules and contract arrangements. This flexibility is crucial for Clubs.

Similarly, expanding compulsory insurance coverage in England to include P&I insurance would undoubtedly increase the number of direct action claims against P&I Clubs. This is not a situation that the Clubs desire. English Courts have attempted to prevent direct action claims by upholding the "pay to be paid" rule favouring P&I Clubs in cases such as *Fanti and the Padre Island*.[163] Therefore, contrary to the international tendency, it does not seem likely that club insurance will be classified as compulsory insurance for P&I insurance shortly in England.[164]

156 International Convention on Civil Liability for Bunker Oil Pollution Damage 2001 (Bunkers Convention).

157 Protocol of 2002 to the Athens Convention relating to the Carriage of Passengers and their Luggage by Sea 1974 (Athens Convention 2002).

158 Nairobi International Convention on the Removal of Wrecks 2007 (Wreck Removal Convention).

159 Martinez and Anrooy, 6.

160 R Bhanu Krishna Kiran, "Liability and Compensation for Oil Pollution Damage: An Examination of IMO Conventions" (2010) 3 *NUJS L Rev* 399, 410.

161 For example, s 85 of the Marine Insurance Act 1906 explicitly acknowledges that the Act is applicable to mutual insurance. Furthermore, any provisions within the 1906 Act that are susceptible to modification through mutual agreement between the parties can indeed be altered by the mutual insurance agreement.

162 Malcolm Clarke and Baris Soyer (eds), *The Insurance Act 2015* (Informa Law from Routledge 2017) 94; David Kendall and Harry Wright, *A Practical Guide to the Insurance Act 2015* (Informa Law from Routledge 2017) 122; Thomas, *Volume Five*, 43.

163 *The Fanti and the Padre Island* [1990] 2 Lloyd's Rep 191. The legal validity of the "pay to be paid" rule was established in the *Fanti and the Padre Island* case. For analysis of the decision, see Chapter 4.

164 For example, the statement from the British Maritime Law Association argues against the necessity of compulsory insurance in the realm of marine insurance, asserting that such an initiative could be detrimental to the sector. See British Maritime Law Association, "The Role of Cargo Owners/Shippers and Marine Insurers in the Quality Shipping Campaign" (1999) https://www.bmla.org.uk/documents/the_role_of_cargo_owners.htm last accessed 30 November 2023.

2. *In Turkish law*

As stated in the book argument, Türkiye's legal policies regarding club insurance are interventionist and prioritize protecting third-party rights. This approach hinders the development of Clubs and club insurance. Because Turkish law opts for a legal policy that expands compulsory insurance practices, the boundaries of third parties' direct action rights are broadened. Consequently, Clubs are more frequently faced with third-party compensation claims. Legal reforms should be made in the context of the relationship between compulsory insurance and club insurance, thereby further supporting the voluntary nature of club insurance to enhance the development of the club insurance industry in Türkiye.

P&I insurance is categorized as compulsory insurance in some situations according to Turkish law. For instance, according to Article 5(1) of the "Regulation on the Requirement to Obtain Insurance Coverage for Vessels against Maritime Claims and Supervision Thereof,"[165] Turkish-flagged ships are required to have "protection and indemnity insurance" against maritime claims.[166] This regulation is a transposition of the provisions of Directive 2009/20/EC of the European Parliament and of the Council dated 23 April 2009[167] regarding the insurance of shipowners for maritime claims into domestic law.[168] As per the regulation, it is a legal obligation for ships meeting specified criteria, such as Turkish-flagged ships of 300 gross tons and above and ships entering or leaving port facilities within Turkish maritime jurisdiction, to obtain protection and indemnity insurance for maritime liens. This regulation outlines the responsibilities and criteria applicable to ships registered under the Turkish Flag and for vessels, irrespective of their flag state, entering or departing from ports, terminals, anchorages, and other port facilities within Turkish territorial waters. The aim is to ensure these vessels acquire insurance coverage for maritime claims and establish guidelines and processes for their oversight.[169]

165 "The Regulation on the Requirement to Obtain Insurance Coverage for Vessels against Maritime Claims and Supervision Thereof" Official Gazette No. 27759 dated 14.11.2010.

166 According to the regulation: Insurance for Maritime Claims: Article 5 – "(1) Shipowners of vessels flying Turkish flag are required to have their vessels insured under a protection and indemnity insurance policy against maritime claims. (2) Shipowners of vessels flying a flag other than Turkish flag are required to have a valid protection and indemnity insurance policy against maritime claims in place when such vessels enter a port facility included within the scope of this Regulation. (3) The insurance referred to in paragraphs 1 and 2 shall cover maritime claims subject to limitation under the framework of 1976 Convention and the Protocol of 1996. The amount of the insurance for each and every ship per incident shall be equal to the relevant maximum amount for the limitation of liability as laid down in the 1996 Convention."

167 Directive 2009/20/EC of the European Parliament and of the Council of 23 April 2009 on the Insurance of Shipowners for Maritime Claims.

168 Aysegul Bugra, "Compulsory Insurance of Shipowners for Maritime Claims" (2012) 12(9) *Shipping & Trade Law* 1.

169 Article 1(1) of "Regulation on the Requirement to Obtain Insurance Coverage for Vessels against Maritime Claims and Supervision Thereof."

Therefore, it is essential to note that within the framework of Turkish law, P&I insurance is mandated for specific risks.[170]

P&I Clubs providing liability insurance can be either Turkish or foreign entities. Another legal regulation that designates P&I insurance as compulsory insurance is Law No. 5312 on the Principles of Intervention in Emergency Situations and Compensation for Damages in the Pollution of the Marine Environment with Oil and Other Harmful Substances (Act 5312).[171] According to Article 8 of this Act, ships of 500 gross tons and above carrying oil and other harmful substances must obtain the insurance required for ships under international agreements to which Türkiye is a party.[172] Besides the obligation to procure insurance, there are also obligations to submit and report documents proving the procurement of this insurance to the relevant authorities. Another legal regulation is the "Regulation on Amendments to the Regulation on the Implementation of the Law on the Development of the Maritime Trade Fleet and the Promotion of Shipbuilding Facilities."[173] According to Article 5(1) of this Regulation, ships meeting the specified criteria must obtain P&I insurance.[174] The conditions for this insurance to be considered valid involve being provided by a P&I Club recognized by the Turkish Ministry of Transport and Infrastructure and the ship with continuous P&I insurance. These conditions are further detailed in the regulation.

These regulations show that in Turkish law, P&I insurance is compulsory for various situations. In addition to provisions requiring certain types of ships to have P&I insurance, there are also regulations governing the supervision of this obligation. Similarly, the obligation to obtain insurance is prescribed for the insured and insurers. In other words, insurance companies operating in the field of compulsory insurance included in this insurance branch cannot refrain from providing this service. For example, an insurance company or P&I Club offering P&I insurance in

170 Nuray Eksi, "Milletlerarası Özel Hukuk Açısından Sigortacıya Doğrudan Başvuru Hakkını Kısıtlayan veya Ortadan Kaldıran Yabancı Yasaların Türk Mahkemelerince Dikkate Alınıp Alınmayacağı" (2015) 4(2) *International Journal of Commercial and Arbitration Law* 31–64, 44.

171 The Principles of Intervention in Emergency Situations and Compensation for Damages in the Pollution of the Marine Environment with Oil and Other Harmful Substances Law No. 5312, Official Gazette No. 25752 dated 11.03.2005.

172 According to Article 8 of the Law No. 5312: "Ships carrying oil and/or other harmful substances that want to enter the application areas are obliged to have one of the financial responsibility documents required from them in accordance with the international agreements to which Türkiye is a party, to report them to the relevant authorities and to show them when requested."

173 The Regulation on the Implementation of the Law on the Development of the Maritime Trade Fleet and the Promotion of Shipbuilding Facilities from the Turkish Ministry of Transport, Maritime Affairs and Communications was published in the Official Gazette No. 29454 dated 23.08.2015.

174 See Article of 5 of the Regulation: "Insurance and class obligation: Article 5(1) To be imported within the scope of this Regulation; a) Ships; 1) Having a permanent P&I insurance issued by one of the P&I Clubs accepted by the Ministry, 2) It must be unconditionally classified from one of the accepted classification societies, 3) Having a valid boat and machinery insurance, it is mandatory. b) Water vehicles; 1) Having P&I insurance issued by one of the P&I Clubs accepted by the Ministry, 2) Having a condition survey report obtained from one of the classification societies accepted by the Ministry. 3) Having a valid boat and/or towing insurance, it is mandatory."

Türkiye must provide insurance services covering the specified risks under Turkish Insurance Law No. 5684.[175] Various monetary penalties are imposed on insurers due to non-compliance with this obligation.[176] Another legal provision prohibiting insurers from avoiding providing compulsory insurance in their respective fields is Article 1483 of the TCC No. 6102.[177] This article explicitly states that insurers cannot refrain from providing compulsory insurance within the scope of their branches, aiming to ensure this obligation bilaterally.[178]

When determining whether P&I insurance falls under the scope of compulsory insurance in Turkish law, we believe it is more accurate to do so within the framework of risk coverage.[179] This is because P&I insurance is explicitly mandated for specific risks and types of ships in the mentioned laws and regulations. For instance, in Act 5312, the obligation to obtain P&I insurance against the environmental risk posed by ships of 500 gross tons and above carrying oil and other harmful substances is explicitly stipulated, and there is no mandatory requirement for obtaining P&I insurance for a ship that does not possess these qualities. Therefore, evaluating within the framework of Turkish law, except for situations where P&I insurance is mandated as compulsory insurance, it should be considered voluntary insurance for other risks and ships.

For Türkiye, which aims to develop club insurance, a more suitable policy would be not to expand compulsory insurance coverage to the detriment of Clubs. Compulsory insurance practices associated with third parties' direct action rights against Clubs increase the economic pressure on Clubs. Undoubtedly, this increased pressure slows down the development of club insurance. Therefore, it is essential to emphasize the pursuit of a legal policy in Türkiye that highlights the voluntary nature of club insurance.

## IV. The Structure of P&I Clubs Sets Club Insurance Apart from Other Insurance Contracts

### *A. P&I Club*

This section will examine how the organizational structure of P&I Clubs distinguishes club insurance from other types of insurance contracts. It implies that the specific features and operations of P&I Clubs, such as their mutual nature, member-driven governance, and collective risk-sharing mechanisms, set them

175 Article 13(1) of Insurance Law No. 5684, published in the Official Gazette dated June 14, 2007, No. 26552.

176 Articles 34(2. b.) and 35(14) of the Law No. 5684.

177 According to Article 1483 of the Law No. 6102: "Subject to the provisions of other legislation, insurers shall not refrain from granting cover for compulsory insurances in the insurance classes, in which they are active."

178 Melis Konfidan, "Deniz Araçları Sorumluluk Sigortası Sözleşmesi (Marine Vehicles Liability Insurance Agreement)" (PhD thesis, Istanbul University Law Faculty 2020) 45.

179 For a similar view, see Acar, *Club Insurance*, 31.

apart from traditional insurance entities. Through an analysis of these structural elements, the research will elucidate how club insurance functions differently from other insurance arrangements, highlighting its distinct characteristics and implications for insured parties.

P&I Clubs are non-profit associations formed by shipowners, with the board of directors managing the Club on behalf of its members. English P&I Clubs have legal personalities and are registered in the companies register, with the applicable laws being the MIA 1906 and the Companies Act 2006.[180]

Members pay a premium based on their ship's tonnage to obtain P&I insurance coverage. The first premium payment is made at entry, and additional premiums are requested later, commonly known as a "call."[181] Some Clubs offer premium plans where a portion of the annual premium is deferred for later payment, referred to as "advance" and "deferred" calls.[182]

At the beginning of each policy year, Club managers assess the income from premiums to be paid by members. If the premium income is insufficient, a premium deficit may occur, resulting in members paying an additional premium, known as a "supplementary call."[183] To effectively manage the Club, managers must set a reasonable premium amount that considers all relevant factors, reducing the number of supplementary calls. However, due to the inherent risks of maritime transport, accurate premium estimation is not always possible, making a supplementary call unavoidable.

If the sum of the premium and investment income collected exceeds the total annual premium at the end of the policy year, the surplus is transferred to the Club's free reserve fund, which can be used for future risks.[184] The status of the Club's free reserve fund is an indicator of its financial strength.

Many English P&I Clubs are registered in offshore centres, such as Bermuda and Luxembourg, and daily operations are conducted in London or other regional offices. The main reason is to avoid heavy tax burdens and financial supervision in England, enabling Clubs to manage their funds independently.[185] Offshore centres enable Clubs to manage their funds more efficiently, but it raises questions about financial transparency and accountability.

P&I Clubs have remained independent in their management system and collaborated with others to share risks against potential damages, forming group P&I Clubs. With reinsurance agreements signed between group Clubs, it has become easier to cover more potential risks. The first group of P&I Clubs was established in 1899 with the Pooling Agreement signed by six English P&I Clubs.[186]

180 Hazelwood and Semark, 9.
181 Varisli, 59.
182 Varisli, 59.
183 Varisli, 59.
184 Lin, 27.
185 Acar, *Club Insurance*, 41.
186 The Standard Steamshipowners' Protection & Indemnity Association (Bermuda) Limited, The Steamship Mutual Underwriting Association (Bermuda) Limited, United Kingdom Mutual Steam

This agreement was later formally established as the International Group in 1979.[187] The International Group Agreement, signed by 13 P&I Clubs in 1999, is still in force today and includes the structure of IGP&I and reinsurance provisions. The IGP&I encompasses three fundamental functions. Firstly, it oversees loss-sharing arrangements, commonly denoted as "pooling," and engages in collective reinsurance of these arrangements. Secondly, it operates as a forum for convening and exchanging viewpoints among the Clubs and their shipowner members concerning shipowners' liability and insurance. Lastly, it assumes the role of a unified representative entity within the industry, facilitating interaction with external stakeholders, including intergovernmental maritime organizations, national governments, worldwide maritime authorities, and the maritime, marine insurance, and reinsurance industries.[188] Currently, over 90% of the world's merchant marine fleet is insured by the International Group of P&I Clubs (IGP&I), today with 12 P&I Clubs[189] being members of IGP&I.[190]

The Clubs maintain continuous communication and engagement with governments, flag state maritime administrations, intergovernmental organizations, maritime and insurance associations, as well as the media and the public through the IG.[191] In this regard, the IGP&I plays a crucial role in lobbying for the global maritime industry on matters concerning shipowners' liability and related marine insurance issues.

For example, among these lobbying activities, the IGP&I maintains constant contact with entities such as flag states, national maritime administrations and institutions, the EU, UN bodies and agencies, International Oil Pollution Compensation Funds, and the International Maritime Organization at the state/regulatory level, influencing their decisions.

Similarly, the IGP&I collaborates closely with international and national shipowners' associations, marine insurance associations, international and national seafarer associations, classification societies, and shipbuilding and equipment

---

Ship Assurance Association (Bermuda) Limited, The Shipowners' Mutual Protection & Indemnity Association (Luxembourg) and The West of England Shipowners Mutual Insurance Association (Luxembourg).

187 Peter Young, *Mutuality, the Story of UK Club* (Granta Editions 1995) Ch. 14.

188 International Group, "About Us" https://www.igpandi.org/about accessed 25 September 2023.

189 On 20 February 2023, North Club merged with Standard Club, resulting in the formation of a new entity known as "NorthStandard." Consequently, the total number of IGP&I members decreased from 13 to 12. See NorthStandard, "The New Name for North and Standard Club – a Guide to Documentation Changes". https://static.igpandi.org/igpi accessed 25 September 2023.

190 American Steamshipowners Mutual Protection and Indemnity Association, Inc., Assuranceforeningen Gard, Assuranceforeningen Skuld, The Britannia Steam Ship Insurance Association Limited, The Japan Shipowners' Mutual Protection & Indemnity Association, The London Steam-Shipowners' Mutual Insurance Association Limited, NorthStandard Limited, The Shipowners' Mutual Protection & Indemnity Association (Luxembourg), The Steamship Mutual Underwriting Association (Bermuda) Limited, The Swedish Club, United Kingdom Mutual Steam Ship Assurance Association (Bermuda) Limited, and The West of England Shipowners Mutual Insurance Association (Luxembourg).

191 International Group, "About Us" https://www.igpandi.org/about accessed 25 September 2023.

manufacturers in the maritime and marine insurance industries, actively participating in decision-making processes.

Hence, international organizations like the IGP&I play a significant role in shaping the legal and regulatory framework of the maritime insurance industry. Their lobbying efforts protect and advance P&I Clubs' interests within the global maritime community. Thus, providing shipowners with comprehensive insurance coverage supports the safe conduct of maritime trade activities. This fact is in line with the book's argument regarding the importance and impact of regulating protective legal policies to ensure the activities and economic stability of P&I Clubs.

The General Council is a significant Club organ that must hold at least one ordinary meeting annually. In addition to these meetings, the General Council has the right to hold extraordinary meetings if any urgent issue needs to be discussed. All members are required to attend ordinary meetings, and each member participating in the General Council has voting rights determined by the total gross tonnage of the ships registered to the Club, as clearly stated in the entry document of the members.[192]

The board of directors is another critical organ of the Club that is responsible for discussing and developing critical issues related to the Club's administration. This organ has the right to spend on all matters related to the administration of the Club, and according to the Club's rules, the board of directors exercises discretionary power in evaluating issues and requests within its authority. Moreover, the board of directors has broad authority to resolve disputes between members and the Club, determine the amount and time of payment of premiums to the Club, manage Club funds, regulate reinsurance relations, audit financial records, and determine policy periods.[193]

The managers are another essential unit of the Club, responsible for implementing decisions made by the board of directors, collecting premiums and contributions, appointing the reporter, conducting insurance activities, maintaining necessary records, and investigating member claims, among other tasks.[194]

One of the crucial elements of P&I Clubs' organizational structure is the role of correspondents. As the local representatives of P&I Clubs, correspondents are responsible for addressing any issues that may arise within their jurisdiction on behalf of Club members. Although not formally agents of the P&I Clubs, correspondents effectively act in their stead when resolving problems encountered by members or ship captains.[195] Additionally, correspondents are crucial in keeping the P&I Clubs apprised of legislative, legal, and technical developments within their respective countries, allowing them to issue relevant circulars and advisory opinions to their members quickly.[196]

192 Alganturk Light, 27.

193 Hazelwood and Semark, 23.

194 Hazelwood and Semark, 28.

195 Guidelines for Correspondents, "International Group of P&I Clubs" (2015) https://static.mycoracle.com/igpi_website/media/article_attachments/Guidelines-for-Correspondents-2015.pdf accessed 29 April 2023.

196 Guidelines for Correspondents, "International Group of P&I Clubs".

In the context of P&I Clubs, preventing loss and damage in marine accidents involving Club members is paramount. In such situations, the speed of the Club's response is crucial to resolve the incident effectively. Correspondents play a key role in facilitating rapid response in these circumstances and must, therefore, be equipped to intervene effectively, efficiently, and expeditiously in maritime accidents occurring within their jurisdiction.

The legal relationship between P&I Clubs and their correspondents is a significant aspect that determines the extent of the correspondent's responsibilities and the extent to which their actions legally bind the Club. Hazelwood suggests that this relationship is not a representation or agency relationship but a form of consultancy.[197] However, this viewpoint is debatable since correspondents can perform various operations by representing the Club and the members in certain situations. Acar contends that if the correspondent had not been authorized to represent the Club, they could not have taken many actions on behalf of the Club.[198] Therefore, the author argues that the legal relationship between the Club and the correspondent should be characterized as a form of representation.

Clarifying this relationship is essential to understand the responsibilities of the correspondent and the extent of their authority in resolving issues and making decisions on behalf of the Club. We advocate that the legal relationship between Clubs and correspondents should not be classified as agency or representation. Clubs aim to expedite the resolution of their members' claims through correspondents worldwide. However, members must notify the Club directly about their claims. Clubs reject notifications made to correspondents as invalid. If Clubs wanted to establish a representation or agency relationship with correspondents, they would do so explicitly through a contract.

Similarly, they would establish rules recognizing members' notifications to correspondents as valid. However, they have chosen not to do so. Clubs refer to the services of correspondents as independent advisory services.[199] This approach aims to eliminate the possibility of holding Clubs liable for damages resulting from the faults of correspondents. Therefore, it is not appropriate to characterize the legal relationship between Clubs and correspondents as one of representation or agency.[200] Correspondents should be recognized as independent advisors, as stated by the Clubs.

197 Hazelwood and Semark, 15.

198 Acar, *Club Insurance*, 54.

199 For example, Shipowners P&I Club describes this relationship on its official website as follows: "Our correspondents act as independent advisers on behalf of our Members and are available to provide direct and immediate assistance in the event of an incident or casualty involving a vessel entered with the Club." See Shipowners P&I Club, "Find Correspondents" https://www.shipownersClub.com/correspondents/find-correspondents/ accessed 13 April 2024.

200 NorthStandard P&I Club explicitly states in the document concerning the correspondent list that correspondents are not agents, in order to avoid characterizing this relationship as a representation relationship. "Correspondents are not agents for service of process upon NorthStandard Limited and NorthStandard EU DAC." See NorthStandard P&I Club, "Our Correspondents" https://north-standard.com/our-correspondents/ accessed 13 April 2024.

### *B. Member*

#### *1. An Overview*

Under this heading, the criteria for becoming a Club member will be examined within the framework of Club rules. Additionally, the discussions in English law regarding the "insurable interest" required to acquire member status will be addressed. Evaluating the criteria that a member must have according to Club rules in the context of Clubs in England will provide a framework on how to position membership status legally for countries aiming to implement England's model.

The term "member" is defined in the Club rules as an individual or entity that owns a ship or a part of it or effects an entry for insurance in the Club.[201] The definition of "owner," in turn, includes a wide range of entities such as owners in partnership, owners holding separate shares, part owners, mortgagees, trustees, charterers, operators, or managers of a ship.[202] Despite the broad definition of "owner," P&I Clubs are not obliged to accept every owner as a member and, therefore, have significant discretion.[203]

The Clubs operate as private companies,[204] thereby abstaining from issuing shares or involvement in public offerings.[205] An inherent implication of this structure is that members do not hold the status of shareholders and are not obliged to contribute capital to the Club. Being constituted as "limited by guarantee," in the event of the Club's liquidation, members' liability is confined to a predetermined amount they commit to guarantee.[206] A company limited by guarantee does not pursue profit, which aligns with the non-profit nature, which is a fundamental rationale for the Clubs adopting this organizational structure.[207] Instead of disbursing profits to members, Clubs internally retain funds or allocate them based on the Club's requirements and the needs of other members. In contrast to company shareholders, Club members do not bear any inherent capital obligations.[208] Instead, their commitment lies in guaranteeing a specified payment if the Club undergoes liquidation

201 See Standard P&I Club, Section N, Rule 26 "Member: every owner or other person who becomes and is for the time being a member of the Club". West P&I Club, Rule 58: "Means a Member for the Time Being of the Association and Includes a Joint Member where the Context so Admits"; Steamship Club's 2020–21, Rule 2; UK P&I Club, Rule 44.

202 See Steamship P&I Club, Rule 2: "Means an owner, owners in partnership, owners holding separate shares in severalty, part owner, mortgagee, trustee, charterer, operator or manager of a ship."

203 Acar, *Club Insurance*, 58.

204 Companies Act 2006, s 4 (1).

205 Community Companies Limited, "What is a Company Limited by Guarantee?" https://www.communitycompanies.co.uk/what-is-a-company-limited-by-guarantee accessed 9 December 2023.

206 Companies Act 2006, s 3 (3): "If their liability is limited to such amount as the members undertake to contribute to the assets of the company in the event of its being wound up, the company is 'limited by guarantee'."

207 International Group of P&I Clubs. "About Us" https://www.igpandi.org/article/about/ accessed 9 December 2023.

208 Acar, *Club Insurance*, 58.

during their membership or within a specified period following the termination of their membership.

In addition, shipowners, charterers, and tenants can also become members of P&I Clubs.[209] This expansion of membership categories can be attributed to the recognition that parties other than shipowners are exposed to risks arising from marine adventure and have an insurable interest, as required by the MIA 1906.[210] The rule booklets of P&I Clubs must include provisions governing resolving any legal disputes between the Club and its members under the applicable state law. English law typically applies to English Clubs.[211]

In summary, the definition of "member" is broad; P&I Clubs acknowledge that parties other than shipowners may have insurable interests and accept lessees, charterers, and others as members. However, they retain the discretion to admit or reject them as members. Members do not participate in the Club's profit distribution. The relationship between the Club and its members, along with members' rights and obligations, is primarily governed by the Club's rulebooks. The principle of mutual responsibility constitutes the foundation of the relationship among Club members, with each member consenting to share potential losses and risks that other members may encounter.[212]

### 2. *Insurable Interest as a Prerequisite for Membership in P&I Clubs*

The insurable interest clause functions as a protective measure against fraudulent or speculative claims, constituting a crucial element in guaranteeing the integrity and endurance of the insurance contract.[213] Therefore, one of the prerequisites for Club membership is that individuals seeking membership must possess an insurable interest.

The insurable interest doctrine constitutes one of the fundamental principles of insurance law.[214] The doctrine establishes that the presence of interest is the basis

209 Murat Yorulmaz, "Deniz Tasimaciligi ve Deniz Sigortalari" (PhD thesis, Marmara University, Istanbul 2009) 173; Alganturk Light, 25; Y. Nejat Incediken, *Gemi İşletme (II) Kulüp Sigortaları, Olayları ve Uygulamaları* (Eko Matbaacılık, Istanbul 1994) 19.

210 In s 5 of the Marine Insurance Act 1906, insurable interest is defined as follows: "(1) Subject to the provisions of this Act, every person has an insurable interest who is interested in a marine adventure. (2) In particular a person is interested in a marine adventure where he stands in any legal or equitable relation to the adventure or to any insurable property at risk therein, in consequence of which he may benefit by the safety or due arrival of insurable property, or may be prejudiced by its loss, or by damage thereto, or by the detention thereof, or may incur liability in respect thereof."

211 For example, Steamship P&I, Rule 48(viii) "These rules and any contract of insurance between the Club and the Member shall be governed by and construed in accordance with English law."

212 Thomas, *Volume Five,* 41.

213 Robert Merkin, Iain Goldrein, and Jonathan Mance, *Insurance Disputes* (3rd edn, Informa 2011), 62; Rhidian Thomas, *Marine Insurance: The Law in Transition* (Informa Law from Routledge 2006) 22; Meixian Song, "Insurable Interest in the Law of Marine Insurance" (2011) 1 *Southampton Student L Rev* 75.

214 Aslıhan Sevinc Kuyucu, "Insurance Contract in CIF Sales and Evaluation of Non-Payment of the Sales Price in Terms of the Insured Interest" (2020) 11(2) *Inonu University Law Review* 724, 731.

for forming an insurance contract, and the validity of such a contract depends on the existence of an insurable interest.[215] The principle of insurable interest posits that the insurance contract is not a contract of indemnity for the property per se but for the interest in the property.[216] However, any risks a ship may encounter while transporting goods from one location to another may damage the interests of individuals with a stake in the cargo. In the event of such damages, only those with an insurable interest in the goods have the right to claim compensation from the insurer.

The compensation amount is determined based on the value of the interest at stake. Those whose interests have been affected due to the loss of the goods have the right to sue the insurer under the contract terms. Nonetheless, to exercise this right, the interest specified in the insurance contract must have incurred damages. Furthermore, for the insurance contract to be legally valid, the insured must have a legal interest in the subject matter of the contract, even in cases where the loss or damage has not yet occurred. This legal interest must have an economic value that is quantifiable in law.[217]

*Lucena v Craufurd*[218] is significant in comprehending the concept of insurable interest.[219] The English Government had confiscated Dutch vessels and their cargo at sea, and the ships disappeared before being brought to England. Before the voyage, the Commissioners of the Admiralty had insured the vessels and cargo. They later filed a compensation claim with the insurer, which was rejected by the latter on the grounds of the Commissioners' lack of insurable interest in the ships and cargo at the time of damage. The House of Lords upheld the insurer's defence, holding that the Commissioners' duties on the ships and cargo would only begin after the ships arrived in England. Therefore, they did not possess insurable interests in the ships and cargo lost before reaching port.

Lawrence J. explained the concept of insurable interest by applying the criteria of "moral certainty" or "factual expectation."[220] He opined that the existence of insurable interest did not solely depend on the legal relationship between the insured and the subject of the insurance. Instead, if a risk arose, it was necessary to determine whether the insured was actually or economically affected by the situation. Hence, the "moral certainty" of profit or loss must be considered, which requires factual investigation rather than legal inquiry. Lawrence's definition of insurable interest was broad. As such, Lord Eldon's definition, which sets narrower boundaries by combining the concept of moral certainty with the existence of fair

215 Merkin and Steele, 25; Malcolm A Clarke, *The Law of Insurance Contracts* (6th edn, Informa Law from Routledge 2019) 45; *Lucena v Craufurd* (1806) 2 B & P (NR) 269; Kyriaki Noussia, "Insurable Interest in Marine Insurance Contracts: Modern Commercial Needs versus Tradition" (2008) 39(1) *Journal of Maritime Law and Commerce* 81–96, 81.

216 Sevinc Kuyucu, 731.

217 Merkin and Derrington, 12.

218 *Lucena v Craufurd* (1806) 2 B & P (NR) 269.

219 Also see *Cumberland Bone Co v Andes Insurance Co 64 Me 466* (1874).

220 Merkin, Goldrein, and Mance, 65.

or legal interest, has been more widely accepted in the doctrine.[221] In *Lucena v Craufurd*,[222] Lord Eldon stated that an insurable interest must constitute an economic interest and be recognized under the law.[223] Thus, not every interest can form the subject matter of an insurance contract. The equivalent of an insurable interest in insurance law is the "insured value." If the interest in the subject matter of the insurance is not legally recognized or has no economic value, the insurance contract in question is considered invalid under English law.[224]

The insurable interest doctrine remains a cornerstone of insurance law, and its proper application is essential for determining the validity of insurance contracts and the ability of insured parties to claim compensation for damages incurred. However, the definition and boundaries of insurable interest have been subject to much debate and interpretation. Lawrence's broad definition is contrasted with Lord Eldon's narrower definition, which requires the interest to have an economic and legal basis.

In English law, it is a fundamental principle that the insured must possess an insurable interest in the subject matter of the insurance.[225] Moreover, a direct and legal relationship between the insured and the insurance subject must exist at the time of the contract's formation and the time of the loss.[226] The absence of an insurable interest renders the insurance contract void. In the landmark case of *Macaura v Northern Assurance Co Ltd*,[227] the House of Lords emphasized that a legal or equitable relationship between the insured and the subject of the insurance is essential to establish an insurable interest. In this case, the insured renewed an insurance policy for timber owned by his company on his behalf. Following the timber's destruction in a fire, the insured claimed compensation from the insurer, but the claim was denied because he had no insurable interest in the property. The House of Lords rejected the insured's argument that he had suffered economic loss due to the timber's destruction, stating that he had no legal or equitable relationship with the timber and, thus, no interest in the insurance subject. Lord Sumner adopted a narrow and technical legalistic approach, concluding that the insured's original legal relationship was with the company, not the timber.[228]

221 Merkin, Goldrein, and Mance, 65; Noussia, *The Principle*, 32.

222 *Lucena v Craufurd* (1806) 2 B & P (NR) 269.

223 In *Lucena v Craufurd*, Lord Eldon said: "In order to distinguish that intermediate thing between a strict right, or a right derived under contract, and a mere expectation or hope, which has been termed an insurable interest, it has been said in many cases to be that which amounts to a moral certainty. However, I have in vain endeavoured to find a definition of that which is fit between certainty and expectation; nor am I to be able to point out in the interest of the moment what it is, unless a right of property, or a right derivable out of some contract about the property, which may be lost in either case upon some contingency affecting the possession or enjoyment of the party."

224 Noussia, "Insurable Interest", 81.

225 Malcolm Clarke, "Insurable Interest in Property in England – a Redundant Rule?" (2010) 2(4) *European Journal of Commercial Contract Law* 205–206, 205.

226 Clarke, "Insurable Interest in Property in England", 206.

227 *Macaura v Northern Assurance Co. Ltd.* [1925] AC 619.

228 *Macaura v Northern Assurance Co. Ltd.* [1925] AC 619.

However, the *Macaura* principle has been criticized for its inflexible and rigid approach, which does not reflect the flexible nature of contemporary commercial practices.[229] A more liberal and flexible approach to determining the existence of insurable interest is advocated by Lawrence J. It is argued that economic interest in insuring the subject matter should establish an insurable interest, provided that interest is lawful. Such an approach would be more consistent with the needs of modern commercial life and the function and necessity of insurance contracts.

The concept of insurable interest has its roots in the marine insurance industry's desire to distinguish itself from wagering contracts.[230] There is a direct link between the nature of marine insurance contracts, indemnity contracts, and the requirement that the insured possess an insurable interest.[231]

One of the most significant judgements of the Court of Appeal addressing the principle of insurable interest is the *Feasey v Sun Life Assurance Co.*[232] The case events unfolded: Steamship Mutual, a P&I Club, insured its members against liabilities towards employees and other individuals injured on board their vessels. When the club approached Lloyd's syndicate to reinsure this risk, the syndicate suggested another policy more suitable under Lloyd's risk codes. Consequently, the club took out a first-party personal accident insurance policy, which stipulated a fixed payment to the club for each death or disability occurring on their members' vessels. Subsequently, a dispute arose; the insurance company alleged that the club lacked an insurable interest in the lives insured under this policy. Given that the case involved life and marine insurance, it was significant to review previous legal precedents.

Lord Justice Waller, the leading judge, determined that the club had an insurable interest and categorized the authorities into four groups. The first group involved Lord Eldon's narrow test, which required a legal or equitable interest in the property. The second group was life insurance, necessitating a legal or pecuniary interest. The third group included situations where the insurance appeared to cover a specific property but, upon proper construction, extended beyond that property to include the insurable interest of the insured. In such cases, the factual expectation test established by Mr Justice Lawrence in *Lucena v Craufurd*[233] was applied. The fourth group encompassed interests that were not even strictly pecuniary, such as policies on a spouse's life, and recognized pervasive interests.

After making these categorizations, Lord Justice Waller concluded that in insuring a specified life, where a pecuniary liability would arise concerning those lives and the intention was to cover that legal liability, this sufficed to establish an insurable interest. Therefore, he broadly interpreted the concept of insurable interest as similar to the pervasive interest decisions, acknowledging the club's pecuniary

229 Noussia, *The Principle*, 33.

230 John Birds, Ben Lynch, and Simon Paul, *MacGillivray on Insurance Law* (15th edn, Sweet & Maxwell 2023) 1–058; Noussia, "Insurable Interest", 81.

231 Noussia, "Insurable Interest", 81; Gurses, 54.

232 *Feasey v Sun Life Assurance Co* [2003] EWCA Civ 885.

233 *Lucena v Craufurd* (1806) 2 B & P (NR) 269.

liability concerning the covered lives and determining that this liability constituted an insurable interest.

Conversely, Lord Justice Ward provided a dissenting opinion, arguing that the club did not possess a sufficient insurable interest.

Ultimately, the concept of "insurable interest" was interpreted contextually in this case. The court concluded that the policy was not a simple life policy but aimed at protecting the Club's interests in the event of a loss. Consequently, it was decided that the club had a pecuniary interest and was entitled to compensation.

Having a legal title to the property over unascertained goods is not a prerequisite for the insured to possess an insurable interest.[234] If the insured has paid the purchase price for unascertained goods, they possess an insurable interest, irrespective of whether they hold ownership over the goods.[235] In *Cumberland Bone Company v Andes Insurance*,[236] this point was emphasized with the following statement:

> If it were essential to the existence of an insurable interest that the assured should have a legal title to the property upon which the insurance is affected, the case would present a different and perhaps more difficult question. But such is not the law. An equitable interest suffices.

This judgement emphasizes the necessity of providing the buyer with an insurable interest upon the payment or part payment of the goods price for a commodity. In scenarios involving the potential loss, damage, or insolvency of the seller, there is a risk that the buyer may not recover the funds expended, serving as sufficient evidence of an insurable interest.[237] This notion references the recent case *Quadra Commodities S.A. v XL Insurance Company SE and Others*.[238] The judgement affirms that, even in cases where ownership of the goods has not been transferred, the payment or part payment of the price generally confers an insurable interest upon the buyer.[239] This affirmation stems from the acknowledgement that the buyer will incur losses in the event of the loss or damage of the goods or the seller's insolvency.[240]

However, there have been suggestions for eliminating the insurable interest requirement and expanding its global reach.[241] The English and Scottish Law

234 Birds, Lynch and Paul, 1–139.
235 *Quadra Commodities S.A. v XL Insurance Company SE and Others* [2023] EWCA Civ 432.
236 *Cumberland Bone Co v Andes Insurance 64 Me 466* (1874).
237 Birds, Lync and Paul, 1–139.
238 *Quadra Commodities S.A. v XL Insurance Company SE and Others* [2023] EWCA Civ 432.
239 *Quadra Commodities S.A. v XL Insurance Company SE and Others* [2023] EWCA Civ 432; Gurses, 70.
240 Birds, Lync, and Paul, 1–139.
241 Robert Merkin, *Reforming Insurance Law: Is There a Case for Reverse Transportation? A Report for the English and Scottish Law Commissions on the Australian Experience of Insurance Law Reform* (Law Commission & Scottish Law Commission, 21 March 2006) http://www.lawcom.gov.uk/docs/merkin_report.pdf accessed 15 May 2023 (Merkin, *Report 2006.*); Bennett, *Marine Insurance*, 74; Merkin and Steele, 51; Noussia, "Insurable Interest", 95; Merkin, Goldrein, and

Commissions revisited the insurable interest doctrine, considering practical issues and criticisms. The Commission initially presented updated proposals on this matter in 2008 and 2011.[242] Later, after evaluating feedback on these proposals, they published a Draft Bill in 2016,[243] which they revised once again, and the Commission released the updated version (Draft Insurable Interest Bill, 2018) in June 2018.[244] However, this draft is specifically designed for life insurance.[245] Life Assurance Act 1774, which is the current regulation, requires the insured to suffer economic loss in the event of another person's death to be able to take out life insurance.[246] In the Draft 2018, the necessity of this financial interest requirement is eliminated, and the economic loss test is expanded.[247] Instead, the insured will have an insurable interest whenever there is a "reasonable prospect" of suffering an economic loss upon the occurrence of the insured event (such as the death, illness, or injury of the insured person).[248] However, marine insurance contracts are excluded from the scope of this draft.[249]

Bennett argues that the insurable interest requirement envisaged in MIA 1906 for marine insurance should not be interpreted narrowly; otherwise, it would contradict the fundamental principles of the insurance requirement.[250] According to the author, if the insured would suffer a loss in the event of the destruction of the goods and is interested in securing the goods, the insurance contract related to this situation cannot be considered a wager, and the insured's insurable interest should be acknowledged.[251] It is incorrect to argue that this situation would encourage the insured to destroy the insured goods to claim compensation deliberately.[252] Merkin and Steele support the idea of reconsidering the insurable interest requirement in

---

Mance, 71; Franziska Arnold-Dwyer, "Taking an Interest in Insurable Interest" (2015) *Lloyd's Maritime and Commercial Law Quarterly* 271; Jianxun Guo, "The Study of Marine Insurable Interest: A Comparison of Laws in China and the United Kingdom" (PhD thesis, University of Exeter 2017) 2.

242 See https://lawcom.gov.uk/project/insurance-contract-law-insurable-interest/ accessed 7 December 2023.

243 Draft Insurable Interest Bill for Consultation (April 2016) https://lawcom.gov.uk/project/insurance-contract-law-insurable-interest/ accessed 7 December 2023.

244 Draft Insurable Interest Bill (June 2018) https://lawcom.gov.uk/project/insurance-contract-law-insurable-interest/ accessed 7 December 2023.

245 Gurses, 59.

246 Merkin and Steele, 119; Life Assurance Act 1774, s 1: "From and after the passing of this Act no insurance shall be made by any person or persons, bodies politick or corporate, on the life or lives of any person, or persons, or on any other event or events whatsoever, wherein the person or persons for whose use, benefit, or on whose account such policy or policies shall be made, shall have no interest, or by way of gaming or wagering; and every assurance made contrary to the true intent and meaning hereof shall be null and void to all intents and purposes whatsoever."

247 Draft Insurable Interest Bill (June 2018), s 2.

248 Draft Insurable Interest Bill (June 2018), s 2 (2).

249 Draft Insurable Interest Bill (June 2018), s 5: "Nothing in this Act has effect in relation to a contract of marine insurance, as defined by section 1 of the Marine Insurance Act 1906".

250 Bennett, *Marine Insurance*, 79.

251 Bennett, *Marine Insurance*, 79.

252 Bennett, *Marine Insurance*, 79.

the context of English law, as it was abandoned in Australia and New Zealand without causing any issues.[253] Noussia argues that strict conditions for determining and establishing insurable interest are no longer necessary.[254] According to the author, imposing stringent conditions to claim compensation from the insurer would be unjustified if the insured has a legitimate economic interest. Instead, the presence of insurable interest should be presumed.[255] We also support the idea that the insurable interest requirement should not be interpreted strictly in marine insurance contracts. This approach aligns with contemporary economic dynamics and commercial practices.

However, Thomas criticizes these approaches.[256] According to the author, despite the restrictive definition of the insurable interest principle in MIA 1906, it does not have a negative impact on commercial life. Most commercial parties can insure all their legitimate risks without restrictions during their commercial activities.[257] The author also contends that insurable interest problems rarely arise from mistakes or misinterpretations by the insured, and dismissing this doctrine is not justified.[258] Instead of eliminating the insurable interest principle, Thomas argues that preserving the existing framework, correcting some misconceptions in its definition, and increasing transparency would be a more appropriate solution. According to him, the insurable interest condition in insurance contracts should be fully preserved and not relaxed. The author criticizes views advocating for eliminating the insurable interest principle, stating that it still serves its purpose today and that abolishing it would not provide the alleged commercial flexibility.[259] In this regard, Thomas's criticisms are not appropriate. Given the rapid developments and changes in the marine insurance industry, commercial life, and technology, it is necessary to adapt to this change legally and introduce flexibility to the insurable interest condition.

The primary purpose served by the insurable interest requirement was to provide legal validity to insurance contracts in the preliminary stages of their emergence and to distinguish them from betting and gambling contracts. The legality and moral validity of insurance contracts are no longer disputed today. Many risks and liabilities can now be the subject of insurance contracts. In English law, where contract freedom is widely accepted, concepts like insurable interest, which are stereotyped and undermine this flexibility, should be revised to adapt to this flexibility. Therefore, considering the presence of a material interest in the insurance contract as sufficient should be considered a solution, especially concerning marine insurance contracts, instead of the insurable interest doctrine. In other words, if there is a commercial relationship between the parties, and it is not explicitly characterized as gambling or

253 Merkin and Steele, 51.
254 Noussia, "Insurable Interest", 95.
255 Noussia, "Insurable Interest", 95.
256 Thomas, *Marine Insurance,* 43.
257 Thomas, *Marine Insurance,* 43.
258 Thomas, *Marine Insurance,* 43.
259 Thomas, *Marine Insurance,* 43.

betting, it should be accepted that the parties have economic interests in the insurance contract without subjecting it to a re-examination of insurable interest.[260]

After touching on the discussions on insurable interest, it is necessary to examine the existence of this condition from the perspective of P&I insurance. As we suggested, the concept of insurable interest in traditional marine insurance contracts should be interpreted flexibly. However, club insurance should be evaluated separately from traditional marine insurance. Accordingly, members' need for an insurable interest should be evaluated more strictly in club insurance. Club insurance is a type with unique rules shaped by these rules. Clubs have established these rules to prioritize the members and the Club's interests to the highest degree. According to Club rules, membership in a P&I Club is contingent upon having an insurable interest. This rule regarding insurable interest serves to protect the common interests of the Club and its members. Therefore, evaluation should be made within the framework of Club rules regarding insurable interest. The principle of insurable interest is strictly applied in Club rules. Those who do not have this interest cannot become members of the Club and cannot benefit from club insurance coverage.

Shipowners must demonstrate a necessity to insure their liabilities against potential losses that may occur during their commercial activities to qualify for membership in P&I Clubs.[261] Adherence to the insurable interest principle dictates that the insurance contract's validity and applicability hinge on the member's ability to demonstrate an insurable interest. This condition applies to all prospective members, covering shipowners and charterers alike. Membership applications undergo a rigorous assessment to ensure compliance with the previously mentioned criteria before entering a P&I Club. The unique operational model and mutuality principle of P&I Clubs make it mandatory for the member to have an insurable interest when entering an insurance contract with the Club. The requirement of an insurable interest is considered a crucial element in maintaining the sustainability and robustness of the insurance contracts between P&I Clubs and their members. Therefore, insurable interest requirements should be safeguarded without being relaxed within the scope of P&I Club insurance contracts.

## V. Entry and Registration Procedures Distinguishing Club Insurance from other Insurance Contracts

### *A. Entry Procedure*

This analysis will be on the entry and registration procedures specific to club insurance, highlighting how these procedures differentiate club insurance from other insurance contracts.

260 For example, the Court of Appeal conducted an examination of insurable interest based on commercial matters in *Glengate-KG Properties Ltd v Norwich Union Fire Insurance Society Ltd.* See *Glengate-KG Properties Ltd v Norwich Union Fire Insurance Society Ltd* [1996] 1 Lloyd's Rep 614.

261 Lin, 44–45.

The "entry" procedure is a critical component of the relationship between a shipowner and a P&I Club, as it involves the registration of the ship to the Club and fulfilling specific entry procedures. The shipowner must accurately report all necessary information to the Club during this phase to ensure the continuation of membership and the benefit from the protection and indemnity services that the Club provides. To regulate this process, P&I Clubs[262] provide detailed information on the admission process, entry procedures, and the information the shipowner must report.[263]

However, the information provided by the shipowner during the entry phase may not be sufficient to determine the risk fully, and further investigation may be required to accurately calculate the risk assessment and the premiums to be paid. The member's previous claim records can be helpful in this regard, and some coverage can be excluded from P&I insurance coverage based on the evaluation of each member's application. Furthermore, the Club managers have the authority to accept or reject the application of an applicant, and they can also amend the contract terms if necessary. The managers may reject an application without providing any reason.

The entry phase is significant for the shipowner to benefit from the protection and indemnity services, and it is also essential for the P&I Club to assess the risk accurately and determine the contract terms.

262 For example, see Steamship P&I Club, Rule 6.

263 Some English P&I Clubs state that the shipowner must report this information to the Club under s 2 of the English Insurance Act 2015. This section of the Act regulates the duty of fair presentation. The foundations of this duty can be found in the *De Costa v Scandret*. In this case, where the insured obtained insurance from the insurer by concealing the suspicious account of his ship, the Lord Chancellor defined the duty of fair presentation with the following words: "The insured has not dealt fairly with the insurers in this case; he ought to have disclosed to them what intelligence he had of the ship's being in danger, and which might induce him, at least, to fear that it was lost, though he had no certain account of it; for if this had been discovered, it is impossible to think, that the insurers would have insured the ship at so small a premium as they have done, but either would not have insured at all, or would have insisted on a larger premium, so that the concealing of this intelligence is a fraud." See *De Costa v Scandret* (1723) 2 P. Wms. 170. According to this case, the duty is that "the party proposing the insurance is obliged to communicate to the insurer all matters that will enable the insurer to determine the extent of the risk they are undertaking to cover." The principles related to the enactment of the IA 2015 were analyzed under the doctrine of the "duty of utmost good faith." The common understanding of the relevant sections of the MIA 1906 was that the duty to disclose and not to misrepresent material facts was an integral part of the duty of good faith. The IA 2015 applies to policies made after 12 August 2016. The Act separates the duty of utmost good faith from the pre-contractual duty to provide information (in the form of disclosure and not misrepresenting material facts). The IA 2015 repealed ss 18–20 of the MIA 1906 and restructured the pre-contractual duty to provide information under the "duty of fair presentation of risk" in Part 2. Furthermore, the IA 2015 altered the phrase in s 17 of the MIA, "A contract of marine insurance is a contract based upon the utmost good faith, and, if the utmost good faith be not observed by either party, the contract may be avoided by the other party," to "A contract of marine insurance is a contract based upon the utmost good faith." See Gurses, 78, 79; *Young v Royal and Sun Alliance Insurance Plc* [2020] CSIH 25.

### B. *The Significance of the Certificate of Entry in the Membership Procedure*

Issuing an entry certificate is a significant step in the P&I Club membership process. The entry certificate is a legal document that outlines the terms and conditions of the insurance coverage, the ship, and its members. The accuracy and completeness of the information in the entry certificate are of utmost importance, as any discrepancies or inaccuracies may result in future disputes between the Club and the member.[264]

The entry certificate is also subject to the English IA 2015, although some Clubs are excluded from specific provisions of this act. The Club rules specify which sections of the Act do not apply to the Club's insurance contract and Club rules.[265] Therefore, the Club managers must carefully review and update the entry certificate so that the members can provide accurate and truthful information.

264 Thomas, "Protection and Indemnity", 34.

265 Eight clubs within the IG P&I (The Britannia Steam Ship P&I; The London P&I; NorthStandard P&I; Steamship Mutual P&I; The United Kingdom Mutual Steam Ship P&I; The West of England Ship Owners P&I; The Shipowners' Mutual P&I) have been affected by the IA 2015 because their rules are subject to English law. Consequently, these clubs have issued a circular concerning the new regulations introduced by the Act. According to this circular, the eight English P&I Clubs have opted to contract out of specific aspects of IA 2015. However, these clubs have agreed to adopt certain provisions of IA 2015 that clarify ambiguous sections of MIA 1906. For instance, the club rule concerning the duty of disclosure as stipulated in MIA 1906 will be replaced by the duty of "fair presentation of the risk" as outlined in IA 2015. This new duty incorporates many features of the existing duty of disclosure. The clubs have incorporated into their rules a provision stating that a member fulfils the duty of fair presentation by disclosing sufficient information to put the club on notice to make further inquiries during the disclosure process. The clubs have recognized that a fair presentation and professional assessment of the risk provide mutual benefits for both members and the clubs, and therefore have included the IA 2015 provision concerning this duty in their rules. Should the insured fail to make a fair presentation, the insurer retains the right to void the policy. Additionally, if the insured's failure to make a fair presentation is deemed innocent or negligent, the insurer has the right to void the policy if it would not have been underwritten had a fair presentation been made. The continuation of the policy will be contingent upon the insurer's decision to proceed with underwriting the risk, despite the relevant information, and will depend on the terms under which the risk would be underwritten or the premium that would be charged. Thus, the remedy of avoidance remains the standard recourse for clubs under the new Act when an insured fails to make a fair presentation of the risk. However, the provisions of IA 2015 related to the breach of the duty of fair presentation have not been included in the club rules by the eight IG members. For example, see London P&I Club Rule: 43.1.1. Emphasizing the importance of proper disclosure in a P&I context and within a mutual club, the eight IG clubs have preserved the MIA 1906 avoidance remedy in their club rules concerning the breach of the duty of fair presentation. Another change introduced by IA 2015 is the prohibition of any insurance contract condition that warrants the accuracy of all pre-contractual statements by the insured. This prohibition nullifies the effect of existing club rules that declare such information to be the "basis" of the insurance contract. This provision is mandatory; thus, any such basis clause has been removed from the rules of the affected eight P&I Clubs. Instead, any inaccuracy in material representations will be addressed in relation to the question of whether the risk was fairly presented. See UK P&I Club, "Circular 15/15: The UK Insurance Act 2015" (UK P&I Club 2015) https://www.ukpandi.com/news-and-resources/club-circulars/2015/circular-1515-the-uk-insurance-act-2015/ accessed 13 August 2024.

Furthermore, any changes to the conditions in the entry certificate must be promptly communicated to the member, and a confirmation receipt indicating the changes and the date of their entry into force must be issued.[266] The entry certificate and confirmation receipt are conclusive evidence and bind the Club and the member.

Given these considerations, it is clear that the entry certificate plays a critical role in the P&I Club membership process. It is essential that the managers and members fully understand the significance of the entry certificate and take all necessary precautions to ensure its accuracy and completeness.

### C. *Procedures for Entry beyond Initial Registration during the Membership Process*

The entry certificate is a critical document that outlines the procedures involved in a member's entry into a P&I Club, along with other related provisions. However, it is not the only document about entry provisions, as the articles of association play an equally crucial role in detailing the functioning of the Club and the relationship between its members.[267] However, since the Companies Act 2006 came into force, companies have been obligated to share their articles of association with members upon request, necessitating that clubs do the same.[268] The articles of association contain more detailed provisions concerning entry procedures, such as membership acquisition, its terms, and results, which members must comply with.

Furthermore, the Club rules provide the most comprehensive information on the relationship between a member and a Club. The rules are typically issued to new members in a rule booklet and are binding on all members.[269] Members must familiarize themselves with the Club rules, as they cannot escape responsibility in a dispute by claiming ignorance. English Courts have ruled that Club rules are binding on members, emphasizing the importance of being well-versed in the provisions contained in the rule booklet.[270] Thus, P&I Club members must review and understand the contents of the entry certificate and the Club's articles of association and rule booklet to ensure compliance with the provisions outlined therein.

## VI. Comparative Analysis and Conclusion

Chapter 1 has shed light on various aspects of club insurance, including its historical foundations, legal frameworks, and evolutionary trajectories in English and Turkish legal domains. These findings have highlighted significant similarities and

266 For example, see Standard Club, Section H, Rule 12.2; Steamship Club, Rule 7/c (iii).

267 Hazelwood and Semark, 39.

268 John Davies, "A Guide to Directors' Responsibilities under the Companies Act 2006" (2007) *Certified Accountants Educational Trust* 69.

269 Hazelwood and Semark, 56.

270 *Volkswagenwerk A.G. and Wolfsburger Transport Gesellschaft M.B.H. v International Mutual Strike Assurance Co. (Bermuda) Ltd* [1977] 2 Lloyd's Rep. 503.

differences characterizing English and Turkish P&I Clubs, emphasizing essential aspects such as structural differences, approaches to legal systems, and entry procedures. Thus, by elucidating aspects like Club structures and membership procedures, this chapter has provided a concrete framework that could guide other countries like Türkiye aiming to develop the club insurance industry, drawing from the English model.

The Turkish P&I insurance company operates with a distinctive structure compared to English P&I Clubs. Unlike English P&I Clubs,[271] the Turkish P&I was established as a public limited company in 2014 to provide robust financial security to the insured.[272] This has led to a lack of deep-rooted historical background, making it new to the market. The establishment of the first and only Turkish P&I insurance company was primarily geared towards meeting the club insurance needs of Turkish-flagged ships and promoting the development of club insurance and marine insurance industries in Türkiye.

The lack of a specific legal framework dedicated to club insurance is a characteristic shared by the Turkish and English legal systems. Marine insurance is regulated under the insurance law of the TCC No. 6102,[273] and this regulation also extends to club insurance. During the drafting of the TCC, a proposed law modelled after the liberal approach of English law and the balance of interests protection feature of German law was presented to reflect the ever-evolving nature of contract law.[274] In other words, while Turkish law is primarily based on English law concerning maritime or land insurance contracts, it adopts German law's principle of protecting the balance of interests of parties and the weak party in direct action cases or disputes related to club insurance.[275] This significantly differs between English and Turkish law regarding club insurance and direct action disputes.[276]

English P&I Clubs have emerged as leaders in the global landscape of club insurance, boasting a rich historical legacy and experience, culminating in the development of Club rules. These rules have cemented the position of English P&I Clubs as prominent providers of club insurance services worldwide. In contrast, shipowners and Turkish-flagged vessels, until 2014, were compelled to procure their club insurance from foreign P&I Clubs. The absence of domestic P&I Clubs or insurers offering such services in Türkiye necessitated this reliance on foreign entities. The establishment of the first Turkish P&I insurance company in 2014 introduced structural distinctions between Turkish and English P&I Clubs,

271 The English P& Clubs operate as private companies limited by guarantee. See https://www.igpandi.org/article/about/ accessed 9 December 2023.

272 These companies are Türkiye Insurance S.A.; Metropole Ltd. Co.; Omur Marine S.A.; Vitsan Marine S.A.

273 Turkish Commercial Code No. 6102.

274 Rayegan Kender, *Türkiye'de Hususi Sigorta Hukuku* (On İki Levha Press, İstanbul 2016) 25.

275 For the General Justification of the Turkish Commercial Code No. 6102, see "Türk Ticaret Kanunu Genel Gerekçesi" http://www.ticaretkanunu.net/turk-ticaret-kanunu-genel-gerekce/ accessed 1 May 2023.

276 Discussions and differences on this issue will be explained in detail in Chapter 4.

encompassing disparities in courts' judgements, entry procedures, and other obligations of parties.

The most notable distinction between the Turkish P&I insurance company and English P&I Clubs is their organizational structure. The Turkish P&I company is not structured as a Club despite providing club insurance services. Instead, it offers this insurance as a classical fixed premium insurance company.[277] However, Turkish law imposes club insurance under the umbrella of mutual insurance. Insurance companies desiring to provide this service based on mutuality must establish themselves as cooperative companies.[278] The Turkish P&I is not established as a cooperative company, so it cannot provide club insurance under the mutuality principle. However, it provides club insurance services with a fixed premium to the insured.

In general, the organizational structure of the Turkish P&I insurance company sets it apart from the English P&I Clubs. In Turkish maritime trade practice, the influences of English law are observed. In contrast, the characteristic of German law, which prioritizes the protection of third parties in resolving marine and club insurance disputes, has been adopted in Turkish law.

Similarly, it is imperative to recognize that notable distinctions exist, particularly concerning the classification of club insurance as either mandatory or voluntary. Turkish law mandates that specific categories of vessels adhere to relevant domestic legislation and international agreements, necessitating compulsory insurance coverage, often provided through club insurance. For instance, vessels transporting hazardous materials transiting the Turkish Strait and ships with a gross tonnage of 300 or more must maintain club insurance, thus rendering it obligatory under Turkish law. In contrast, English law does not impose domestic legal obligations regarding club insurance, except those dictated by international treaties. While club insurance is a customary practice in many jurisdictions, it is not legally compulsory in most cases. In English law, the execution of insurance contracts, including club insurance, is regarded as voluntary, affording such agreements protection against legislative interference, thereby upholding the autonomy of contracting parties.

The first query of Chapter 1 evaluated the feasibility of the English model by examining the similarities and differences in the Club rules, legal nature, and entry procedures of Turkish and English P&I Clubs, which regulate their structural aspects. The analysis shows that these structural differences will not prevent Türkiye from following England's P&I Clubs model. Even though the Clubs have some structural variations, they can be overcome. Additionally, Clubs in both countries offer P&I insurance coverage for common risks. This chapter also underscored the intrinsic advantages of the Club structure within classical English P&I Clubs, characterized by its flexibility, financial prowess, and extensive membership. Internal and arbitration mechanisms are employed to resolve disputes, expediting the

277 Turkish P&I, "About Turk P&I" https://www.turkpandi.com/en/about-turk-p-i/about-turk-p-i accessed 1 May 2023.

278 Goktug Burucuoglu, "Kulup Sigortasi (P&I) Cercevesinde Esyanin Ziyai Veya Hasari Halinde Teminatin Kapsami" (Master thesis, Ankara University Law Faculty 2019) 27.

efficacy of Club rules. In contrast, Turkish P&I Clubs, nascent in their inception and operating on a fixed premium basis, exhibit limitations in flexibility and broad discretion when contrasted with their English counterparts. Therefore, Türkiye must model the structural features of English P&I Clubs and make Clubs legally more flexible.

The second query addressed the potential advantages of Türkiye adopting the policies of English law prioritizing the application of Club rules. Developing club insurance within a nation necessitates establishing a solid legal framework that safeguards the interests of Clubs operating within that jurisdiction. English law, characterized by the principle of freedom of contract, affords Clubs a high degree of autonomy in framing their rules and negotiating contracts with members. English Courts typically refrain from intervening in disputes between Clubs and members, provided that the agreed-upon rules fall within the purview of freedom of contract. This legal framework is conducive to the development of Clubs.

Conversely, while embracing the principle of freedom of contract, Turkish law operates within a narrower scope than its English counterpart. Turkish law permits restrictions on freedom of contract when the protection of the weaker party in insurance law is warranted. Contracts imposed upon a party without the opportunity for negotiation or modification may be rendered invalid under Turkish law. The context of club insurance necessitates that Turkish P&I align its rules and contracts with insurance and contract law. The liberal approach of English law to club insurance is one of the main factors behind the leading position of English P&I Clubs globally. Therefore, Türkiye must adopt a more flexible legal approach within the framework of club insurance to foster its development. As stated in the main argument of the book, there is a need for legal reform in Türkiye to implement a legal policy close to the English model, prioritizing contractual freedom and giving legal validity to Club rules.

These inquiries inquired into the specific legal regulations under English law that diverge from Turkish law and favour the fortification of the legal infrastructure of P&I Clubs. They also explored the feasibility of adopting such regulations within Turkish law. While prevailing legal regulations in Turkish law and the current legal framework of Turkish P&I insurance models pose challenges in directly emulating the English P&I insurance model and its legal framework, these obstacles can be overcome through legislative reform. In order to advance P&I insurance in Türkiye, a policy that aligns with the English model, provides flexibility to Clubs, and minimizes legal intervention should be pursued.

The regulations and judicial precedents governing the protection and operations of P&I Clubs in English law offer a more advantageous environment for these entities than in Turkish law. English law distinctively treats P&I insurance as a specialized category, diverging from its treatment of other insurance types. In contrast, Turkish law assimilates P&I insurance into the broader framework of insurance law, subject to the overarching principle of protecting the weaker party. P&I Clubs in Türkiye are not granted unique legal privileges, as Turkish law aims to safeguard the weaker, like third parties. This distinction has posed considerable challenges in developing the P&I insurance industry within Türkiye.

While English law provides an advantageous legal foundation for P&I Clubs, comprehensive legal reform will inevitably be imperative to facilitate its transference to Turkish law or its application to Turkish P&I Clubs, considering the potential contraventions of Turkish insurance and contract law principles. The advancement of club insurance in Türkiye necessitates the construction of a legal framework tailored to the industry's specific requirements and intricacies. This undertaking calls for meticulous research and examination of the challenges encountered by Turkish P&I, as well as the practical cultivation of club insurance within Türkiye.

In conclusion, the structural differences between Clubs in Türkiye and those in England should not be considered a barrier to adopting the English model. These structural disparities stem from the corporate structuring of Clubs in Türkiye. Moreover, similarities in the entry procedures and functioning of organs among Clubs facilitate the modelling process. However, England has incentivized its P&I Clubs to maintain a leading position in the club insurance industry by granting them significant legal privileges and assurances. Nevertheless, Türkiye has been slow in taking steps to develop club insurance. Due to Turkish law being bound to a framework that protects the insured, legal privileges have not been granted to Clubs. Türkiye must change this legal policy through legislative reform to advance club insurance.

# 2 Covered Risks and Termination Conditions of P&I Club Insurance

## I. Introduction

This chapter provides a detailed examination of the insurance coverage offered by P&I Clubs, emphasizing the distinctions between club insurance and other forms of marine insurance. The discussion focuses on the extent of coverage, termination of insurance contracts, and the comparability of English and Turkish P&I Club rules. By scrutinizing English P&I Club rulebooks, which serve as a primary source of guidance on the scope and cessation of club insurance, this chapter aims to clarify the structure and operation of P&I insurance.

A conceptual framework is introduced to illustrate the risks covered under P&I insurance, particularly if Turkish P&I Clubs adopt the English model. While certain risks are commonly included in P&I insurance across most English Clubs, individual Clubs retain the discretion to expand their coverage scope. This chapter discusses these standard risks and their variations among different Clubs. Examining the risks covered and the termination of membership contributes to a comprehensive understanding of this insurance system and underscores its importance in ensuring the secure conduct of maritime trade activities.

This analysis provides a foundation for assessing whether Türkiye should implement a legal framework aligned with the English model. By doing so, it offers practical insights for legislative improvements and highlights the necessity of legal reform in club insurance regulation.

### *A. The Importance of Comprehensive Insurance Coverage Provided by Club Insurance in Conducting Maritime Trade Activities*

This analysis will emphasize the significance of the comprehensive insurance coverage provided by club insurance in facilitating maritime trade activities. It will highlight how club insurance plays a crucial role in offering financial protection and risk management support to shipowners engaged in maritime trade, thus contributing to such activities' smooth and secure conduct.

When explaining the risks and limitations covered by P&I Club insurance, English Club rules will be a reference. According to the rules of the P&I Clubs, unless otherwise agreed between members and Directors, the Club provides insurance

DOI: 10.4324/9781003628897-2

coverage to its members for various liabilities, costs, and expenses. However, these liabilities, costs, and expenses must be related to the registered ship's entry into the Club and operation.

One of the arguments of the book is that the prioritization of the application of Club rules in English law is a significant factor in developing this insurance. While examining the rules of coverage provided by Clubs, this chapter will demonstrate that these rules sometimes exclude specific provisions of English laws. Clubs' flexibility is supported by English law, which prioritizes Club rules over statutory law. Therefore, Clubs can freely determine the risks covered by insurance. This flexibility is crucial for Clubs to sustain their activities and remain economically strong.

In summary, while this chapter is informative and descriptive, its primary purpose is to demonstrate how English P&I Clubs can freely determine the scope of insurance coverage and how English law encourages this freedom through Club rules. It will also emphasize the importance of comprehensive club insurance coverage for maritime trade activities. The aim is to provide concrete support for the book's argument advocating that the country's legal policies should protect club insurance.

### *1. Liability to Seamen*

The definition of a seafarer in the context of P&I Club rules pertains to any individual employed as part of a ship's complement, including the master and apprentices, under the crew agreement terms or another contract of service or employment to serve on board an entered ship.[1] P&I insurance covers indemnity liabilities of the entered ship[2] concerning the death, personal injury, or illness of any seafarer, as well as medical, funeral, and other mandatory expenses relating to such death, personal injury, or illness.[3] Moreover, the insurance extends liability coverage for damages or compensation for loss or damage to the seafarer's belongings, as well as return and replacement costs incurred due to the seafarer's death, personal injury, illness, or desertion.[4]

The legal relationship between the seafarer and the member is subject to the state law in which they operate.[5] The member's liability and indemnity limit are also determined under that state's law. In other words, the P&I Club assesses each

1 Steamship P&I Club, Rule 2. In addition, the Club refers to the seafarer definition in Maritime Labour Convention 2006. The seafarer definition in the Article 2/1(f) of the Convention is: "Seafarer means any person who is employed or engaged or works in any capacity on board a ship to which this Convention applies."

2 Entered ship means according to Club rules: "A ship which has been entered in the Association for insurance." See UK P&I Club, Rule 44/Definitions.

3 Britannia P&I Club, Rule 19/1; West of England P&I Club, Rule 2, Section 1; UK P&I Club, Rule 2, Section 2–3; Standard P&I Club, Section C, Rule 3.1.1; Steamship P&I Club, Rule 25; North of England P&I Club, Rule 19/1; Shipowners' P&I Club, Rule 2/1; The London P&I Club, Rule 9.3.

4 The London P&I Club, Rule 9.3.

5 Acar, *Club Insurance*, 119; Christopher Hill, *Maritime Law: Lloyd's Practical Shipping Guides* (6th edn, Routledge 2014) 394.

member's responsibility to the seafarer by following the applicable law governing this legal relationship. Liability is based on negligence under English law, which governs the relationship between seafarers and members. The member is held accountable not only for their fault but also for the fault of the seafarers. In summary, English law imposes a strict liability regime on shipowners.[6]

### 2. *Liability to Passengers*

Passengers who travel on an entered ship under a contract of carriage for reward are defined by Club rules as individuals who are not engaged or employed in any capacity related to the business or operation of the insured vessel.[7] The P&I insurance these Clubs provide covers several risks such passengers may encounter. The coverage typically extends to hospital and funeral expenses, medical support benefits, and other costs incurred due to the passenger's illness, injury, or death. Compensation for damaged personal belongings and baggage is also generally included. However, the insurance does not cover goods such as cash, negotiable instruments, precious metals, or objects of a rare or precious nature.[8]

Regarding the amount of passenger coverage, P&I Clubs have established specific rules, referring to the 1974 Athens Convention on the Carriage of Passengers and their Luggage by Sea[9] and the Protocol of 2002. "The 1974 Convention" provides a liability regime for carriers regarding damage to passengers on the ship.[10] The carrier is liable for any damage or loss caused to a passenger due to fault or neglect during carriage activities.[11] However, the carrier's liability for causing such damage without fault or negligence may be limited within specific limits defined by the Convention. Initially, many countries did not widely accept the Convention because the liability limits were considered too low.[12] Subsequently, the 2002 Protocol[13] increased the liability limit per passenger.[14]

The most significant regulation introduced in the 2002 Protocol relates to compulsory insurance and certification. The Protocol requires carriers to have

6 Hill, 398.

7 Shipowners' P&I Club, Rule 67; Steamship P&I Club, Rule 2: "Passenger means any person carried on board the entered ship pursuant to a contract for carriage"; Britannia P&I Club, Rule 2: "Passenger: A person carried on board an Entered Ship by virtue of holding a ticket of passage."

8 North of England, Rule 19/17(e)(G); Shipowners' P&I, Rule 2, Sections 1,2 (C).

9 Athens Convention relating to the Carriage of Passengers and their Luggage by Sea (PAL) 1974.

10 Baris Soyer, "Sundry Considerations on the Draft Protocol to the Athens Convention Relating to the Carriage of Passengers and Their Luggage by Sea 1974" (2002) 33 *Journal of Maritime Law and Commerce* 519, 521.

11 International Conference on the Revision of the Athens Convention Relating to the Carriage of Passengers and Their Luggage by Sea, 1974, LEG/CONF.13/11 (30 August 2002) http://rosaeg.no/erikro/WWW/corrgr/dipcon/11.pdf accessed 30 April 2023.

12 This limit of liability was set at 46,666 Special Drawing Rights (SDR) per carriage.

13 Protocol of 2002 to The Athens Convention Relating to The Carriage of Passengers and Their Luggage by Sea, 1974.

14 Increased to 250,000 SDR per passenger.

compulsory insurance covering damages and losses to passengers on ships. Under Article 4bis of the Protocol, the carrier must have compulsory insurance to meet the strict liability limits established by the Convention for passengers' death and personal injury. P&I Clubs often provide this compulsory insurance,[15] but the carrier must have compulsory insurance to meet the strict liability limits established by the Convention for passengers' death and personal injury. P&I Clubs often provide this compulsory insurance.[16] During the Convention negotiations, the IGP&I requested a reduction in the limits of compulsory insurance, stating that they were too high and difficult to meet. However, the International Maritime Organization did not accept this proposal, and the limits were not reduced.[17]

The importance of compulsory insurance and certification in P&I Clubs has become increasingly apparent, particularly in direct action cases. When compulsory insurance is legally required, third parties who have suffered damages have the right to claim directly to the insurer. In conclusion, P&I Clubs are subject to direct action claims from passengers and are responsible for indemnifying them for any resulting damages. This regulation is essential in facilitating compensation for third-party losses and damages. However, the situation is not the same for P&I Clubs, as this compulsory insurance arrangement significantly increases their liability, given the likelihood of direct action claims from third parties.

Suppose passenger damages result from "war, hostilities, civil war, insurrection, or a natural phenomenon of an exceptional, inevitable, and irresistible character" or the negligence or defect of third parties. In that case, the carrier is relieved of liability, provided they can prove the situation.[18] Additionally, different systems have been developed under the 2002 Protocol, taking the principles of liability and compensation from conventions relating to environmental pollution as examples to make it easier to compensate passengers. Consequently, a strict liability regime has been introduced instead of a fault-based liability in a shipping incident.[19] This means that the carrier's liability to passengers increases, and they are liable within

15 According to Article 4bis of the 2002 Protocol: "When passengers are carried on board a ship registered in a State Party that is licensed to carry more than twelve passengers, and this Convention applies, any carrier who actually performs the whole or a part of the carriage shall maintain insurance or other financial security, such as the guarantee of a bank or similar financial institution, to cover liability under this Convention in respect of the death of and personal injury to passengers. The limit of the compulsory insurance or other financial security shall not be less than 250,000 units of account per passenger on each distinct occasion."

16 Athens Convention relating to the Carriage of Passengers and their Luggage by Sea (PAL), "International Maritime Organization" https://www.imo.org/en/About/Conventions/Pages/Athens-Convention-relating-to-the-Carriage-of-Passengers-and-their-Luggage-by-Sea-(PAL).aspx accessed 30 April 2023.

17 Protocol of 2002 to the Athens Convention Relating to the Carriage of Passengers and Their Luggage by Sea, 1974, "International Maritime Organization" https://www.imo.org/en/About/Conventions/Pages/Athens-Convention-relating-to-the-Carriage-of-Passengers-and-their-Luggage-by-Sea-(PAL).aspx last accessed 30 April 2023.

18 Articles 4(1)(a), (b) Protocol to Amend the Athens Convention Relating to the Carriage of Passengers and their Luggage by Sea 1974 (Athens Protocol 2002).

19 Soyer, "Athens Convention", 530.

certain limits for damages caused by their negligence. According to the 2002 Protocol, a "shipping incident" includes a "shipwreck, capsizing, collision, or stranding of the ship, explosion, fire in the ship, or defect in the ship." However, Soyer criticizes this definition, emphasizing its insufficiency, which can lead to uncertainty when damage is caused by the defective behaviour of more than one person. For instance, if an inadequate crew cannot extinguish a fire from a cigarette thrown by a passenger on the ground, the damage will result from both the crew's and the passenger's fault. However, it will be challenging to determine whether this event is considered a "shipping incident."[20] Moreover, Soyer argues that the definition of "defect in the ship" is too narrow and restrictive, and its limits should be more specific. The 2002 Protocol defines "defect in the ship" as

> any malfunction, failure, or non-compliance with applicable safety regulations in respect of any part of the ship or its equipment when used for the escape, evacuation, embarkation and disembarkation of passengers; or when used for the propulsion, steering, safe navigation, mooring, anchoring, arriving at or leaving berth or anchorage, or damage control after flooding; or when used for the launching of life-saving appliances.[21]

Soyer's views on this issue are apt as defining the boundaries of the "shipping incident" and "defect in the ship" definitions contained in the Convention is critical to determining liability and the limit of compensation payable.

Another regulation stipulated in the Convention relates to the certificate requirement. This requirement applies to liabilities arising from war and terrorism risks as well as maritime and other non-war risks.

The International Group of P&I Clubs has stated that they do not cover the risks of war and terrorism and cannot provide insurance regarding the Convention's regulations.[22] They also do not provide insurance as a "War Risk Blue Card" to meet obligations arising from such risks under the Convention.[23] As such, particular purpose insurers often provide "War Risk Blue Cards."[24] "Non-War Passenger Blue Cards" are among the guarantees the International Group of P&I Clubs covers.

In summation, P&I insurance covers liability to passengers and is regulated by international conventions. These conventions have mandated compulsory

20 Soyer, "Athens Convention", 525.

21 Articles 4(5)(c) Protocol to Amend the Athens Convention Relating to the Carriage of Passengers and their Luggage by Sea 1974 (Athens Protocol 2002).

22 Acar, *Club Insurance*, 111.

23 Athens Protocol 2002 in a Nutshell, "Gard" (20 October 2020) http://www.gard.no/web/updates/content/20740184/athens-protocol-2002-in-a-nutshell accessed 30 April 2023.

24 For example, Shoreline Passenger Solutions (SPS) provides the war insurance that shipowners must have in accordance with the Athens Convention 2002 by issuing the War Blue Card ("Blue Card"). See Shoreline Passenger Solutions (SPS), https://www.shoreline.bm/solutions/passenger-solutions/ accessed 30 April 2023.

insurance for passenger damage, allowing for direct action lawsuits against P&I Clubs, the insurance providers, for passenger compensation claims.

### *3. Coverage for the Collision with Another Ship*

Collisions between ships can result in significant damages, including ship and cargo damage, environmental pollution, general average, and wreck removal liabilities.[25] The *de Vaux v Salvador* judgement of the Court of King's Bench was a ground-breaking ruling that paved the way for hull insurance coverage of collision damages. Before this judgement, collisions were considered among the perils of the seas, and damages arising from the collision were compensated based on procedures set out in maritime codes.[26] However, the application of these rules[27] could lead to unfair consequences.[28] The *de Vaux v. Salvador* ruling rejected the idea that collision liability should be assessed under the "perils of the seas" framework and recognized that the Court does not uphold some rules on collision.[29]

Despite this landmark judgement, liability insurance for collision damages was not legally accepted at the time, but collision liability was added to the risks covered by hull insurers.[30] Currently, hull insurance remains the primary insurance that covers the liability arising from collisions.[31] However, this insurance only covers a portion of the damages,[32] leaving shipowners to seek additional insurance to cover

25 Hill, 283; Baughen, 270; Acar, *Club Insurance*, 118; Bennett, *Marine Insurance*, 396.

26 Merkin and Steele, 66.

27 For instance, under the former Admiralty rule, in cases where both parties were at fault in a collision, the damages incurred by the vessels were apportioned equally between them. See Bennett, *Marine Insurance*, 396.

28 Reginald Godfrey Marsden and J. William Mansfield, International Marine Conference Washington, A Treatise on The Law of Collisions at Sea, With an Appendix Containing the International Regulations for Preventing Collisions at Sea, and Local Rules for the Same Purpose in Force in the Thames, Mersey, and Elsewhere, also the Regulations Approved at the Washington International Maritime Conference (3rd edn, Stevens and Sons Limited 1891) 61.

29 Merkin and Steele, 67; Reynardson, 466.

30 Merkin and Derrington, 35.

31 International Hull Clauses (IHC) 2003 cl 6.1: "The Underwriters agree to indemnify the Assured for three fourths of any sum or sums paid by the Assured to any other person or persons by reason of the Assured becoming legally liable by way of damages for 6.1.1 loss of or damage to any other vessel or property thereon 6.1.2 delay to or loss of use of any such other vessel or property thereon 6.1.3 general average of, salvage of, or salvage under contract of, any such other vessel or property thereon, where such payment by the Assured is in consequence of the insured vessel coming into collision with any other vessel." Accordingly, hull insurance covers only a certain part of the liability arising from the collision, not the whole. See http://www.fortunes-demer.com/documents%20pdf/polices%20corps/Etrangeres/Royaume%20Uni/International%20Hull%20Clauses%202003.pdf last accessed 30 April 2023.

32 The Hull International Clauses of 2003 provide coverage for three-fourths of the liability arising from collision incidents. Nevertheless, the insured may opt to pay an additional premium to secure coverage for the full liability. It should be noted, however, that the 2003 Clauses have not gained widespread acceptance due to their stringent provisions against mechanical breakdown, latent damage, and fraudulent claims. Notably, while prior versions of the Clauses (adopted in 1983 and

the remaining damages.[33] P&I insurance is an essential policy that covers damages not covered by hull insurance[34] and the remaining 1/4 loss[35] without being limited to the insured value.[36]

P&I insurance covers a range of damages, including loss or damage to goods carried on board due to the collision,[37] damages caused by the collision during the loading or unloading of goods, and damages resulting from delayed delivery of goods and loss of use due to collision.[38] Additionally, P&I insurance covers the member's liability for damages arising from the late cargo delivery.[39] In cases where the liability of at least one of the vessels for collision damage is not limited by law, the settlement of the hull and Club insurers with each other is based on cross-liability.[40] This approach determines the fault rate between the ships and calculates who is liable for the damage they suffered based on that rate.[41]

While the cross-liability principle may seem confusing, insurers argue that it results in more accurate and fair outcomes than single-liability. Both hull and Club insurers prefer the cross-liability principle when calculating collision liability.[42] However, it is worth noting that this approach still has limitations and may not always result in a fair outcome for all parties involved. Therefore, it is crucial to

---

amended in 1996) do not explicitly provide for fourth-fourths coverage against collision, insurers may still offer such coverage to policyholders who opt to pay an additional premium. For detailed information, see Merkin and Steele, 58.

33 Susan Hodges, *Cases and Materials on Marine Insurance Law* (Cavendish 1999) 535; Hazelwood and Semark, 5; Noussia, *The Principle*, 68; Bennett, *Marine Insurance*, 398; Gurses, 260.

34 For example, the insured vessel, wrecks, removal or disposal of obstructions, cargoes, or any other things whatsoever, and the cargo or other property on, or the engagements of, loss of life, personal injury, or illness are not covered by hull insurance.

35 But in practice, hull insurers also provide insurance for the remaining one quarter, provided that the insured pays an additional premium.

36 Soyer, *Warranties*, 116.

37 West P&I, Rule 2 Section 9(B); UK P&I, Rule 2 Section 10(B); Steamship P&I, Rule 25/v(b); Standard P&I, Section C, Rule 3.6.3.

38 West P&I, Rule 2 Section 9(A); UK P&I, Rule 2 Section 10(A); Steamship P&I, Rule 25/v(a); Standard P&I, Section C Rule 3.6.1.

39 Shipowners' P&I, Rule 2 Section 7.

40 West P&I, Rule 2 Section 9(C/d); UK P&I, Rule 2 Section 10(C/d); Steamship P&I, Rule 25/v(e); Standard P&I, Section C, Rule 3.6.6; The London P&I, Rule 9.13.2.3.

41 To explain with an example, ships X and Y collide with equal fault rate (1/2). The total loss on ship X is £1,000, and it is £2,000 on ship Y. X is liable for half of the loss of Y, while Y is liable for half of the loss of X. X claims £1,000 loss of himself and 3/4 of half of Y's loss from his hull insurer. However, X's insurer has a subrogation right for £500 against Y, which is liable for half of X's loss. Y also claims £2,000 loss of himself and 3/4 of half of X's loss from his hull insurer. Y's insurer also has a subrogation right for £1,000 against X, which is liable for half of Y's loss. Club insurers, on the other hand, cover 1/4 of half of the losses of both ships (Half of the loss is calculated because the fault rate of the ships is equal). In this case, X's Club insurer pays 1/4 of the £1,000 portion of the loss incurred on Y's ship. Y's Club insurer will also pay 1/4 of the £500 on X's ship. For similar examples, see Gurses, 261; Acar, *Club Insurance*, 126; Hodges, 537.

42 Hodges, 536; Gurses, 261.

continually evaluate and update collision liability policies to ensure fair and equitable outcomes for all parties involved in collisions between ships.

### 4. *Coverage for Towage Costs*

P&I insurance is designed to provide coverage for the costs and liability that may arise from the towage of a vessel by a member or from the towage of the member's entered ship by another vessel.[43] The coverage is subject to various conditions that must be met by the member, such as the notification of the towage contract to the Club in advance and the payment of an additional Call or premium, if required.

The Club rules specify the situations in which towage coverage is offered. This includes cases where it is conducted as part of a contract for entering or leaving a port or for manoeuvring within the port as part of routine trading activities. However, it is essential to note that hull insurance must not cover the liability, and the Club must approve the towage contract.

Moreover, the coverage provided by the Club is also contingent upon several other conditions.[44] For instance, the entered ship must be habitually towed from port to port or place. If it is specially designed for towage purposes or later used in this way, this must be notified to the Managers at the time of entry or conversion. The Managers must also approve the towage contract, and the member must have paid or agreed to pay the additional call or premium requested by the Club.

The regulation of towage activities on the high seas is significant in the maritime industry. To this end, international agreements such as TOWCON[45] and TOWHIRE[46] have been developed to govern the commercial industry's terms and conditions of ocean towage. These agreements ensure that the parties involved in towage operations know their rights and obligations.

The TOWCON agreement, which operates on a lump-sum payment system, is widely considered the most current version of the international ocean towage agreement. The latest edition, TOWCON 2008, has been widely adopted by Clubs[47] and industry participants. Similarly, the TOWHIRE agreement, based on a daily hire basis and developed by the Baltic and International Maritime Council (BIMCO), is essential for commercial towage operations.[48]

43 According to the Club rules, provided the towage coverage in the following cases: "(i) under the terms of a contract entered into for the purpose of entering or leaving port, or manoeuvring within the port during the ordinary course of trading in; (ii) in the ordinary course of trading of an Entered Ship which is habitually towed from port to port or from place to place." See Britannia P&I, Rule 19/4(A); Shipowners' Club, Rule 2, Section 10(A); North of England, Rule 19/15(a).

44 Shipowners' Club, Rule 2, Section 10(D/iv); Steamship P&I, Rule 25/ix(d).

45 International Ocean Towage Agreement Lump Sum (TOWCON).

46 International Ocean Towage Agreement Daily Hire (TOWHIRE).

47 North of England, Rule 19/15(B); Shipowners' Club, Rule 2, Section 10(D); Standard P&I, Section C, Rule 3.10.2(4).

48 For detailed information about these agreements, see Baatz, 256.

However, it should be noted that the TOWCON and TOWHIRE agreements are not designed to regulate port towing operations. While these agreements have been developed to provide a degree of certainty and predictability in ocean towage, the scope of their application is limited to the commercial industry.

Towage contracts typically share liability using the "knock-for-knock" principle.[49] This rule, mainly from the insurance industry, states that every insurer must cover damages to insured vehicles,[50] regardless of the insured party's fault.[51] Until the 1960s, this principle governed automobile accidents in England, compelling drivers to bear their damages in accidents or purchase first-party insurance.[52] However, this system was later abolished in the context of England's vehicle insurance.[53]

In different segments of the general maritime industry, such as oil and gas companies and towage contracts, the "knock-for-knock" principle continues to be employed today.[54] It has become widespread, especially in the oil and gas industry.[55] Under a towage contract based on this principle, the owners of the entered ship and the owners of the towing vessel are entirely responsible for any loss or damage to their property.[56] Consequently, the parties do not have the right to make any claims against each other. While this principle simplifies the allocation of risks and liabilities among the parties involved in towing operations, there is always a risk of it being inappropriate or unfair, particularly when one party has significantly more bargaining power than the other.[57]

P&I Clubs accept these types of contracts.[58] However, "knock-for-knock" contracts can be complex in some cases. Therefore, Clubs often recommend using towage contracts published by BIMCO[59] for their members.[60] Additionally, due to

49 UK P&I Club, "POST-CASUALTY TOWAGE: The risks and the process required to maintain P&I coverage" https://www.ukpandi.com/media/files/imports/13108/briefings/23321-towage_guidance_note.pdf accessed 14 December 2023.

50 John Birds, "Motor Insurers and the Knock for Knock Agreements" (1978) 41 *The Modern Law Review* 201, 202; Merkin and Steele, 129.

51 Baatz, 257.

52 Richard Lewis, "Insurer's Agreements Not to Enforce Strict Legal Rights: Bargaining with Government and in the Shadow of the Law" (1985) 48 *Modern Law Review* 275, 285–286.

53 Lewis, "Insurer's Agreements Not to Enforce Strict Legal Rights".

54 Gideon Parchomovsky and Endre Stavang, "Contracting Around Tort Defaults: The Knock for Knock Principle and Accident Costs" (2013) 14 *The CREE Centre, Working Paper* https://www.jus.uio.no/ifp/english/research/news-and-events/events/knock_for_knock_stavang_cree_wp_14_2013.pdf 8 accessed 14 December 2023.

55 Parchomovsky and Stavang, "Contracting Around Tort Defaults".

56 Parchomovsky and Stavang, "Contracting Around Tort Defaults".

57 Kristoffer Svendsen, Endre Stavang, and Greg Gordon, *Knock-for-Knock Indemnities and the Law: Contractual Limitation and Delictual Liability* (Informa Law from Routledge 2023) 169.

58 UK P&I Club, "Post-Casualty Towage: The Risks and the Process Required to Maintain P&I Coverage" https://www.ukpandi.com/media/files/imports/13108/briefings/23321-towage_guidance_note.pdf accessed 14 December 2023.

59 See the latest edition of the ocean towage contract published by BIMCO, "TOWCON 2021" https://www.bimco.org/contracts-and-clauses/bimco-contracts/towcon-2021 accessed 14 December 2023.

60 BIMCO, "TOWCON 2021".

the risk of imposing heavy obligations on members, these contracts based on the "knock for knock" principle must undergo Club approval.[61]

### 5. *Coverage for Cargo Liability*

Cargo liability is one of the key areas covered by P&I insurance, but the extent of coverage varies based on the Clubs' discretion. The coverage for goods can be expanded or narrowed by the Clubs depending on their interpretation of the applicable liability rules. Clubs follow the Hague[62] or Hague-Visby Rules[63] to determine the member's liability for cargo damage resulting from the contract of carriage. However, Clubs may not cover liability under more stringent agreements such as the Hamburg Rules,[64] which impose strict liability on the carrier.[65] The Clubs' reluctance to cover cargo liability under more stringent liability rules can be attributed to the increased burden of coverage they would have to bear.[66]

The Clubs' coverage for cargo liability is also subject to certain conditions, such as the requirement for a clear causal link between the damage to the goods and the ship's operation.[67] Deviations from the agreed-upon voyage or adventure are generally not covered,[68] except in certain circumstances where the Club may privately accept such deviations.[69] Additionally, P&I insurance does not typically cover rare and valuable goods such as rare metals or stones, bank notes, other forms of currency, and bullion.[70]

Moreover, the coverage for cargo liability is not static, as Clubs continuously update their rules to adapt to technological and economic developments. The Clubs' authority to determine the scope of the coverage they provide for cargo losses or damages according to each situation and claim means that the extent of coverage can

61 North of England, Rule 2(1); Standard P&I, Section C, Rule 3.10.2; Steamship P&I, Rule 25/ix(d/d); The London P&I, Rule 23.2.1.2; UK P&I, Rule 2 Section 13(C/d).

62 International Convention for the Unification of Certain Rules of Law relating to Bills of Lading ("Hague Rules") (signed 25 August 1924).

63 International Convention for the Unification of Certain Rules of Law relating to Bills of Lading ("Hague-Visby Rules") (signed 25 August 1924; revised Brussels, 1968).

64 United Nations Convention on the Carriage of Goods by Sea ("Hamburg Rules") (signed 31 March 1978, entered into force 1 November 1992).

65 Standard P&I, Section C, Rule 3.13.3(1); Shipowners' Club, Rule 2, Section 14(E/i); Steamship P&I, Rule 25/xiii(d/i); West P&I, Rule 2 Section 16(C/a); UK P&I, Rule 2 Section 17(D/a); Britannia P&I, Rule 19/17(G/i).

66 Ilian Djadjev, *The Obligations of the Carrier Regarding the Cargo: The Hague-Visby Rules* (Springer 2017) 38.

67 Sjur Brækhus and Alex Rein, *Handbook of P&I Insurance* (2nd edn, Assuranceforeningen Gard, Arendal 1979) 173.

68 Burucuoglu, 87.

69 Standard P&I, Section C, Rule 3.13.3(2); Shipowners' Club, Rule 2, Section 14(E/iii); Steamship P&I, Rule 25/xiii(d/iii); West P&I, Rule 2 Section 16(C/d); UK P&I, Rule 2 Section 17(D/b); Britannia P&I, Rule 19/17(G/ii).

70 Steamship P&I, Rule 25/xiii(d/iv).

vary depending on the circumstances.[71] Furthermore, Clubs may require payment of a premium or additional call to increase the scope of the coverage provided.

Overall, while P&I insurance coverage for cargo liability can offer protection against potential losses, the scope and extent of the coverage provided by Clubs can vary depending on the liability rules, conditions, and circumstances, highlighting the importance of carefully reviewing the insurance policy's terms.

### 6. *Coverage for Pollution Risks*

One of the most crucial aspects of protection offered by P&I Clubs is the liability arising from pollution. P&I insurance covers the member's liability for damages and expenses from the release, discharge, or contamination of oil or other substances from the entered ship without any geographical limitations. Notably, P&I insurance covers the member's liability not only for pollution arising from oil but also for pollution from any substance. Moreover, the Club assumes all legal liability arising from pollution damages without distinguishing between national legal regulations or international agreements. The Club provides insurance against pollution, regardless of the country or agreement, in which the member is liable for pollution damage as per national or international legislation.

However, if the member's entered ship is included in the definition of "relevant ship"[72] as defined in the STOPIA[73] and TOPIA[74] agreements, the member must agree to be a party to these agreements[75] for the duration of their membership period, to avail of pollution coverage provided by the P&I Club.[76] If the member wishes to exercise their right to withdraw from these agreements and the Club does not give written consent, then the member cannot take advantage of the pollution coverage provided by the Club.[77] However, it is pertinent to note that the Club has

71 Some Clubs Provide P&I insurance coverage under the same conditions as the rules applied to the traditional paper "bill of lading" in electronic trading with systems adopted by the International Group. For example, Standard P&I, Section C, Rule 3.13.3(5).

72 According to the STOPIA 2006 and TOPIA 2006 Clause III/ B, the relevant ship's definition is as follows: "A Ship shall be eligible for Entry in the scheme if: (1) it is of not more than 29,548 Tons; (2) it is insured by a Club; and (3) it is reinsured through the Pooling arrangements of the International Group. Such a ship is referred to herein as a 'Relevant Ship'."

73 Small Tanker Oil Pollution Assurance Agreement 2006 (as amended 2017).

74 Tanker Oil Pollution Assurance Agreement 2006 (as amended 2017).

75 The Small Tanker Oil Pollution Assurance Agreement 2006 (STOPIA) outlines the requirements for shipowners to make payments to the 1992 Fund. These payments serve to regulate the financial implications of the limitation of liability provisions set forth in the 1992 International Convention on Civil Liability for Oil Pollution Damage (1992 CLC) for spills arising from tankers with a gross tonnage of less than 29,548 GT. On the other hand, the Tanker Oil Pollution Assurance Agreement 2006 (TOPIA) stipulates that shipowners must provide compensation to the Supplementary Fund for 50% of the compensation it pays out for pollution damage resulting from tankers in States that are party to the 2003 Supplementary Fund Protocol.

76 Bundock, 557.

77 Standard P&I, Section C, Rule 3.8.7; Shipowners' Club, Rule 2 Section 9(F/G); Steamship P&I, Rule 25/vi(f/iv); West P&I, Rule 2 Section 11(E/d); UK P&I, Rule 2 Section 12(c); Britannia P&I,

broad discretion regarding whether to provide cover to the member despite the latter's decision to withdraw from the agreements.

In summary, while the P&I Club provides comprehensive coverage for pollution liability, the Club's discretion regarding whether to cover the member despite the latter's withdrawal from the relevant agreements may have significant implications for the member. Therefore, it is significant for the member to carefully consider their decision to withdraw from these agreements and its potential impact on their coverage.

### 7. *Coverage for Wreck Removal Liabilities*

Contemporary maritime law systems have established regulations that permit certain entities, such as coastguards and port or lighthouse authorities, to undertake the removal of wrecks that pose a navigation hazard.[78] In England, for instance, the Merchant Shipping Act 1995, Sections 252[79] to 254, delineate the rules on wreck removal. These regulations empower the relevant entity to take charge of the removal process while giving them the authority to recover the costs incurred by the shipowner.[80] Under English law, the ownership of a wrecked vessel is retained by the shipowner at the time of the sinking, stranding, or abandonment, and they are therefore liable for the costs associated with the removal of the wreck.

The P&I Clubs offer coverage for wreck removal liability, which encompasses costs and expenses incurred from removing, destroying, lighting, or marking the wreckage. The coverage also includes any damage sustained by the cargo onboard, and the Clubs provide comprehensive insurance services that cover such damages.[81] However, the value of any recovered cargo is typically subtracted from the total costs incurred. The liability must be legally required to provide wreck removal coverage or the costs incurred by the authorities must be reimbursed by the shipowner. Additionally, the Club must approve the wreck removal contract before the coverage is extended.[82]

---

Rule 19/12(F/(vi/a); The London P&I, Rule 9.15.1.6; North of England P&I, Rule 19/13(C).

78 Baatz, 264.

79 According to the Merchant Shipping Act 1995 Section 252, of the powers of harbour and conservancy authorities in relation to wrecks are as follows: "(a) to take possession of, and raise, remove or destroy the whole or any part of the vessel and any other property to which the power extends; (b)to light or buoy the vessel or part of the vessel and any such other property until it is raised, removed or destroyed; and (c)subject to subsections (5) and (6) below, to sell, in such manner as the authority think fit, the vessel or part of the vessel so raised or removed and any other property recovered in the exercise of the powers conferred by paragraph (a) or (b) above; (d)to reimburse themselves, out of the proceeds of the sale, for the expenses incurred by them in relation to the sale."

80 Section 253 of the Merchant Shipping Act 1995 stipulates that expenses incurred by authorities for wreck removal may be recovered from the individual who owned the vessel at the time of the vessel's sinking, stranding, or abandonment.

81 Standard P&I, Section C, Rule 3.11; Shipowners' Club, Rule 2 Section 12; Steamship P&I, Rule 25/xi; West P&I, Rule 2 Section 14; UK P&I, Rule 2 Section 15; Britannia P&I, Rule 19/13; The London P&I, Rule 9.18; North of England P&I, Rule 19/14.

82 The London P&I, Rule 9.18.1; Shipowners' Club, Rule 2 Section 12/D(iv/a); UK P&I, Rule 2 Section 15/D(d/i).

### 8. *Coverage for Quarantine Expenses*

The spread of epidemics through maritime transport poses a significant risk, making it necessary to quarantine ships to prevent further transmission. With the outbreak of the Covid-19 pandemic,[83] many ships were subjected to quarantine measures.[84]

P&I insurance typically covers the costs incurred due to quarantine and related direct expenses. In Club rules, these costs are often specified as

> Quarantine and disinfection expenses and the net loss to the owner (over and above such expenses as would not have been incurred but for the outbreak) in respect of the cost of fuel, insurance, wages, stores, provisions and port charges.[85]

The coverage provided by P&I insurance includes these expenses. However, it is essential to note that if the member knowingly proceeds to a port where quarantine is required and incurs costs, the Club may not provide coverage for these expenses.[86]

### 9. *Coverage for Unrecoverable General Average Contributions*

The general average is a fundamental concept in maritime law that aims to allocate the costs of extraordinary sacrifices and expenses incurred to protect a vessel and its cargo during a sea voyage.[87] The York-Antwerp Rules,[88] widely accepted and applied worldwide, guide the allocation of these costs between the shipowner, cargo owners, and parties entitled to freight. For the general average to be applicable, the expenses and sacrifices must be voluntary and reasonable, and there must be a complete or partial recovery of the ship or cargo.[89]

In some countries, such as the United Kingdom, the York-Antwerp Rules only apply if explicitly included in contracts.[90] Standard hull and machine insurance usually provide coverage for the general average. However, in certain circumstances, the value of the ship may be higher than the amount covered by the hull policy.[91] In such cases,

83 COVID-19, or Coronavirus disease 2019 as it is called, is a highly contagious disease caused by SARS-CoV-2, which creates severe acute respiratory syndrome in humans. It first appeared in Wuhan, Hubei province, China, in 2019. Later, the disease spread worldwide, leading to the COVID-19 pandemic. See World Health Organization, https://www.who.int/health-topics/coronavirus#tab=tab_1 accessed 20 December 2020.

84 For example, Norwegian Cruise Line Holdings, MSC Cruises, Disney Cruise Line, Royal Caribbean, Carnival Cruise Line, Princess Cruises, Celebrity Cruises, etc.

85 See COVID-19 claims FAQs (ukpandi.com) accessed 20 December 2020.

86 Standard P&I, Section C, Rule 3.12.

87 Leon S Felde, "General Average and the York-Antwerp Rules" (1952–1953) 27 *Tulane Law Review* 406; Noussia, *The Principle*, 111; Baughen, 311; Hodges, 734.

88 York-Antwerp Rules 2016, https://comitemaritime.org/work/york-antwerp-rules-yar/ accessed 30 April 2023.

89 Marine Insurance Act 1906, c 41, s 66(4); Noussia, *The Principle*, 112.

90 Baughen, 311.

91 Baatz, 451.

P&I insurance can indemnify the remaining costs that the standard hull policy cannot cover.[92] Nevertheless, it is crucial to note that if the costs exceed the value of the recovered ship or cargo, the Club only provides coverage up to the insured value.[93]

Moreover, the Club's insurance covers the general average share, extraordinary costs, or recovery fee share that the insured cannot collect from the cargo owner or any other relevant party due to a violation of the contract of carriage.

In summary, the comprehensive coverage provided by Clubs against various risks, such as the general average, ensures the safe conduct of maritime trade activities. Since Clubs provide these coverages based on the principle of mutuality, they must also consider the interests of all their members and the Club itself. Therefore, Clubs have significant discretion when providing insurance coverage to a member. The scope of this insurance may vary depending on each member and each event. The flexibility afforded to Clubs is a key distinguishing feature that sets them apart from other marine insurers.

### *10. Coverage for Fines*

P&I insurance also includes coverage against fines and penalties imposed on members by domestic and foreign government authorities.[94] This coverage encompasses fines related to customs, immigration, and pollution, as specified in the Club rules.[95]

However, it should be noted that coverage may not be provided if the member is found guilty of engaging in illegal activities such as overloading their ship or illegal fishing.[96] The rules of most English clubs make this clear.[97] The P&I insurance may cover other fines and penalties not explicitly mentioned in the Club rules, subject to the Club's discretion.

### *11. The Omnibus Rule Facilitating the Expansion of Insurance Coverage*

One of the most crucial Club rules demonstrating the flexibility in the insurance coverage provided to members is the "omnibus rule."[98]

92 Standard P&I, Section C, Rule 3.14, 3.15; Shipowners' Club, Rule 2 Section 15; Steamship P&I, Rule 25/xiv, xv; West P&I, Rule 2 Section 17; UK P&I, Rule 2 Section 19; Britannia P&I, Rule 19/18; The London P&I, Rule 9.20; North of England P&I, Rule 19/18.

93 North of England P&I, Rule 19/18(a).

94 Hugh S Meredith, "Fines, Penalties, and Other Miscellaneous Liabilities; Expenses of Defense; General Conditions and Exclusions; Grounds for Cancellation; Second Seaman's Policy; Club Letters of Guarantee or Undertaking" (1968–1969) 43 *Tulane Law Review* 602.

95 Standard P&I, Section C, Rule 3.16; Shipowners' Club, Rule 2 Section 19; Steamship P&I, Rule 25/xvi; West P&I, Rule 2 Section 21; UK P&I, Rule 2 Section 22; Britannia P&I, Rule 19/19; The London P&I, Rule 9.23; NorthStandart P&I, Rule 19/19.

96 Meredith, 603.

97 Standard P&I, Rule 3.16/4; UK P&I, Rule 2 Section 22/E(a); Britannia P&I, Rule 19/19(E); North of England P&I, Rule 19/19(f/D).

98 The London P&I Club Rule 9.28. "Omnibus Rule 9.28.1: Liabilities, losses, costs and expenses incidental to the business of owning, operating or managing Ships which and to such extent as the

Clubs provide insurance for many risks to their members. However, the liabilities and risks a shipowner requires insurance cover are not fixed. Due to the dynamic nature of these risks, broader insurance protection may be necessary. These risks that need to be covered by P&I Club rules may not be specified. Therefore, Club rules and Clubs must be flexible enough to respond to the changing needs of shipowners. Clubs typically provide this flexibility through the "omnibus" rule included in their rules. With this rule, Club managers have the discretion to make decisions based on the situation and provide insurance coverage to their members for risks not covered in the Club rules.

This rule entails the Club's voluntary payment for insurance claims by members that are not explicitly covered or entirely excluded from the scope of coverage the Club provides relating to the operation and management of the ship. The purpose of this rule is to provide members with broader insurance coverage. The Club is not required to provide any justification when providing this coverage.[99] Additionally, the Club can determine the amount of insurance coverage at its discretion.[100]

The flexibility afforded by this rule is a significant advantage in swiftly providing insurance services. Furthermore, this aspect distinguishes club insurance from other types of insurance.

### B. *Exclusions and Limitations of P&I Club Insurance Covers*

#### *1. The Exclusions*

Clubs exclude certain risks from their insurance coverage, which are explicitly detailed in their rules. The reasons behind the exclusion of these risks may vary among different Clubs. Other types of insurance may cover some of the excluded risks, while others may require additional premiums to be included. In general, the risks that are excluded from the club insurance can be categorized as follows:

> a) the member's liabilities arising from the transport of hazardous materials, smuggling, or illegal activities; b) claims for compensation resulting from double insurance; c) the member's liabilities for unpaid rent, fuel, or cargo in case of chartering the ship; d) liabilities covered by hull insurance, unless the Club decides otherwise; e) damages caused by war, civil war, rebellion, etc; f) the member's liability for errors in the classification of the ship;

---

Members' Committee in its sole discretion shall consider fall within the scope of this Class, 9.28.1.1 PROVIDED that there shall be no recovery which is expressly excluded by other provisions of these Rules, save to the extent that those members of the Members' Committee present when the claim is being considered are unanimous that such exclusion should be overridden in the particular circumstances of the case."

99 Thomas, "Protection and Indemnity", 36.

100 Acar, *Club Insurance*, 205.

and g) the member's liability for damages caused by wilful misconduct or unseaworthiness.[101]

It should be noted that this list is not exhaustive, and other risks may be excluded from this insurance coverage.[102] However, the previously mentioned risks are the most significant and standard exclusions that all Clubs apply.[103] Clubs meticulously specify these exclusions to avoid ambiguity and ensure their members know the risks not covered by their insurance policies.

*2. The Limitations*

Clubs may exclude certain risks and set specific limitations on their coverage. In addition, the Club's liability is limited to the same rate if the liability of an entered vessel is limited by law. This means that Clubs do not assume any responsibility for amounts exceeding the legal liability of the entered ship.[104] Another restriction concerns the tonnage of the entered vessel. If the shipowner enters less than the total tonnage of the ship into the Club, they can only claim compensation at the rate of the entered tonnage unless the Club agrees to special conditions.

The coverage for the member's liability arising from oil pollution in club insurance is also subject to limitations. The Club's liability for oil pollution is limited to the amount determined by the Managers under the prevailing conditions unless it is limited to a lower amount. Unless the Managers decide otherwise, this limit will apply to all claims arising from any oil contamination incident related to the entered ship.

As of 2020, most Club Managers have set a limit of US $1,000 million per each entered ship-related incident for the shipowner's liability arising from oil pollution.[105] Clubs do not provide coverage for sums exceeding this limit.

Club insurance liability limit also covers liability to passengers and shipowners. The member's liability to passengers and shipowners is limited to a certain amount per policy year, as determined by the Club. For instance, for policies issued in 2020, the total liability for all claims arising from an incident is restricted to US $2,000 million for passenger liability, and the limit for liability to passengers and seafarers is set at US $3,000 million for each entered ship.[106] These limits are determined by the Club Managers and are updated each policy year.

101 Standard P&I, Section D, Rule 4.1; Shipowners' Club, Part 5; Steamship P&I, Rule 18; West P&I, Part II; UK P&I, Rule 5; Britannia P&I, Part IV; North of England P&I, Part 4.

102 For other exclusions examples, see; Shipowners' Club, Part 5 Rules 23 between 32; Steamship P&I, Rule 11/vi; West of England P&I, Rules 12 between 19; UK P&I, Rule 5; Britannia P&I, Rules 20–21; The London P&I, Rule 15; NorthStandart P&I, Rules 23 between 28.

103 UK P&I Club, "Circular 02/23: War Risks P&I Excess Cover" (17 February 2023) https://www.ukpandi.com/news-and-resources/circulars/2023/circular-02–23/ accessed 20 December 2023.

104 Standard P&I, Section F, Rule 6.2.1; Steamship P&I, Rule 18/i; West P&I, Part II, Rule 7(2); UK P&I, Rule 5(B/i); Britannia P&I, Part IV, Rule 27(1) North of England P&I, Part 4, Rule 22(1).

105 Standard P&I, Section F, Rule 6.5.1; Shipowners' Club, Part 5, Rule 21A; Steamship P&I, Rule 18/ii(f); West P&I, Part II, Rule 7(3); UK P&I, Rule 5(B/ii); North of England P&I, Part 4, Rule 22(3).

106 Standard P&I, Section F, Rule 6.6, 6.7, 6.8; Shipowners' Club, Part 5, Rule 21D; Steamship P&I, Rule 18/ iv(b); West P&I, Part II, Rule 7/ (5); UK P&I, Rule 5(B)iii; Britannia P&I, Part IV,

## II. Termination Types Distinguishing Club Insurance from other Insurance Contracts: Termination, Cancellation, and Cesser

### *A. Introduction*

This section will explore specific cases of termination that differentiate club insurance from other types of insurance contracts. Examining these termination cases will highlight the unique aspects of club insurance regarding contract termination, demonstrating how it differs from conventional insurance agreements.

English P&I Clubs have extensively regulated the insurance coverage provided to members and the termination of membership in their Club rules. The Clubs have freely determined these rules at their discretion. Therefore, Clubs can terminate their insurance contracts with members under the circumstances specified in the Club's rules. The Club rules governing these termination cases can be freely asserted against members due to the liberal approach of English law.

### *B. Termination*

The Club rules provide for several types of ending insurance, each with different legal consequences. One such type is "termination," which takes effect at the end of the insurance period. The policy renewal date in club insurance is fixed for 20 February each year. The Club or member may terminate the insurance by giving written notice 30 days before this date.[107] Upon termination of the insurance with a "termination notice," the Club's liability for protection and indemnity against the members ceases for events occurring after the termination date. However, the Club remains liable for member claims arising from events before the termination date. It is incumbent upon the member to pay the premiums and contributions they owe, even if the insurance has expired.

### *C. Cancel*

Another form of insurance termination in club insurance is cancelling insurance due to the member's non-payment of premiums or contributions.[108] The cancellation of insurance carries significant implications that are retroactively applicable.[109] Specifically, the Club's liability to the member's claims is nullified from the moment of cancellation, retroactively erasing any claims to events occurring before the cancellation date. Conversely, the member remains responsible for

Rule 27(2)(B); North of England P&I, Part 4, Rule 22(4/b).

107 Standard P&I, Section J, Rule 16.1, 16.2; Shipowners' Club, Part 6, Rule 45; UK P&I, Rule 28; The London P&I, Rule 30.

108 Standard P&I, Section J, Rule 17.3; Shipowners' Club, Part 6, Rule 48; Steamship P&I, Rule 37; West P&I, Part IV, Rule 39; UK P&I, Rule 28; Britannia P&I, Part VI, Rule 33(1); The London P&I, Rule 30(1).

109 Acar, *Club Insurance*, 89.

paying any premiums or contributions owed to the Club even after insurance cancellation. Therefore, the member's liability persists following the cancellation and does not cease immediately, as with the Club's liability. In brief, "cancel" is a mode of ending club insurance that has a retrospective impact and burdens the member.

### *D. Cesser*

The cessation of insurance, also known as "cesser," is a type of termination that becomes effective in the future due to specific events, such as the death or insolvency of the member, a conviction, or a finding of mental incapacity.[110] If the member is a company, the insurance will cease upon the dissolution or insolvency of the company. Despite some similarities with the termination of insurance, cessation has distinct legal consequences.[111] In the case of the cesser, the Club's liability is extinguished concerning events after the cesser date while remaining intact for previous events. Conversely, the member remains liable for any unpaid premiums and contributions related to prior years. The member's obligation to pay premiums and contributions ceases for the remainder of the policy period.

## III. Comparative Analysis and Conclusion

Chapter 2 provided a framework based on English P&I Club rules for countries needing legal reform regarding club insurance by examining the scope, exceptions, and limitations of club insurance.

Common principles emerge when the coverage and termination conditions in Turkish and English P&I Clubs' rules are compared. These similarities facilitate Türkiye's emulation of England in developing club insurance. The flexibility in the rules of English P&I Clubs regarding coverage and termination and the Clubs' discretion in these matters provides significant advantages. For example, Clubs can expand or restrict this insurance coverage while considering the economic interests of all members and the Club itself. Similarly, coverage provided to one member may not be extended to another. The broad discretion of clubs and the minimal intervention of English law in club rules are crucial factors in developing club insurance in England. Therefore, the book supports the argument that countries with a more flexible legal policy regarding club insurance will see faster development in this industry. This chapter has shown that coverage rules can vary based on Clubs' discretion. This chapter's detailed inclusion of these rules has illustrated this flexibility concretely.

110 Standard P&I, Section J, Rule 17.1; Shipowners' Club, Part 6, Rule 46/1(A); Steamship P&I, Rule 35; West P&I, Part IV, Rule 38; UK P&I, Rule 29; Britannia P&I, Part VI, Rule 33(1), 33(2); North of England P&I, Part 6, Rule 37.

111 Acar, *Club Insurance*, 87.

Despite the distinction of Turkish P&I functioning as a state-supported insurance entity, it still deviates from the traditional Club model by offering club insurance services through a fixed premium structure. Nevertheless, parallels exist between English and Turkish P&I Clubs regarding application acceptance, insurance termination procedures, and the scope of covered risks. These similarities are evident in Club rules regulating the termination and entry procedures, with both systems reflecting harmonious risks and excluded risks. Concerning the scope of risk coverage, Turkish P&I rules are similarly structured to English P&I Club regulations, covering relevant risk categories and excluding similar hazards. Core coverage areas include liabilities to seafarers, passengers, and third parties, collisions with other vessels, pollution claims, towage operations, salvage liabilities, quarantine expenses, cargo-related liabilities, separable general average contributions, the vessel's general average proportion, and fines. The rules governing Turkish P&I coverage reflect those found in English P&I Club regulations, rendering a comprehensive description unnecessary.

While Turkish P&I was not initially established as a traditional Club, it has implemented rules resembling those observed in English P&I Clubs concerning application procedures and evaluations. Following the assessment of applications, Turkish P&I undertakes to provide club insurance services to individuals meeting the prescribed criteria. Termination of insurance is similarly regulated as in English P&I Clubs, resulting in the cancellation of coverage alongside the non-transfer of premiums, akin to retroactively terminating insurance services. Scenarios involving the insured's death, mental incapacity, or insolvency terminate insurance coverage, impacting the continuation of services. Regardless of the circumstances resulting in termination, members remain responsible for previously paid premiums.

The comparison of English P&I Clubs and Turkish P&I Corporation reveals differing historical developments, legal frameworks, the legal stances of relevant parties, and the legal frameworks governing club insurance. Despite these differences, significant parallels emerge regarding the rules regulating the risks assumed by club insurance and the termination and entry procedures for members. These similarities are facilitating factors for this modelling. However, differences in the legal policies of English and Turkish law regarding club insurance, particularly in court judgements and insurance law principles, can be viewed as obstacles to this modelling. Overcoming these obstacles will be achievable in Türkiye through new legislation concerning club insurance. Such legislation should facilitate the adoption of the non-interventionist and liberal legal approach of English law in club rules, strengthening the club insurance industry in Türkiye. To this end, adherence to the liberal values of English law from the legal perspective of P&I insurance in Türkiye will accelerate industry protection and advancement.

In conclusion, a comparison with the English model has been made to support the need for legal reform in club insurance in Türkiye and to make this framework more concrete. This comparative analysis has focused on the similarities and differences between English and Turkish P&I Clubs, particularly regarding the insurance coverage and termination rules of club insurance. This chapter has demonstrated that transferring English Club rules to Turkish P&I rules is technically feasible, but Turkish law must be reformed to encourage this modelling. This legal reform should be carried out within a framework of non-interventionist and liberal legal policies. However, this legal reform should be limited to club insurance. Club insurance should be classified separately from traditional liability and maritime insurance. Thus, a legal reform specific to club insurance, compatible with the English legal model, should be implemented.

# 3 Rights and Obligations of the Parties in English and Turkish P&I Clubs

## I. Introduction

This chapter explores the regulatory framework governing the rights and obligations of parties in P&I Club insurance and the extent to which these rules contribute to the economic stability of Clubs. The discussion focuses on the English legal approach, which has played a crucial role in shaping and reinforcing Club rules, thereby enabling the sustainable development of club insurance in England. Analyzing English court decisions alongside Club rulebooks provides an understanding of how legal structures support the operational strength of Clubs.

A comparative perspective is employed to assess the feasibility of adopting similar legal principles in Türkiye. The potential for reforming Turkish law to align with English P&I Club rules is considered, particularly regarding the regulation of rights and obligations. This analysis evaluates how implementing such reforms could enhance the Turkish club insurance system and contribute to its overall development.

A key issue examined in this chapter is the role of Club rules in restricting third-party claims through direct action mechanisms. By regulating members' rights and obligations, Clubs establish legal defences against third-party claims, ensuring that indemnification obligations remain enforceable only within the scope of Club rules. English law recognizes these restrictions, and their legal implications are examined in detail.

The chapter concludes with a comparative analysis of Turkish and English P&I Club rules, offering insights into potential legal reforms that could strengthen the Turkish club insurance framework. The findings presented in this section provide a foundation for assessing whether the English model offers an effective solution for Türkiye and other jurisdictions aiming to enhance their club insurance systems.

## II. Analyzing Rules Regarding Members' Rights and Obligations that Highlight the Flexibility of English P&I Club Rules

### *A. The Rules Regarding Members Rights*

Chapter 3 will explain how the rules of English P&I Clubs are formulated to preserve the Clubs' economic strength while regulating the parties' rights and obligations.

DOI: 10.4324/9781003628897-3

The rules governing the rights and obligations of members will be examined first to present these concrete analyses. Subsequently, it will be observed that the rules concerning the Clubs are formulated not as obligations but as services that the Club will provide at its discretion. This preference means Clubs provide insurance coverage to their members not as an obligation but as a service. In this sense, Clubs have significant discretion in providing insurance coverage to their members. The reason for this flexibility is not to avoid providing insurance coverage to members.

On the contrary, Clubs offer insurance to their members for many risks. Clubs formulate these rules to assert defences against third parties. Especially in cases where third parties utilize their right of direct action, Clubs can assert against third parties all the defences they could assert against members, thanks to these rules. The protective approach of English law prioritizing the application of Club rules strengthens the position of Clubs against third parties even more.

The third chapter will support these arguments with concrete examples while discussing these rights and obligations and English court judgements. In summary, members' rights in club insurance are essential to shaping the relationship between members and the Club. These diverse rights include the right to vote, contract assignment, premium refund, and technical and legal support. However, the scope and application of these rights may vary depending on the specific rules and regulations of the Club.

### *1. Right to Vote*

In English P&I Clubs, the right to vote is a common feature regulated in the Clubs' partnership agreements or bylaws. The allocation of voting rights is based on various criteria, such as tonnage or the number of registered ships. It aims to ensure a fair representation of the members in decision-making processes. For instance, in the bylaws of the UK P&I Club, managers and members who pay fixed premiums have one vote for each ship. In comparison, members with mutual premium insurance have one vote for each registered vessel with a tonnage of 1500 or more tons, and a member vote regardless of the number of ships for registered vessels with a tonnage of fewer than 1,500 tons.[1] However, certain restrictions exist, such as excluding insurers reinsured by any of the companies from the right to vote.[2] Furthermore, in cases where a registered vessel is entered into the Club by multiple members, only one member can exercise the right to vote.

The allocation of voting rights is crucial in ensuring a democratic and equitable representation of the members in the Club's management. However, more prominent members with greater tonnage or more registered ships may be in a more advantageous position than other members.[3]

1 Bye-laws United Kingdom Mutual Steam Ship Assurance Association Bye-laws 2011(UK P&I Club, Bye-laws 2011), Rule 12/C.

2 UK P&I Club, Articles of Association 2020, Article 17/C.

3 Alganturk, 131; Hazelwood and Semark, 75; Acar, *Club Insurance*, 49.

As a result, Clubs can introduce different voting systems and rules to prevent such imbalances and promote the Club's effectiveness. Therefore, the allocation of voting rights plays a significant role in shaping the power dynamics between the Club and its members, and it is essential to analyze the specific rules and regulations in place to determine their fairness and equity.

### 2. *Right to Assign the Contract*

When regulating the rules regarding members' rights, Clubs operate with an understanding that prioritizes the Club's and other members' common interests. For example, although the contract assignment is stipulated as one of the member's rights in the Club rules, the exercise of this right is subject to the written approval of the Club.[4]

Obtaining written consent from the Club at the time of contract assignment is suitable as it only provides its members insurance protection. The absence of such a requirement could expose the Club to increased responsibility, which it seeks to avoid. Consequently, any assignment of the contract without the written consent of the Club shall be deemed invalid, and the person taking over the contract cannot make any claims against the Club.[5] However, the Managers may exercise discretion and accept such an assignment under certain circumstances.[6]

If the transfer is deemed invalid, the insurance contract will expire, and the member must pay the unpaid premiums for previous periods. Moreover, the assignee who takes over the contract without written consent cannot make any claims against the Club based on the contract.

### 3. *Right to Legal Support*

The Club rules grant the member the right to legal support services to address any disputes that may arise with third parties. As the member's liability is covered by club insurance, the Clubs must provide legal support to the member. This provision directly serves the interests of the Clubs, as they are responsible for compensating any losses caused by the liability of the members. By offering legal support and advocacy services, the Clubs can potentially reduce the member's liability, eliminate it, or reach a settlement with a third party. This, in turn, can reduce the compensation the Club must pay the member. The provision of legal support services to the member by the Club is a crucial element of the club insurance contract, as it protects the interests of both the member and the Club.

4 Britannia P&I Club, Rule 42/1; West of England P&I Club, Rule 37/1; UK P&I Club, Rule 15/A; Standard P&I Club, Section H, Rule 14.1; Steamship P&I Club, Rule 41; North of England P&I Club, Rule 47; Shipowners' P&I Club, Rule 43/1; The London P&I Club, Rule 26.1.

5 George W Nowell, "Marine Protection & Indemnity Policy Annotations Project: Assignments" (MLA Special Report, Maritime Law Association of the United States, San Francisco, Summer 2001) 95.

6 Britannia P&I Club, Rule 42/1; West of England P&I Club, Rule 37/1; UK P&I Club, Rule 15/A; Standard P&I Club, Section H, Rule 14.1; Steamship P&I Club, Rule 41; North of England P&I Club, Rule 47; Shipowners' P&I Club, Rule 43/1; The London P&I Club, Rule 26.1.

*4. Right to Claim Premium Refund*

The Club rules also provide the right to claim a premium refund to the members. However, the circumstances under which a member can claim this right are limited and must be specified in the Club rules. Specifically, the member may be entitled to a partial refund of the premium paid if a registered vessel remains without cargo in a safe harbour or place for 30 or more consecutive days, subject to Manager's discretion.[7] To claim this right, the member must notify the Club in writing within three months of the relevant policy year; otherwise, the right to refund is forfeited. This rule is designed to ease the premium burden on members by mitigating the loss of earnings from extended docking without cargo.

This section has highlighted the central rights of members outlined in Club rules. Clubs have the discretion to vary the scope of these rights for each member. It emphasizes that Club rules regarding members' rights are structured to safeguard the interests and economic strength of the Club. The authority of Clubs to obtain written approvals and their discretion in approving the use of these rights reinforce this strength. These rules are standardized across all English P&I Clubs, and the superior position of Clubs over their members is also recognized by English law.

***B. The Rules Regarding Members Obligations***

Under this heading, Chapter 3 will discuss Clubs' rules regarding their members' obligations and significant judgements from English courts regarding these rules. This review will demonstrate that Clubs, primarily when regulating members' obligations, depart from the general principles of English insurance law and establish stricter rules against members. It will also clarify English law's approach, which gives legal validity to these Club rules and recognizes that club insurance differs from other insurance types. These findings and analyses will strengthen the argument of the book that countries aiming to enhance club insurance should adopt a legal policy that prioritizes the enforcement of Club rules.

*1. Payment of the Calls and Premiums*

One of the central obligations of the member in club insurance is the prompt and complete payment of calls and premiums to the Club. For example, The Standard P&I Club requires its members to pay all premiums and other sums in the manner and time determined by the board.[8] This obligation is standard across Clubs, as

7 Britannia P&I Club, Rule 13; West of England P&I Club, Rule 48/1; UK P&I Club, Rule 27; Standard P&I Club, Section K, Rule 18.8; Steamship P&I Club, Rule 33; North of England P&I Club, Rule 15; Shipowners' P&I Club, Rule 56; The London P&I Club, Rule 37.1.

8 Standard P&I Club, Rule 18.1/18.2 is as follows: "Members who have entered the Club in respect of any policy year, not being a closed policy year, other than on fixed premium terms, each other against liabilities which they or any of them may incur or become liable to share and contribute to the funds

the regular and timely payment of premiums and calls is essential to ensure Clubs' uninterrupted and smooth operation. Indeed, the rules regarding the payment of premiums and calls are meticulously arranged in Clubs, as failure to pay may disrupt the provision of necessary coverage to the members, compromising the objectives of club insurance. Disputes concerning the payment of premiums are resolved under these rules, either in court or arbitration.

One of the distinctive features of club insurance is its unique call collection system, which differs from the collection methods used by conventional insurers. The system is based on the principle of mutuality, where members must participate in the Club's expenses by paying the calls decided by the Club.[9] These calls are distinct from premiums charged by conventional fixed-premium insurers, as Clubs based on mutual insurance provide coverage to their members without profit,[10] and the amount of premium is determined by considering the risk analysis of the entered vessel, such as its tonnage, age, and class.[11] Consequently, the amount in premiums paid by each member may differ, and the premium calculation is adjusted to the entered vessel's essential characteristics, ensuring that each member pays a fair and appropriate amount.[12] The principle of mutuality is, therefore, a defining feature of club insurance, and it underpins the system of call collection, which ensures that Clubs can operate effectively and provide their members with the necessary coverage.

The MIA 1906 stipulates that premium articles do not apply to mutual insurance. According to Article 85(2) of the MIA 1906,[13] the provisions of the law do not apply to mutual insurance, but a substitute arrangement may be agreed upon in place of the premium. This arrangement aims to differentiate club insurance from traditional insurance contracts and reduce legal interference with the Club's rules by exempting club insurance established based on the mutuality principle from the premium provisions of the law. This exemption is advantageous for Clubs as it enables them to enforce their rules more efficiently and provides a flexible area of action. Since the premium provisions of the law do not apply to club insurance, the obligations of members to pay premiums are determined based on Club rules and judgements. Hazelwood supports the regulation that premium-related provisions of the law do not apply to Clubs, arguing that the calls contained in Club rules are not equivalent to premiums but can be regarded as similar.[14]

---

of the Club required to meet: (1) all its liabilities and other outgoings, actual or anticipated; (2) all provisions of the board deems it expedient to make. Members agree to pay all premium and other sums determined by the board, in such manner and at such time as the board may require."

9 Hazelwood and Semark, 103.

10 Noussia, *The Principle*, 6.

11 Alganturk, 137.

12 Burucuoglu, 45.

13 Marine Insurance Act 1906, s 85(2): "The provisions of this Act are not applying to mutual insurance, but a guarantee or other arrangement may be agreed upon, may be substituted for the premium."

14 Hazelwood and Semark, 103.

According to Hazelwood, premiums represent the insurer's price to assume the insured's liability. In club insurance, however, members agree with the Club to contribute to the payment of losses arising from a member's liability and make payments to the Club based on this agreement.[15] Therefore, in classic insurance contracts, the insured enters a contract only with the insurer regarding their liability, and the premiums paid do not aim to cover the losses of others.[16] In club insurance, on the other hand, members' payments of calls to the Club are based on mutual assistance. As a result, members are responsible not only for losses that may arise from their liability but also for losses related to the liability of other members, as they are obliged to pay these calls. The board of managers requests that members pay these calls specified in Club rules using payment methods determined by rules.[17] These calls establish a fund to cover any member's compensation claims, the Club's expenses, and all other costs. Therefore, the "premium/call" payment represents one of the most crucial obligations of members in Club rules.

Since the obligation to pay premiums to the Club is solely the responsibility of the member who holds the entry certificate and is a party to the contract, the Club is accountable solely to the member based on its rules. Hence, if an insurance agency registers a member with the Club, the only person who can claim compensation against the Club is the individual listed as a member on the entry certificate. Representatives or other ship partners who are not Club members are not obliged to pay premiums, nor do they have any rights against the Club. In *Montgomerie v. UK Steamship*,[18] for instance, Wright J. ruled that

> Where a person contracts as agent for a principal contract is the contract of the principal and not that of the agent; Prima facie at common law the only person who may sue is the principal, and the only person who can be sued is the principal.[19]

Therefore, it has been established that joint owners of a ship registered with the Club cannot be held accountable for unpaid premiums since they are not included in the entry certificate as members. Moreover, this case implies that the Club is solely responsible to its members, and no one other than the member can sue based on the policy, nor can the Club demand that non-member joint shipowners pay premiums.[20]

In the context of club insurance, members must fulfil their obligation to pay premiums and calls, failure of which results in sanctions as outlined in Club

15 Hazelwood and Semark, 103.

16 Noussia, *The Principle*, 6.

17 Britannia P&I Club, Rule 11; West of England P&I Club, Rule 43; UK P&I Club, Rule 19; Standard P&I Club, Section K, Rule 18.1; Steamship P&I Club, Rule 10; North of England P&I Club, Rule 12; Shipowners' P&I Club, Rule 50; The London P&I Club, Rule 32.

18 *Montgomerie v United Kingdom Mutual Steamship Association* [1891] 1 QB 370.

19 *Montgomerie v United Kingdom Mutual Steamship Association.*

20 *The United Kingdom Mutual Steamship Ass'n Association v Nevill* [1887] 19 QBD 110 (CA).

rules. These sanctions may include the member having to pay interest, losing insurance coverage, and the Club being absolved of liability and terminating the contract, making it challenging for the member to obtain coverage from another Club.[21]

In classic insurance contracts, the insurer's liability to the insured arises regardless of the payment of the premium, and paying premiums is not considered a condition precedent.[22] If the insurer does not indemnify the damage caused by the risk without receiving payment for the premiums, it must specify this in the contract. Thus, the insurer can terminate the contract due to non-payment, and the insured forfeits the right to claim compensation. Club insurance policies clearly outline this point in their rules, and members must pay premiums and calls on time and in full to benefit from the insurance provided by the Club.[23]

The general principle in English law is that failure to pay premiums alone does not terminate the contract unless explicitly stated in the policy.[24] In *Pacific & General Insurance Co Ltd v Hazell*,[25] Moore-Bick J supported this principle by stating that the insured's failure to pay the premium alone is not a just cause for the termination of the contract. However, suppose the insurer wants to terminate the contract due to non-payment. In that case, the policy must clearly state the time of payment of the premium as the essential element of the contract.[26]

On the other hand, clubs have practices that are contrary to the general principle. Club rules clearly state that they can withdraw from the contract if the member violates the premium payment obligation.[27] Therefore, the Club can terminate the contract at its discretion. The consequences of contract termination include the

21 Britannia P&I Club, Rule 12(8); West of England P&I Club, Rule 32; UK P&I Club, Rule 23; Standard P&I Club, Section K, Rule 20.1.1; Steamship P&I Club, Rule 37; North of England P&I Club, Rule 17; Shipowners' P&I Club, Rule 54; The London P&I Club, Rule 35.

22 Gurses, 188.

23 Britannia P&I Club, Rule 12(8); West of England P&I Club, Rule 32; UK P&I Club, Rule 23; Standard P&I Club, Section K, Rule 20.1.1; Steamship P&I Club, Rule 37; North of England P&I Club, Rule 17; Shipowners' P&I Club, Rule 54; The London P&I Club, Rule 35.

24 In *Fenton Insurance Co Ltd v Gothaer Versicherungsbank*, Potter J states as follows: "In cases concerned with insurance, where accounts are rendered and paid through the medium of brokers and/or underwriting agents and delays in payment are not infrequent, it seems to me that one could rarely, if ever, infer a repudiatory intention under a treaty of this kind by reason of non-payment of balances simpliciter (by way of distinction from a failure persisted in despite receipt of demands and/or protests)." See *Fenton Insurance Co Ltd v Gothaer Versicherungsbank VVAG* [1991] 1 Lloyd's Rep 172.

25 *Pacific & General Insurance Co. Ltd v Hazell & Ors* [1997] LRLR 65 (QB Com Ct).

26 Gurses, 189.

27 For example, West of England P&I Club, Rule 39/2 states that: "If the Member fails to pay the Demanded Sums in full on or before the Deadline: (ii) the Association shall immediately cease to be liable and shall not thereafter become liable to that Member for any loss, damage, liabilities, costs or expenses whatsoever in respect of any or all vessels at any time entered by him, irrespective of whether insurance of such vessels terminated by reason of this or any other Rule or at any previous time for any other reason, or whether the events giving rise to such loss, damage, costs, expenses or liabilities occurred before or after termination and whether any claim by the Member against the Association was made before or after the Deadline."

removal of the registered vessel from the insurance coverage and the member's inability to claim compensation for previously claimed damages. The timely and complete payment of calls and premiums is crucial for the Clubs to conduct insurance protection and other services without interruption. The strict implementation and regulation of these rules serve to protect and strengthen the insurance provided to members. These rules have been renewed and strengthened over time, with English law recognizing their validity and enforceability based on judicial outcomes.[28] This has contributed to the solid economic infrastructure and power of English Clubs, with their system for paying premiums and calls being put on a valid legal basis and running smoothly.

In summary, while English law has a general principle that failure to pay premiums alone does not result in insurance contract termination, Clubs have a practice contrary to this principle. Strict regulation and implementation of rules related to the timely and complete payment of premiums and calls are essential to protect and strengthen the insurance provided to members. English law has recognized this, contributing to English Clubs' solid economic infrastructure and power. As emphasized in the book argument, countries such as Türkiye, which seek to advance the club insurance industry, should embrace a policy reflective of the English legal approach. The foundational principles of insurance law in Türkiye also apply to club insurance. Hence, Turkish law recognizes the legal authority of Club rules as far as they align with these principles. The book argument advocates for revising this approach in Türkiye and comparable nations striving to bolster the club insurance industry.

### 2. *The Strict Implementation of Members' Duty of Disclosure in Club Rules*

#### A. AN OVERVIEW

The duty of disclosure holds significant importance in English insurance law, yet club insurance is subject to stricter regulation for members than general insurance law principles. Despite reforms in English law to ease this obligation, such changes have not been integrated into Club rules. Initially, this section will examine the practices and reform initiatives concerning the duty of disclosure under English law. Subsequently, it will elucidate the Club's approach to this matter as outlined in their rules. This demonstration will highlight how Clubs can exercise their rules freely within the liberal approach of English law. As the book argues, this flexibility

28 Clubs have established regulations to ensure that their members fulfil their obligations to pay premiums and calls, by implementing these regulations as a conditional precedent or warranty for the member's entitlement to compensation. The issue of whether a Club rule constituted a penalty clause was debated in Padre Island, but it was determined that the violating party was not required to pay the other party. Since this judgement, penalty clauses have been expressly included in Club rules for violations of the rules related to the payment of premiums. For instance, Rule 12(6) of the Britannia P&I Club's rules provide for such penalty clauses. *The Padre Island* [1987] 2 Lloyd's Rep 529, as decided by Saville J, is a relevant authority in this regard.

is paramount for English Clubs to conduct their operations and effectively uphold their global leadership positions.

The duty of disclosure is a fundamental principle of insurance law, which requires insureds to provide complete and truthful information to insurers about the risks they seek to insure.[29] This duty is based on Lord Mansfield's definition of good faith in *Carter v Boehm*.[30] In this case, Lord Mansfield emphasized that good faith prohibits either party from concealing relevant information, leading the other party into a contract based on false assumptions.[31]

The insured possesses the most detailed and accurate information about the risks they seek to insure. Therefore, their declarations are the basis for the insurer's assessment of the risk and the determination of the terms of the insurance contract.[32] The insurer relies on the information provided by the insured to decide whether to provide coverage and the amount of premium to be charged.[33] Therefore, the insured's duty of disclosure is crucial in ensuring that the insurer can make an informed decision and accurately assess the risks involved.

In *Carter v Boehm*,[34] the court additionally held that in cases where the insured neglects their duty of disclosure, either by supplying incomplete or false information, the insurer reserves the right to void the contract on the grounds of fraud.[35] This judgement[36] clarified the obligations of both insureds and insurers. It established a fair balance between the duty of disclosure of the insured and the obligation of the insurer to investigate.[37] While there have been many legal debates about the definition and implementation of utmost good faith, Lord Mansfield's decision has continued to influence insurance law.

Under the duty of disclosure, the insured is responsible for providing all material facts to the insurer before the contract is signed without the insurer's need to investigate.[38] The insured's representative must also disclose relevant information

29 Law Commission and Scottish Law Commission, Insurance Contract Law: Misrepresentation, Non-Disclosure and Breach of Warranty by the Insured, LCCP No 182, SLCDP No 134 (2007) para 12.27; Law Commission and Scottish Law Commission, Insurance Contract Law: Business Disclosure; Warranties; Insurers' Remedies for Fraudulent Claims; And Late Payment, LCCP No 353, SLCDP No 238 (July 2014) para 7.21; Peter MacDonald Eggers and Sir Simon Picken, *Good Faith and Insurance Contracts* (4th edn, Informa Law 2018) 41; Thomas, *Volume Four*, 15; Gurses, 80.

30 *Carter v Boehm* (1766) 3 Burr 1905.

31 Lord Mansfield described good faith in this case as follows: "Good faith forbids either party concealing what he knows privately, to draw the other into a bargain, from his ignorance of that fact, and his believing the contrary." See *Carter v Boehm* (1766) 3 Burr 1905, 1910.

32 Baatz, 436; Yiqing Yang, "The Past and Future of Utmost Good Faith: A Comparative Study Between English and Chinese Insurance Law" (PhD thesis, University of Exeter 2017) 100.

33 Dina Esmaeil M Abuzaid, "Reform of the Doctrine of Utmost Good Faith: A Comparative Study between the UK and Saudi Arabia" (PhD thesis, University of Stirling 2018) 126.

34 *Carter v Boehm* (1766) 3 Burr 1905.

35 *Carter v Boehm* (1766) 3 Burr 1905, 1909–1910.

36 *Carter v Boehm* (1766) 3 Burr 1905, 1909–1910.

37 Robin Pearson, "*Carter v Boehm*: Facts and Context" (2016) 20 *Insurance Law Journal* 19.

38 *Pan Atlantic Insurance Co Ltd v Pine Top Insurance Co Ltd* [1995] 1 A.C. 501; Eggers and Picken, 233; Robert Merkin, *Colinvaux's Law of Insurance* (11th edn, Sweet & Maxwell 2017) para 6–003.

they and the insured possess.[39] In addition to disclosing material information, the insured must also answer the insurer's questions honestly and accurately and refrain from making false statements.[40]

The good faith rule on insurance contracts is applied more stringently in insurance law than in contract law in England.[41] This is because it obligates one party to disclose material facts that the other party does not know, distinguishing insurance law from contract law.[42] Therefore, insureds must comply with their duty of disclosure to ensure that insurers can make informed decisions about the risks they undertake to insure.

### B. DUTIES OF DISCLOSURE AND UTMOST GOOD FAITH UNDER THE MARINE INSURANCE ACT (MIA) 1906

Until the adoption of the IA 2015, the duties in insurance contracts, such as the duty of disclosure, fair presentation, and not to misrepresent material facts, were analyzed under the doctrine of "utmost good faith" within the framework of the MIA 1906.[43] The primary reason for examining how the regulations on the duty of disclosure were structured in the MIA 1906 is that, in contemporary times, English P&I Clubs continue to outline the framework of this duty in their Club rules, excluding it from the IA 2015 regulations and maintaining alignment with the MIA 1906.[44] Due to the more stringent regulations in the MIA 1906 compared to the IA 2015, Clubs are still revising their rules in line with the provisions of the MIA 1906.[45] Clubs attach particular importance to the consequences of non-compliance with the duty of disclosure to effectively protect the interests of their members and the common interests of the Club under the principle of mutuality. Therefore, we will first examine the duty of disclosure within the framework of the MIA 1906 and then discuss the changes in the IA 2015.

The duty of disclosure and utmost good faith was regulated between Sections 17 and 20 of the MIA 1906.[46] The fundamental purpose of these provisions was to ensure

39 Semin Park, "Analysis on the Current Interpretations of the Duty of Disclosure in English Insurance and Marine Insurance Contracts" (PhD thesis, University of Bristol 1996) 13.

40 Germano, 758.

41 Peter Macdonald Eggers, "The Development of the Law of Remedies for an Unfair Presentation of the Risk" in D. Rhidian Thomas (ed), *Marine Insurance: Volume Five* (Informa Law 2014) 113.

42 Gurses, 80.

43 Gurses, 79.

44 Britannia P&I Club, Rule 6(2)(ii); West of England P&I Club, Part II, Rule 21(2)(a); UK P&I Club, Rule 7(D/E); NorthStandard P&I Club, Section 2, Rule 6(2)(a); Steamship P&I Club, Rule 6(ii)(c); Shipowners' P&I Club, Rule 10B (ii); The London P&I Club, Rule 43.1.1(i).

45 For example, according to West of England P&I Club, Part III, Rule 21(2)(a): "The following provisions of the Insurance Act 2015 ("the Act"), shall be excluded from the Rules and any contract of insurance made by the Association as follows: (a) Section 8 of the Act shall be excluded. As a result, any breach of the duty of fair presentation shall entitle the Association to avoid the policy, regardless of whether the breach of the duty of fair presentation be innocent, deliberate or reckless."

46 Sections 17, 18/1, and 20/1 of Marine Insurance Act 1906 state: 17: "A contract of marine insurance is a contract based upon the utmost good faith, and, if the utmost good faith be not observed

transparency and honesty in insurance relationships and to guarantee that both parties to the contract had access to all relevant information.[47] Accordingly, the insured was obligated to provide the insurer with complete and accurate information before signing the contract,[48] a duty applicable to all insurance contracts, including marine and club insurance.[49] The MIA 1906[50] stipulated that in case of non-compliance with these obligations, the contract would not automatically become void; instead, the insurer could exercise the right to avoid the contract.[51] The exercise of this right by the insurer resulted in the contract being treated as if it had never existed, relieving the insurer of the obligation to pay insurance compensation.

In the MIA 1906, regarding the duty of the insured to provide information pre-contract, the information to be provided to the insurer covered details that would affect the insurer's acceptance of insurance, the terms of insurance, and the amount of the premium.[52] It was essential that this information not be mispresent.[53] If the insurer claimed that the insurance contract terms were affected by the insured's breach of this obligation, the burden of proof rested on the insurer.[54] Concerned about the potential heaviness of this burden of proof for the insurer, the possibility of the insured's non-compliance with the duty of information disclosure affecting the insurance contract was conceptually kept broad.[55] In such cases, it was accepted that the policy could be cancelled from the beginning of the contract.[56]

In the MIA 1906, the duties of disclosure and utmost good faith were regulated to continue throughout the policy period, just as they did pre-contract. During this period, the insured was required to disclose material facts to the insurer without misrepresenting them. Otherwise, insurers had the right to repudiate or avoid the policy.[57]

---

by either party, the contract may be avoided by the other party." 18/1: "Subject to the provisions of this section, the assured must disclose to the insurer, before the contract is concluded, every material circumstance which is known to the assured, and the assured is deemed to know every circumstance which, in the ordinary course of business, ought to be known by him. If the assured fails to make such disclosure, the insurer may avoid the contract." 20/1: "Every material representation made by the assured or his agent to the insurer during the negotiations for the contract, and before the contract is concluded, must be true. If it be untrue the insurer may avoid the contract."

47 Eggers and Picken, 60.

48 Bennett, *Marine Insurance*, 103.

49 Thomas, *Volume Five*, 100.

50 Section 17 of the Marine Insurance Act 1906.

51 Merkin and Steele, 53; Soyer, *Warranties*, 324; Gurses, 391; Acar, *Club Insurance*, 318.

52 Gurses, 79.

53 Gurses, 79.

54 Bennett, *Marine Insurance*, 120.

55 Bennett, *Marine Insurance*, 120; Robert Merkin, *Reforming Insurance Law: Is There a Case for Reverse Transportation? A Report for the English and Scottish Law Commissions on the Australian Experience of Insurance Law Reform* (Law Commission & Scottish Law Commission, 21 March 2006) http://www.lawcom.gov.uk/docs/merkin_report.pdf accessed 15 May 2023.

56 Merkin, *Report 2006*.

57 Merkin, *Report 2006*.

While these obligations were mutually regulated in the MIA 1906, disputes in English law arose more from the insured's non-compliance with these obligations.[58] Again, the sanction attached to the insurer's breach of this obligation was the right to avoid the contract. Merkin emphasized that the practical utility of the insured's exercise of this right was limited.[59] The author also mentioned that English courts take a more rational approach when assessing the duties insurers must follow throughout the contract period based on the duty of utmost good faith. In other words, the duty of utmost good faith paved the way for rationally assessing other obligations based on objective criteria.[60]

Merkin criticized the MIA 1906 for not sufficiently clarifying the limits of the insured's obligations in this area, the ambiguity of compensation issues, courts applying a rationality-based test rather than a reasonable test for this obligation, and, consequently, the inability to speak of a practice favourable to the insured.[61] Merkin's criticisms are particularly valid when viewed from the insured's perspective. Because the MIA 1906 did not clearly define the limits of the principle of utmost good faith within the framework of the insured's obligations, the insured faced the constant risk of the insurer cancelling the policy.[62] The severe sanctions in the Act led to unfair consequences in the event of the insured's non-compliance with obligations. Therefore, reconsidering and reorganizing these sections of the Act in reform efforts was a well-founded step.

### C. DUTY OF DISCLOSURE UNDER THE INSURANCE ACT (IA) 2015

As previously indicated, under English law, under MIA 1906 Section 17, the parties to a marine insurance contract were obligated to adhere to the principle of utmost good faith during contract negotiations. This meant that the parties were required to observe the utmost good faith in establishing the contract, disclosing all relevant information about the contract, and conveying any circumstances that could affect the risk to the other party.[63] However, with the enactment of the IA 2015 on 12 August 2016, specific provisions regarding the duty of disclosure under MIA 1906 were abolished.[64] In this context, the IA 2015 applies provisions concerning pre-contractual disclosure duty similarly to other non-marine insurance, including coverage for maritime risks.[65]

The IA 2015 has repealed some portions of MIA 1906 Section 17. While MIA 1906 Section 17 granted the right to avoid the contract to parties in the event of a

58 Thomas, *Volume Five*, 102.
59 Merkin, *Report 2006*.
60 Merkin, *Report 2006*.
61 Merkin, *Report 2006*.
62 Thomas, *Volume Five*, 101.
63 Richard Aikens, "Has the Principle of 'Utmost Good Faith' in Marine Insurance Law Become Like the Cheshire Cat – Now You See It and Now You Don't?" in Ozlem Gurses (ed), *Research Handbook on Marine Insurance Law* (Edward Elgar Publishing 2024) Ch 3, 51.
64 Sections 18, 19, and 20 of MIA 1906 were abolished.
65 Jia and Zhao, *Maritime Law*, 63.

breach of the utmost good faith principle by one of the parties, the repercussions for a party's non-compliance with this principle in the context of a contract under the IA 2015, as outlined in Section 14(3) under the heading "Good Faith,"[66] differ from those under MIA 1906. In this scenario, the right of avoidance for the parties has been eliminated, and alternative sanctions have been introduced. Consequently, while the general interpretive principle of good faith has been retained, it is no longer a standalone enforcement tool.[67]

The IA 2015 emphasizes the pre-contractual duty of the insured to present the risk to the insurer fairly.[68] The duty of fair presentation has been reformulated and harmonized within the framework of the IA 2015. By designing a dialogue mechanism between the insured and the insurer,[69] the Act ensures the active participation of the insurer in the underwriting process.[70] During the Law Commission's reform efforts, it was asserted that an approach requiring the active involvement of the insurer in the underwriting stage would be the best practice for the insurance market.[71] The IA 2015 has enshrined and encouraged this practice in legislation, undoubtedly motivating more insurers to adopt such practices.[72] Simultaneously, the Law Commission underscored the importance of the insured fully meeting the pre-contractual duty of fair presentation of risks.[73] According to the Commission, the insured often possesses more information about the risk of being insured than the insurer.[74] Therefore, encouraging a complete and transparent exchange of information before entering an insurance contract is crucial. According to existing law, the responsibility to disclose information to the insurer lies with the prospective insured. Section 3(4) of the IA 2015 anticipates that the insured's disclosure will be deemed a fair presentation in two cases:

> (a) disclosure of every material circumstance which the insured knows or ought to know, or (b) failing that, disclosure which gives the insurer sufficient information to put a prudent insurer on notice that it needs to make further enquiries for the purpose of revealing those material circumstances.[75]

66 IA 2015, s 14(1) Good faith: "Any rule of law permitting a party to a contract of insurance to avoid the contract on the ground that the utmost good faith has not been observed by the other party is abolished." S 14(3)(a): "in s 17 of the Marine Insurance Act 1906 (marine insurance contracts are contracts of the utmost good faith), the words from, 'and' to the end are omitted."

67 Thomas, *Volume Five*, 99.

68 IA 2015, s 3.

69 Merkin, *Report 2006*.

70 English and Scottish Law Commissions, "Insurance Contract Law: Business Disclosure; Warranties; Insurers' Remedies for Fraudulent Claims; and Late Payment" (Law Com No 353, Scot Law Com No 238, 2014) para 5.54.

71 Law Commissions Report 2014, para. 3.3.

72 Rui Zheng, "Marine Insurance Law Reform in China: Experiences from the UK" in Shengnan Jia and Lijun Liz Zhao (eds), *Commercial and Maritime Law in China and Europe* (Informa Law from Routledge 2023) 87.

73 Law Commissions Report 2014, para. 3.1.–3.3.

74 Law Commissions Report 2014.

75 Insurance Act 2015, ss 3(4)(a) and 3(4)(b).

In case of a breach of the duty of disclosure under MIA 1906 Section 17, avoidance of the contract was considered a severe sanction, leading to the termination of the contract from its inception.[76] With the enactment of the IA 2015, this practice has been altered, and various sanction options have been adopted instead.[77] Accordingly, the IA 2015 has narrowly tailored the "avoidance" right to exceptional circumstances. For the insurer to rescind the contract, it is a prerequisite that the breach qualifies as a "qualifying breach."[78] In other words, it is not sufficient for the undisclosed matter to be significant only in the eyes of a prudent insurer; it must also have influenced the final decision of the contracting insurer.[79] In cases where the breach is not based deliberately or recklessly, if it is apparent that the insurer would have entered the contract under different terms or at a higher premium, the insurer cannot exercise the right to rescind.[80] Instead, the insurer will have the option to continue the contract under new conditions or, in the event of the occurrence of the risk, will be entitled to compensation, considering the ratio between the premium that should have been paid and the premium paid.

In summary, Section 21(2) of the IA 2015 has entirely repealed the provisions of MIA 1906 governing the duty of disclosure under Sections 18, 19, and 20. However, the IA 2015 has not fundamentally altered the utmost good faith duty in marine insurance contracts covered by MIA 1906. The first sentence, stating that the insurance contract under Section 17 of MIA 1906 is based on utmost good faith, has been preserved, while the second sentence, allowing the other party to render the contract void in case of a breach of this principle by one of the parties, has been abolished. The provisions of the IA 2015 relating to the duty of fair presentation of the risk do not apply to consumer insurance. For consumer insurance, this duty is regulated by the Consumer Insurance (Disclosure and Representations) Act 2012, which came into force on 6 April 2013. According to this act, the insurers' right to void the policy due to a consumer's misrepresentation has been abolished. In other words, the act does not impose a disclosure obligation on consumers. However, insurers retain the right to void the policy in two instances. The first is if the consumer has committed fraud. The second is if the consumer has not provided reasonable answers to the questions, the insurer would not have entered into the insurance contract had it known the truth. The Act 2012 prohibits pre-contractual consumer statements from constituting warranties, subjecting them only to misrepresentation principles.[81] Additionally, a remedy for a breach of a policy term should only be available if the breach was ongoing when the loss occurred. The common law rule

76 Aikens, 57.
77 Aikens, 57.
78 According to IA 2015, s 8(5): "A qualifying breach is deliberate or reckless if the insured (a) knew that it was in breach of the duty of fair presentation, or (b) did not care whether or not it was in breach of that duty."
79 Gurses, 88.
80 Gurses, 137.
81 Merkin and Steele, 55.

that a breach of warranty retroactively and automatically terminates the coverage does not apply to consumer insurance.[82]

After reviewing, English P&I Clubs and the International Group have decided not to enforce these sanctions.[83] In this regard, Clubs have accepted the decision to retain the regulation envisaged under MIA 1906 Section 17 regarding sanctions.

## D. DUTY OF DISCLOSURE UNDER ENGLISH P&I CLUBS' RULES

This section will illustrate how the stringent regulation of the duty of disclosure in Club rules surpasses that of legal requirements. Doing so will reinforce the book's argument that English law prioritizes the enforcement of Club rules and underscores the necessity of this approach for Clubs to uphold their operations and safeguard their economic resilience.

English P&I Clubs continue to delineate the framework of the duty of disclosure in their Club rules, still relying on the provisions of MIA 1906. The Clubs argue that this obligation has not been adequately addressed in the context of club insurance under IA 2015. The duty of disclosure for members in the context of club insurance has a more significant impact than other insurance contracts. This is because, under the principle of mutuality in club insurance, members are expected to consider the interests of other members and the Club, requiring them to act more diligently. Due to the stricter regulations and consequences of non-compliance with this obligation in MIA 1906 compared to IA 2015, Clubs have preferred to revise their rules under the provisions of MIA 1906. Therefore, under this heading, we will examine the duty of disclosure for members within the framework of Club rules shaped by MIA 1906.

In club insurance, the duty of disclosure is of particular importance since the mutual nature of the insurance implies that each member is responsible to the other. It is, therefore, crucial to prevent any increase in this responsibility by ensuring that all necessary information is reported fully to the Club. The Club's risk analysis and call calculations rely heavily on the information and explanations provided by the members.[84] Hence, the duty of disclosure is considered one of the most significant obligations of members in club insurance.

The Club's rules contain specific provisions for the duty of disclosure, which members must fulfil during the application process and throughout their membership.[85] Members must inform the Club of all issues related to their ships and covered risks to enable the Club to calculate the correct calls they must pay. They are also obligated to notify the Club without delay of any changes after accepting

82 Merkin and Steele, 56.

83 Britannia P&I Club, Rule 6(2); West of England P&I Club, Part III, Rule 21/d-22; UK P&I Club, Rule 7; Standard P&I Club, Section M, Rule 23.4; Steamship P&I Club, Rule 6(ii); Shipowners' P&I Club, Rule 36B; The London P&I Club, Rule 5.2.1; 5.2.2.

84 Yvonne Baatz and others, *Maritime Law* (Informa Law 2014) 435; Germano, 816.

85 West of England P&I Club, Part III, Rule 21/d; UK P&I Club, Rule 7.

their membership.[86] The Club's rules enumerate specific changes that the member must report, such as management, flag, classification society, government authority responsible for ship certification for the trade-in question, crew nationality, trading or operating area, or nature of trade or operation.[87] However, changes that affect the reduction or increase of risk must also be reported to the Club, regardless of whether they are explicitly listed in the rules.[88]

Non-fulfilment of the duty of disclosure may result in the Club's termination of the member's entry on the vessel and changes to the member's premium grade or entry conditions.[89] In extreme cases, a breach of the duty of disclosure may even deprive the Club of the coverage it provides. However, it is worth noting that while the Club rules state that membership may be terminated if the member fails to fulfil this obligation, such sanctions are rarely imposed in practice.[90] Instead, Clubs tend to increase the number of calls that must be paid and amend the members' premium grades and entrance conditions.

Hazelwood argues that the disclosure provisions of the MIA 1906 are not in line with the specific nature of mutual P&I insurance and are not feasible for the Clubs.[91] According to Hazelwood, the Clubs have chosen to remain silent on this issue, which raises questions about their approach to the duty of disclosure. However, he finds the Club's approach inappropriate and criticizes it. One of the main differences between traditional insurance and club insurance is the relationship between the insured and the insurer.[92] In traditional insurance, the insurer may refrain from contracting if the insured does not disclose or misrepresent essential information that can be considered essential for the insurer under MIA 1906. In club insurance, members are insured, and insurers must disclose more comprehensive information.[93] According to the author, Club rules must be more comprehensive than the disclosure provisions of MIA 1906.

Hazelwood also criticizes the timing of the disclosure duty. While issuing an entry certificate in Clubs shares similarities with the policy arrangement of traditional insurers, this process is insufficient to determine when the contract between the Club and the member is assigned. The entry certificate can sometimes be issued after the insurance start date. Therefore, according to Hazelwood, uncertainty may also occur regarding the timing of the disclosure duty, as the

86 Hazelwood and Semark, 36.

87 The main aspects of these changes that the member must notify the Club of are listed in the Club rules as follows: "Management, flag, classification society, government authority responsible for ship certification for the trade-in question, nationality of crew, trading or operating area or nature of trade or operation."

88 Britannia P&I Club, Rule 6(2); West of England P&I Club, Part III, Rule 21/d-22; UK P&I Club, Rule 7; Standard P&I Club, Section M, Rule 23.4; Steamship P&I Club, Rule 6(ii); Shipowners' P&I Club, Rule 36B; The London P&I Club, Rule 5.2.1; 5.2.2.

89 The London P&I Club, Rule 5.2.5; Noussia, *The Principle*, 41.

90 Acar, *Club Insurance*, 286.

91 Hazelwood and Semark, 32.

92 Hazelwood and Semark, 33.

93 Hazelwood and Semark, 33.

stage at which the contract will be deemed concluded for club insurance is not specified in the law.[94]

We disagree with Hazelwood's criticisms because Club rules impose a stringent obligation on members even in their current state. Expanding the basic information that Clubs can demand from members makes it difficult for members to fulfil this obligation. Furthermore, it is worth noting that the Club's rules clearly state the information requested by the Club regarding club insurance.[95] At the same time, Clubs are not obliged to accept the shipowner as a member, even if they have fulfilled their disclosure duty, as the Clubs have discretion over whether to accept the shipowner as a member. Therefore, regulating the duty of disclosure more comprehensively than MIA 1906 will not provide a significant practical benefit to Clubs.[96]

In summary, the duty of disclosure is an essential obligation in insurance contracts, and it is particularly critical in club insurance due to its mutual nature. Members must fulfil this obligation fully to enable the Club to calculate the correct calls they must pay, and failure to do so may result in significant consequences. Despite the severe consequences of breaching the duty of disclosure, Clubs tend to impose lenient sanctions.

The approaches to the duty of disclosure in English law, Club rules, and related reform efforts have been analyzed under this heading. These analyses are crucial as they demonstrate the prominence of Clubs' flexibility and freedom in shaping their Club rules in England. The legal policies in English law that grant freedom to the club insurance industry are pivotal for developing this industry. This fact underscores the book's argument, which emphasizes the necessity of legal policies that encourage the implementation of Club rules to enhance the club insurance industry.

### 3. *Rules Governing Members' Obligations to Adhere to Benefit from the Insurance Coverage Provided by Clubs: Warranties*

This title will examine the specific rules, known as warranties, that members must comply with to access the insurance coverage offered by Clubs. In Club rules, another significant obligation for members is the requirement to adhere to warranties. Clubs have regulated this obligation as strictly as the duty of disclosure. Despite legal reform efforts regarding warranties in English insurance law, Clubs have not integrated these regulations into their rules. This is because the reforms aimed at mitigating warranty terms in law.

This section will examine the reform process concerning warranties in England and the Club's approach. Thus, it will demonstrate the influence of the liberal approach of English law on Clubs' ability to apply their Club rules flexibly. This

94 Hazelwood and Semark, 33.

95 Britannia P&I Club, Rule 6(2); West of England P&I Club, Part III, Rule 21/d-22; UK P&I Club, Rule 7; Standard P&I Club, Section M, Rule 23.4; Steamship P&I Club, Rule 6(ii); Shipowners' P&I Club, Rule 36B; The London P&I Club, Rule 5.2.1; 5.2.2.

96 Acar, *Club Insurance*, 286.

discussion will also underscore the necessity of legal policies that encourage the implementation of Club rules to enhance the club insurance industry.

### A. WARRANTIES WITHIN THE FRAMEWORK OF THE MARINE INSURANCE ACT 1906

In the context of MIA 1906, warranties[97] were designed to define and limit the risks assumed by insurers.[98] If the risk presented to insurers was not the actual risk encountered, it was believed that insurers had the right to absolve themselves of future liabilities.[99] However, this concept has been misused over time. By the mid-20th century, insurers began demanding guarantees from the insured on various matters, most of which were warranties that did not affect the insurance assessment decision.[100] For example, the warranty for paying marine premium instalments on specific days had become widespread, which did not impact the insurance value.[101]

Express warranties included commitments by the insured regarding the accuracy of a specific situation, regardless of its relevance to the risk and whether it influenced the insurer's assessment decision.[102] The term "warranty" was not mandatory if the parties' intentions were clear.[103] All warranty statements in insurance contracts, except for marine insurance, must be explicit.[104] However, implicit warranties related to the suitability and legality of maritime activities are still included in contracts, as has been the case in maritime law.[105]

Before delving into the changes introduced by the reform efforts, it is necessary to examine how MIA 1906 regulated the issue of warranties. Warranties play a crucial role in determining the limits of risk that insurers are willing to assume, as they are promises or commitments made by the insured in insurance contracts that must be complied with.[106] Before the IA 2015 regulations, breach of a warranty

97 For detailed information, see Jonathan Gilman and others, *Arnould: Law of Marine Insurance and Average* (20th edn, Sweet & Maxwell 2023) para 19–01; Paul Reed, *Construction All Risks Insurance* (3rd edn, Sweet & Maxwell 2021) para 12–049; Hugh Evans, KC Roger Stewart, and Kieran Lee Marshall (eds), *Jackson & Powell on Professional Liability* (9th edn, Sweet & Maxwell 2023) para 8–067; Terry O'Neill and Jan Woloniecki, *The Law of Reinsurance* (5th edn, Sweet & Maxwell 2021) para 6–151.

98 Merkin, *Report 2006*.

99 MacGillivray on Insurance Law, para 10–022.

100 Merkin, *Report 2006*

101 Merkin, *Report 2006*.

102 Law Commission and Scottish Law Commission, "Insurance Contract Law: Business Disclosure; Warranties; Insurers' Remedies for Fraudulent Claims; And Late Payment" (Law Com No 353, Scot Law Com No 238, 2014) para 13.4.

103 Law Commission and Scottish Law Commission, "Insurance Contract Law: Business Disclosure; Warranties; Insurers' Remedies for Fraudulent Claims; And Late Payment"; MacGillivray on Insurance Law, para 10–029.

104 MacGillivray on Insurance Law, para 10–032.

105 MacGillivray on Insurance Law, para 10–031; 10–032.

106 Thomas, *Marine Insurance*, 25; Hazelwood and Semark, 195; Hill, 56; Soyer, *Warranties*, 3; Gurses, 100. According to the s 33(1) of the Marine Insurance Act 1906: "A warranty, in the following sections relating to warranties, means a promissory warranty, that is to say, a warranty by

in contract law and marine insurance law were treated differently under the MIA 1906.[107] In marine insurance, a breach of warranty by the insured immediately freed the insurer from liability under the insurance contract, regardless of whether the breach was related to a substantial element of the contract or whether there was a causal link between the breach and the accident.[108]

Under Section 33(3) of the MIA 1906, the insured was obligated to adhere to the warranties stipulated therein, irrespective of whether such warranties were directly associated with the risk covered by the insurance contract.[109] In the event of a breach of any warranty outlined in the policy, the insurer was absolved from liability under the provisions of the MIA 1906. This exemption was predicated on the insurer's explicit condition that the assumption of the risks delineated in the policy hinged upon the insured's strict compliance with the specified warranties.

In *Good Luck*,[110] the House of Lords confirmed that the insurer was relieved of liability when the insured breached their commitment to notify the insurer before entering a war zone, and the ship was subsequently attacked and damaged. However, breach of warranty did not automatically terminate the insured's obligations, such as paying premiums, which remained valid until fulfilled.[111]

Under the provisions of the MIA 1906, the insurer could avoid liability from the date of the violation, even if the insured had remedied the breach or there was no causal link between the breach and the resulting damage.[112] Furthermore, if a warranty were issued in the policy, it bound the insured, even if they were unaware of its existence or content.[113]

The MIA 1906's approach to breach of warranty has been criticized for being too harsh on the insured and not considering the nature of the breach or the underlying risk.[114] In response to these criticisms, the English and Scottish Law Commissions have proposed reforms to restore the balance of interests and justice between

---

which the assured undertakes that some particular thing shall or shall not be done, or that some condition shall be fulfilled, or whereby he affirms or negatives the existence of a particular state of facts."

107 MacGillivray on Insurance Law, para 10–085; *HIH Casualty & General Insurance Ltd v Axa Corporate Solutions (formerly Axa Reassurance SA)* [2002] EWCA Civ 1253.

108 Bennett, *Marine Insurance*, 536.

109 MIA 1906 s 33(3) stated that: "A warranty, as above defined, is a condition which must be exactly complied with, whether it be material to the risk or not."

110 *Bank of Nova Scotia v Hellenic Mutual War Risk Association (Bermuda) Ltd (The Good Luck)* [1992] AC 233 (HL).

111 Gurses, 112, 113.

112 Hyeon Kim, "Warranty and the Pay-to-Be-Paid Rule in Korea" (2012) 43 *Journal of Maritime Law and Commerce* 566.

113 Alastair Owen, *The Law of Insurance Warranties: Flawed Reform and a New Perspective* (Informa Law from Routledge 2021) 14.

114 Thomas, *Marine Insurance*, 30; Hazelwood and Semark, 195; Soyer, *Warranties*, 303; Owen, 214; Gurses, 120.

the insured and the insurer.[115] The IA 2015 has introduced reforms to address these concerns by introducing proportionate remedies for breach of warranty and allowing for a causal link between the breach and the loss to be considered in determining liability. These reforms have been crucial in addressing the flaws in the previous regulations and ensuring more significant equity in the system, though some areas remain of criticism.[116]

### B. REFORMS CONDUCTED BY THE ENGLISH AND SCOTTISH LAW COMMISSIONS AND WARRANTIES WITHIN THE FRAMEWORK OF THE INSURANCE ACT 2015

The concerns regarding the potential misuse of warranties under the MIA 1906 have laid the foundation for reform efforts in the United Kingdom. During the reform discussions, the English and Scottish Law Commissions emphasized that insurers should always adhere to their ethical obligations and act diligently and willingly in doing what is right.[117] Otherwise, reliance by insurers on non-compliance with warranties unrelated to losses could lead to unfair consequences for policyholders and brokers. On the other hand, the Australian Law Commission pointed out that insurers often continued working with policyholders, even in cases where they could be released from liability due to breaches of warranty, showing a commitment to their responsibility.[118] Similarly, insurers claimed that non-compliance with warranties unrelated to losses was rare and, in such cases, was usually due to the insured's failure to fulfil their duties.[119]

Contrary to this defence, lawyers consulted by the Australian Commission asserted that insurers frequently abused warranty provisions in practice, providing concrete data to support their claim.[120] Considering the discussions and criticisms in the reform process in Australia, the English and Scottish Commissions acknowledged that unilaterally and unfairly leaving the regulation to the insurer's conscience was not appropriate. Therefore, a reform in warranty provisions was deemed necessary, focusing on eliminating uncertainties and explicitly stating the consequences of warranty breaches in policies.[121] The Commission emphasized the need to soften the harsh consequences envisaged in MIA 1906 in the event of warranty breaches, suggesting methods such as providing the insured with the opportunity to remedy the breach or accepting causation links.[122]

115 Law Commission and Scottish Law Commission, "Insurance Contract Law: Misrepresentation, Non-Disclosure and Breach of Warranty by the Insured" (Law Com No 292, Scot Law Com No 194, 2007) para 7.6; Law Commission and Scottish Law Commission, "Insurance Contract Law: Business Disclosure; Warranties; Insurers' Remedies for Fraudulent Claims; and Late Payment" (Law Com No 353, Scot Law Com No 238, 2014) para 14.11.

116 Owen, 237.

117 Law Commission Report 2014, para 1.28.

118 Australian Law Reform Commission, Review of the Marine Insurance Act 1909 (ALRC Report No 91, 2001) para 9.26.

119 Australian Law Reform Commission, Review of the Marine Insurance Act 1909, para 9.27.

120 Australian Law Reform Commission, Review of the Marine Insurance Act 1909, para 9.26.

121 Law Commission Report 2014, para 1.28.

122 Law Commission Report 2014, para 12.1.

After the recognition of the need for reform in insurance warranties and breaches, this requirement was examined by the English and Scottish Law Commissions. As a result of the reform efforts, new regulations were introduced in the United Kingdom through the IA 2015. New Zealand and Australia had implemented warranty-related legislative reforms earlier than the United Kingdom. Although there were acknowledged deficiencies in Australia's and New Zealand's approaches, it was asserted that these did not pose significant problems in practice. Among these deficiencies, it was mentioned that the Australian Insurance Contracts Act blurred the boundaries of warranty provisions within the scope of contracts, representing an unnecessarily complex and faulty approach.[123] On the other hand, Owen argued that the reforms in New Zealand, as outlined in the Insurance Law Reform Act, exhibited an approach contrary to balancing the interests of the insured and insurer, skewing this balance in favour of the insured.[124]

Nevertheless, unlike Australia or New Zealand, the Law Commission chose not to follow more favourable approaches to the insured in England. While leveraging the experiences of Australia and New Zealand and legal commission reviews in this field, the Commission adopted a unique legal approach. As a result, the reform efforts for warranty breaches and other provisions found their place in the IA 2015.

The Law Commission's discussions on warranty provisions have centred on two crucial aspects of express warranties in marine insurance, which have since been revised. The first change relates to the requirement of a causal link between the breach of warranty and resulting damage. Under the new regulations, an insurer may only escape liability if a clear causal connection between the violation and the resulting harm can be established. If no such connection exists, the insurer cannot evade responsibility.[125]

The second significant amendment introduced by the IA 2015 is Section 10, which allows the insured the opportunity to rectify any breach of warranty. If any of the warranties in the insurance policy are unfulfilled, coverage will be suspended until the insured fulfils the warranty. If the warranties can be fulfilled and are completed by the insured, the insurer's coverage liability will commence. However, the insurer will not be liable for any damage resulting from the breach of warranty before it was fulfilled. Nevertheless, the insurer must pay damages when the warranty is fulfilled.[126]

The provisions within the IA 2015 suggesting the suspension of the breach of warranty and the elimination of fundamental conditions of the warranty are appropriate.[127] Simultaneously, the provisions proposing that the suspension be

123 Owen, 238.
124 Owen, 238.
125 Law Commission Report 2014, para 14.11.
126 IA 2015, s 10.
127 Owen, 239–240.

limited to specific risk categories should be cautiously approached. Nevertheless, there are several deficiencies and flaws in the warranty provisions of the IA 2015. For instance, Section 11[128] of the Act may lead to increased uncertainty and litigation, as it regulates non-material terms and their validity concerning the insured's request.[129] If insurers include terms unrelated to the risk in the policy, they cannot rely on these terms to reject the insured's claim. These warranty terms must be of a nature that reduces the risk of loss at a specific type, place, or time to be valid. However, contract terms defining the risk are outside the scope of Section 11.

While most provisions result from meticulous consideration, the inclusion of warranties in Section 11 of the statute at the last minute and its complete exemption from parliamentary scrutiny constitute the source of this deficiency.[130] Owen attempts to demonstrate that Section 11 leaves the law in a state of uncertainty.[131] The argument suggests that effective reform should address warranties and other provisions to exclude insurers from liability, such as exclusion clauses, terms, and conditions within the insurance policy.[132] For example, it is unlikely that all exclusion clauses are subject to Section 11, which requires violating a contract provision. Similarly, the relationship between Section 11 and conditions precedent is unclear.[133] Although the Law Commission has taken a clear stance on causation, there are risks associated with Section 11(3) not creating an effective causal link, resulting in a complex and uncertain outcome. The Commission has argued against evaluating the consequences of the breach without considering what happened.[134] However, adopting a more explicit causation approach could be more favourable.

In general, all reform initiatives related to warranty provisions in IA 2015 are a significant step in addressing most issues in this regard. However, a crucial aspect to consider when applying these provisions is that these reforms should not interfere with the privity nature of the contract between the parties. Owen suggests that the court consider the contract's scope to prevent this.[135] If the dispute falls outside the scope of the policy, the solution should primarily involve causation. Flexibility

128 IA 2015, s 11: "Terms not relevant to the actual loss (1) This section applies to a term (express or implied) of a contract of insurance, other than a term defining the risk as a whole, if compliance with it would tend to reduce the risk of one or more of the following – (a) loss of a particular kind, (b) loss at a particular location, (c) loss at a particular time. (2) If a loss occurs, and the term has not been complied with, the insurer may not rely on the non-compliance to exclude, limit or discharge its liability under the contract for the loss if the insured satisfies subsection (3). (3) The insured satisfies this subsection if it shows that the non-compliance with the term could not have increased the risk of the loss which actually occurred in the circumstances in which it occurred. (4) This section may apply in addition to section 10."

129 Arnould: Law of Marine Insurance and Average, para 19.05.

130 Arnould: Law of Marine Insurance and Average, para 19.05; Owen, 239.

131 Owen, 239.

132 O'Neill and Woloniecki, *The Law of Reinsurance*, para 6–153.

133 O'Neill and Woloniecki, *The Law of Reinsurance*, para 6–153; Owen, 239.

134 Law Commission Report 2014, para 18.39.

135 Owen, 240.

in applying IA 2015 provisions should be used to adapt to the specific conditions of the insurance contract when resolving disputes, allowing the court to use flexibility and discretion to prevent harsh decisions on insurers.

### C. WARRANTIES UNDER THE FRAMEWORK OF THE RULES OF THE ENGLISH P&I CLUBS

The Clubs have established strict rules concerning warranties to ensure members comply. These warranty provisions are a crucial element of the Club's insurance contract, and any breach of these rules may result in the Club being relieved of its obligation to provide insurance coverage from the date of the violation. The significance of the violation is immaterial, as any breach of warranty can be grounds for the Club to refrain from liability. Nonetheless, Clubs may exercise discretion in practice and impose various sanctions in response to a breach of warranty. Instead of terminating the contract, the Club can raise the members' premiums.[136]

While the IA 2015 mitigated the consequences of warranty breaches, Clubs have clarified that Sections 10 and 11 of the Act will not be enforced in disputes between the Club and the member.[137] Despite the reform of the MIA 1906, Club rules remain more stringently regulated than existing legal regulations concerning warranty breaches. Most member obligations are stipulated as warranties in the Club rules to ensure they exercise more outstanding care in fulfilling their responsibilities to each other and the Club.[138] Clubs also use warranty violations as leverage against third parties, especially in compensation claims.

The warranties in the Club rules are often used to protect the Club's interests and may serve as an obstacle to third parties' claims. In general, Clubs that do not terminate their members' contracts in case of a breach of warranty can deny compensation claims made by third parties based on the members' failure to fulfil the warranties. For Clubs, this flexibility is crucial to sustain their operations. For instance, if a third party exercises the right of direct action against the Club, the Club has the right to assert all defences arising from Club rules against the third party. If a member fails to fulfil an obligation stipulated as a "warranty" in the Club rules, the Club can refuse to compensate the third party by invoking this. Clubs retaining this power serve the purpose of prioritizing the interests of both their members and the Club itself. Therefore, English law prefers not to interfere with

136 Burucuoglu, 47.

137 Britannia P&I Club, Rule 3(5); West of England P&I Club, Part III, Rule 21/2(b),(c); UK P&I Club, Rule 5/L-ii(b),(c); Standard P&I Club, Section A, Rule 1.5.2/(2),(3); Steamship P&I Club, Rule 7/iv-(a),(b); Shipowners' P&I Club, Rule 10B/(ii),(iii); North of England P&I Club, Rule 6(2)-(b),(c); The London P&I Club, Rule 43.1.1/(ii),(iii).

138 Britannia P&I Club, Rule 3(5); West of England P&I Club, Part III, Rule 21/2(b),(c); UK P&I Club, Rule 5/L-ii(b),(c); Standard P&I Club, Section A, Rule 1.5.2/(2),(3); Steamship P&I Club, Rule 7/iv-(a),(b); Shipowners' P&I Club, Rule 10B/(ii),(iii); North of England P&I Club, Rule 6(2)-(b),(c); The London P&I Club, Rule 43.1.1/(ii),(iii).

the content of Club rules. This approach encourages Clubs to maintain their economic resilience against third-party compensation claims and promotes the development of the club insurance sector.

As a result, the analysis in this section aligns with the book's argument, highlighting the crucial role of law policies that uphold the enforcement of Club rules in fortifying the club insurance industry.

### *4. Other Obligations of Members in the Club Rules*

This chapter highlights the various obligations that members of an insurance Club must comply with, in addition to premium payment, the duty of disclosure, and warranties. To benefit from the Club's insurance coverage, the member must promptly notify the Club of any incidents requiring liability during the insurance contract period and the claims made by third parties.[139] Failure to notify within the stipulated period may result in the member being unable to access the insurance coverage.

Moreover, the member must provide all information and documents related to the claims for compensation to the Club, its appointed experts, or lawyers and allow them to be audited and copied.[140] The member must also keep the Club informed of any developments, changes, and expenses related to their responsibilities under the club insurance. Suppose the member settles with third parties or accepts liability without the Club's approval. In that case, they will be liable to pay the costs or expenses incurred as compensation to the Club in the amount determined by the Managers.[141]

The Club rules also stipulate other obligations that members must comply with, such as notifying the Club of any changes that may affect the premium amount to be paid, such as changes in vessel registration details.[142] Failure to comply with these obligations may lead to the termination of the insurance coverage provided and the contract.

Members must adhere to these obligations, as failure to do so may result in severe consequences, including being unable to access the insurance coverage provided by the Club. Additionally, non-compliance with the Club rules may result in the member incurring additional costs or expenses and, in severe cases, may lead to the termination of the insurance contract.[143] It is, therefore, essential for members to fully understand their obligations and adhere to them to avoid any adverse consequences.

139 Britannia P&I Club, Rule 30(1); West of England P&I Club, Part III, Rule 24/1(a); Standard P&I Club, Section G, Rule 7.1.

140 Britannia P&I Club, Rule 30(3); West of England P&I Club, Part III, Rule 24/1(c); Standard P&I Club, Section G, Rule 7.5.

141 Britannia P&I Club, Rule 31(2); West of England P&I Club, Part III, Rule 24/2; Standard P&I Club, Section G, Rule 7.6.

142 Britannia P&I Club, Rule 31(4A); West of England P&I Club, Part III, Rule 24/1(e); Standard P&I Club, Section G, Rule 7.8.

143 For example, see Standard Club, Section H, Rule 12.2; Steamship Club, Rule 7/c (iii).

## III. English P&I Clubs' Rules Regarding Clubs' Rights and Obligations and the Importance and Advantages of Flexibility in these Rules for Clubs

### A. Introduction

In this section, the analysis will focus on exploring the rules concerning the rights and obligations of Clubs, emphasizing the significance and benefits of flexibility in these rules for Clubs. This analysis will show that in the Club rules, the obligations of Clubs are structured not as obligations in a real sense but as services provided to members at the Club's discretion. For example, if a member breaches their obligations, the Club reserves the right to abstain from providing these services. This distinction's significance lies in reinforcing Clubs' superior position over their members. To minimize losses, each member must adhere to the instructions provided by the Club. This obligation is a requirement of the mutuality principle in addition to members' obligations to each other.

The Club fulfils its services if a member complies with the necessary instructions. These services include claims handling, providing a letter of guarantee, paying insurance compensation, and other extraordinary expenses. Clubs have the freedom to provide these services to each member within the framework of their discretionary authority. For example, a Club has the authority to accept one member's request for a guarantee while rejecting a similar request from another.

The flexibility in the application of Club rules and the discretion of the Club are protected by English law. The legal approach of English law, which prefers not to intervene in the content and implementation of Club rules, facilitates the operation of club insurance activities. This approach will be concretely demonstrated in this section through the rules regarding the obligations and services of English Clubs and English court judgements.

### B. The Claims Handling Procedure Specific to Clubs and the Advantages of this Procedure

This title will examine the Clubs' unique claims-handling process and highlight its benefits. One of the areas where the distinctive character of club insurance stands out is claims handling.[144] It is crucial and necessary for Clubs to operate flexibly to address their members' claims effectively and quickly. Thanks to this flexibility, Clubs ensure that claims are resolved immediately. Therefore, as argued in the book, the legal policies of countries towards Clubs should be regulated in a way that preserves this flexibility, providing Clubs with significant ease and advantage in carrying out these activities.

144 Britannia P&I Club, Rule 30; West of England P&I Club, Part II, Rule 7; UK P&I Club, Rule 36; Standard P&I Club, Section G, Rule 7; Steamship P&I Club, Rule 31; Shipowners' P&I Club, Part 4, Rule 8; North of England P&I Club, Rule 33; The London P&I Club, Rule 18.

Club members operate and trade ships for profit. Therefore, encountering any casualty or event[145] while operating a ship can disrupt these activities, resulting in a loss of earnings. P&I Clubs offer their members comprehensive claims handling services to minimize the risks of potential loss of profits and commercial reputation. This service protects members against legal liabilities and seeks to minimize the fiscal impact of claims in terms of liability and cost. Clubs's services are much more comprehensive and practical than other marine insurers. To support members, Clubs provide legal advisors and ensure that urgent measures are taken through experts. They also collect evidence of resulting damage and execute technical and legal procedures. Additionally, the Club's ability to handle these claims quickly and effectively ensures the stability of the Club's economic management.[146]

However, meeting members' claims is not regulated as a traditional Club debt or obligation. They have significant discretion in this regard, and members must fully comply with the requirements and obligations set out in the Club's rules.[147] Failure to comply with these rules may result in Clubs using their discretion to meet only a portion of the claims or avoid meeting them altogether.[148] However, it is worth noting that Clubs meet the members' claims except in exceptional cases, such as non-payment of premiums.[149]

Despite Clubs having the authority to meet their members' claims, the reason for performing all necessary actions on behalf of the members is to avoid taking any liability towards third parties.[150] Therefore, any losses incurred in this process and the liability towards third parties officially belong to the member. Clubs have arranged these rules to prevent third parties from claiming compensation from the Club in direct action cases.[151]

The expenses incurred by the Club in this process are made in the member's account and name, and the Club is not obliged to compensate the member unless otherwise stated in the policy. Additionally, Clubs can file a lawsuit on behalf of the member for compensation for any damage,[152] and this process is conducted in the member's best interest.[153]

145 Clubs have not explained the concepts of "casualty" and "event." The reason for this is the danger that if these concepts are defined, the scope of events that need to be reported may be narrowed. Because it is difficult to determine in advance which event will generate a claim, the limits of this scope should not be drawn.

146 Hazelwood and Semark, 308.

147 Britannia P&I Club, Rule 30; West of England P&I Club, Part II, Rule 7; UK P&I Club, Rule 36; Standard P&I Club, Section G, Rule 7; Steamship P&I Club, Rule 31; Shipowners' P&I Club, Part 4, Rule 8; North of England P&I Club, Rule 33; The London P&I Club, Rule 18.

148 Hazelwood and Semark, 307.

149 Hazelwood and Semark, 307.

150 Bennett, *Marine Insurance*, 709.

151 Hazelwood and Semark, 308; Acar, *Club Insurance*, 376.

152 *Groom v Crocker* [1939] 1 KB 194 (CA).

153 Bennett, *Marine Insurance*, 709.

### *C. Letters of Undertaking Provided by Clubs and their Importance in Maritime Trade Activities*

This heading will analyze the Club rule governing the provision of letters of undertaking services to members and exemplary English court judgements resolving disputes in favour of Clubs regarding this rule. This analysis will support the book's arguments that Club rules are structured to protect Club interests and that English law encourages this approach.

The P&I Clubs offer their members a range of securities, including letters of undertaking (LOUs) and letters of guarantee (LOGs), to secure the release of arrested vessels.[154] These securities are widely accepted in many maritime jurisdictions and ports around the world, and the strong economy of the Clubs has accelerated their acceptance and reputation.[155] Providing such securities is critical for members to continue their trade activities without interruption, as the arrest of a member's vessel can result in significant financial losses. In such cases, the Club immediately issues an LOU to the member, preventing further damages. The arrangement of LOUs also serves the purpose of looking after the Club's interests, as the Club undertakes to compensate the members for events within the insurance coverage and seeks to minimize any resulting losses.[156]

The decision to provide security to shipowners is entirely at the discretion of the directors of the Clubs. In other words, it is not a debt or obligation of the Club to provide such securities to members. The Club is not obliged to accept a member's claim for an LOU or LOG, and this issue is clearly stated in the judgements made by the High Court. For example, the *FSL-9 PTE Ltd and Norwegian Hull Club*[157] revolve around providing security to their members by P&I Clubs. The case arose from a dispute between the owners and charterers of the chemical tanker FSL New York and the P&I Club, where the Club provided a letter of undertaking (LOU) as security for the cargo loss suffered by the vessel. However, the owners subsequently demanded an increase in the security amount, citing the "liberty to apply" provision in the LOU, which allows either party to seek a court order concerning the security. The Club declined to comply with the owners' request, bringing the dispute before the High Court.

The case's heart was whether the P&I Club could be compelled to increase the security amount. The owners claimed that the security provided was inadequate and requested an increase, while the Club argued that it had provided sufficient security and was not obligated to increase it. The High Court ruled that the Club could not be forced to increase the security amount, as the LOU was a contractual agreement between the parties, and the liberty to apply provision did not confer an unlimited right to seek additional security.

154 Hill, 117; Hazelwood and Semark, 247.

155 Paul Myburgh, "P&I Club Letters of Undertaking and Admiralty Arrests" (2018) 18(4) *CML Working Paper Series* 3 http://law.nus.edu.sg accessed 8 May 2023.

156 Myburgh, "P&I Club Letters of Undertaking and Admiralty Arrests", 2.

157 [2016] EWHC 1091 (Comm).

The *FSL-9* underscores the complexities involved in determining the adequacy of security provided by P&I Clubs and the limitations on the ability of parties to seek additional security under LOUs. The case also highlights the importance of clear and precise drafting of LOUs to avoid ambiguity and potential disputes. This judgement will significantly reduce cases brought with confidence in the liberty to apply the provision. The Club's LOU service to its members is often viewed as an "act of friendship,"[158] and the provision of security is granted at the Club's discretion. As such, shipowners must understand the limited scope of the liberty to apply provision and the discretionary nature of the P&I Club's security provision.

In the event of an arrest of the member's ship, the member should contact the Club's managers directly rather than Club representatives or correspondents, as the discretion to provide the necessary security for the ship's release belongs to the Club managers.[159] Outside the Club's discretion, providing security to the member is subject to other conditions in the Club's rules. These conditions include that the arrested vessel was registered to the Club at the time of the incident causing damage, that the loss was caused by the risks covered by the insurance provided by the Club to that member, that the member is legally responsible for this damage, that the member must not have unpaid premium debt, and that the class of the ship entered must not have changed.[160] The Club may agree to provide securities to its members upon request if these terms are met.

These securities, provided through LOUs, are increasingly important in the maritime industry and continue to be widely used. Judgements of the English Courts have also strengthened the legal basis of LOUs, increasing the validity and reliability of these securities.[161] For example, due to the English Court of Appeal's judgement in the *Atlantic Confidence*,[162] it was legally accepted that LOUs issued by the Club could be used to create a limiting fund. This decision undoubtedly played a significant role in expanding the use of LOUs issued by the Club and improving its credibility.

## *D. The Claim Payment Procedure Specific to Clubs and the Importance of Key Club Rules Related to this*

### *1. An Overview*

Under this heading, we will examine the Club rules concerning Clubs' obligations to recover members and the English court judgements reflecting disputes arising

158 *Gregory Maritime Ltd v Thos R Miller & Son, United Kingdom Mutual Steamship Assurance Association Ltd, and United Kingdom Freight, Demurrage and Defence Association Ltd* [1966] 1 Lloyd's Rep 296.

159 Hazelwood and Semark, 256.

160 KX Li, "Acceptability of P&I Club Letter as Security" (2000) *International Journal of Shipping Law, Part 2* 78; Alganturk, 174; Burucuoglu, 41.

161 Myburgh, "P&I Club Letters of Undertaking and Admiralty Arrests", 20; Eleni Melekou, "The P&I Club Letters of Undertaking as a Modern Form of Security for the Release of Arrested Ships" (Master thesis, Queen Mary University of London 2016) 59.

162 *Kairos Shipping Ltd v Enka & Co LLC (The Atlantic Confidence)* [2014] EWCA Civ 217.

from implementing these rules. This analysis will also scrutinize the "pay to be paid" rule, which is highly significant for Clubs. The process leading to the acceptance of this rule in English law and the impact of Clubs during this process will be elucidated. These analyses will strengthen the book's argument by demonstrating the significant contribution of legal policies that validate Club rules to developing the club insurance sector.

Another feature distinguishing Clubs from other insurers is their aim to achieve the best cost and time for the Clubs and members during the claims payment process rather than seeking a fair outcome. Therefore, Clubs adopt a pragmatic approach to assessing facts and law. The objective of achieving the best economic outcome for both the member and the Club stems from Clubs operating according to the principle of mutuality.

P&I Clubs provide insurance coverage for various risks faced by shipowners. If a member's liability arises due to the occurrence of a covered risk, the Club's insurance policy comes into effect, and the member is indemnified up to certain limits, provided that the terms and conditions specified in the Club's rules have been fulfilled. The right of members to seek recovery from the Club is stipulated in the Club rules as a privilege granted to the member. Therefore, if the member meets the conditions outlined in the Club rules, the Club must compensate the member. These conditions include the fact that the incident requiring compensation must fall under the purview of the Club's insurance policy and that the member's ship must have been registered with the Club before the incident occurred. Additionally, the member must have fulfilled all other obligations specified in the Club rules, including paying all the necessary premiums.[163]

The Club rules regulate members' recovery not as a debt of the Club but within the framework of the rights possessed by the members. However, we will consider this within the Club's scope of services because this member claim is fulfilled at the Club's discretion. The Clubs make decisions regarding member recovery considering the Club's and other members' collective interests. They advocate the principle of "mutuality," asserting that each member has a responsibility towards one another and that the common interests should be upheld. For example, Club rules contain important provisions regarding the "pay to be paid" and "discretion" rules, which are crucial for the Club to indemnify the member. The "pay to be paid" rule ensures that the Club will only pay the member if the member has first paid any amount owed to a third party. The "discretion" rule gives the Club the discretion to determine whether to indemnify the member, even if the conditions for compensation have been met. In addition to these rules, other Club rules cover aspects such as the amount of compensation payable, the timing of payment, and the Club's right to the successor to the member's rights.

In summary, P&I Clubs provide insurance coverage for a range of risks shipowners face. However, the Club's obligation to indemnify a member is subject to specific conditions outlined in the Club's rules. These conditions include "pay to be

163 Acar, *Club Insurance*, 399; Burucuoglu, 42.

paid," payment of premiums, and fulfilling other obligations. Additionally, even if all these obligations are met, the Club reserves the right to refuse indemnification under the "discretion" rule. The flexibility afforded by this rule is crucial for Clubs to sustain their economic activities. Legal policies should support this flexibility to preserve the P&I insurance industry.

### 2. *"Pay to be Paid" Rule and Discretion of the Club*

#### A. AN OVERVIEW

Club insurance is commonly categorized as liability insurance, but its specific characteristics, as stipulated in Club rules, bring it closer to indemnity insurance.[164] Indemnity insurance requires the insured party to indemnify the third party before claiming from the insurer. Unlike liability insurance, this places a condition precedent on the insured. The "pay to be paid" rule is a central feature that defines club insurance as indemnity insurance. According to this rule, Club members must first indemnify third parties if they are responsible for their losses and then claim this indemnification from the Club following the Club rules.[165]

The "pay to be paid" rule is included in the rules of all P&I Clubs.[166] Although the language used by each Club in their rule books may differ, the essence of the rule is to make a member's right to recover from the Club subject to certain conditions.[167] In most cases, these conditions stipulate that the member must unconditionally discharge any liability, costs, or expenses from their funds, not by loan or otherwise, before claiming the Club. This rule is based on the idea that the Club's obligation to indemnify its members arises from specific conditions.[168] The member must, therefore, indemnify the third party before requesting compensation from the Club. This means that third parties who suffer damage from a legally liable member do not have the right to claim compensation from the Club.

While several conditions must be met for the Club to compensate the member, there are exceptions where these rules do not apply. Sometimes, the Club has broad "discretion" to compensate a member. The current circumstances of each event are

164 Hazelwood and Semark, 335.

165 Colin de la Rue, Charles Anderson, and Jonathan Hare, *Shipping and the Environment* (3rd edn, Informa Law from Routledge 2023) 824; Hyeon Kim, "Warranty and the Pay-to-Be-Paid Rule in Korea" (2012) 43 *Journal of Maritime Law and Commerce* 574.

166 See Britannia P&I Club, Rule 5(1); West of England P&I Club, Part II, Rule 10; UK P&I Club, Rule 5/A; Standard P&I Club, Section F, Rule 6/15; Steamship P&I Club, Rule 12; Shipowners' P&I Club, Part 5, Rule 16; North of England P&I Club, Rule 20; The London P&I Club, Rule 3.1.1.

167 For example, the UK P&I Club's Rule 5/A regulates this rule as follows: "Unless the Directors in their discretion otherwise, it is a condition precedent of an Owner's right to recover from the funds of the Association in respect of any liabilities, costs or expenses that he shall first discharged or the same out of funds belonging to him unconditionally and not by way of loan or otherwise."

168 Mile Phillips and Teah Sloan, "The 'Pay to be Paid' Rule – A Protected Right?" (2015) *Maritime Risk International* 1.

considered when determining whether certain conditions need to be met. For example, a final court order may not be required in cases where the member's liability to the third party can be determined clearly without one.[169] Another exceptional case is when cargo owners claim indemnification based on a letter of undertaking issued by the Club in case of cargo damage. If the letter of undertaking indicates that the Club is liable for the claim, the member is not expected to meet the "pay to be paid" condition. Finally, if an agreement is reached without delay with the third party who suffered losses, the Club may agree to indemnify it based on discretion. In such a case, the member must no longer comply with the "pay to be paid" rule.

The "pay to be paid" rule has been a subject of discussion by the English and Scottish Law Commissions[170] during the amendment process of the Third Parties (Rights Against Insurers) Act 2010, which replaced the previous 1930 Act. The Commission has recognized that this rule is used in P&I Club insurance; however, some representatives have raised concerns regarding its application by mutual insurers. The Commission sought the opinion of consultants to evaluate how this rule should be revised, and it has proposed reforming the law to prevent insurers from relying on "pay to be paid" rules.

In the *Fanti and Padre Island*,[171] the club could use the "pay to be paid" rule as a defence. This rule requires the insured to settle the claim with the third party to have the right to claim the insurance money from the insurer. However, if the insured becomes insolvent, they cannot pay the third party's claim. Consequently, to satisfy the "pay to be paid" rule, the claimant, who succeeds to the insured's rights under the 1930 Act, would have to pay the claim themselves first and then seek reimbursement from the insurer. Legally, this is an impossible situation. Despite this impossibility, the House of Lords accepted the Club's defence based on the "pay to be paid" rule.

The House of Lords ruled that when a third party steps into the assured's position under the 1930 Act, the third party must be considered as a member of the P&I Club. Therefore, the third party had to ensure that certain conditions necessary for the Club's obligation to settle the claim were fulfilled.

Furthermore, the House of Lords determined that the 1930 Act could not override the rules of the respective P&I Clubs. Thus, the judgement specified that a third party's direct action right was only possible if the club rules did not contain a "pay to be paid" clause. If the club rules included the "pay to be paid" condition, which required the member to pay the claim first and then seek reimbursement from the Club, the third party was bound by the same rule.

This case highlighted that a third party suffering damage due to the wrongdoing of an insolvent shipowner could not, under English law, directly sue the P&I Club because of the "pay to be paid" rule. Consequently, under English law, insolvency

169 Hazelwood and Semark, 336.

170 Law Commission and Scottish Law Commission, "Third Parties Rights Against Insurers" (Law Com No 272, Scot Law Com No 184, July 2001) paras 5.37, 59–62.

171 *The Fanti and the Padre Island* [1991] 2 AC 1.

nullified a claimant's right to directly seek compensation from the P&I Club for the wrongdoing of the shipowner or charterer.

However, Lord Justice Goff warned the Clubs not to use this rule against claims for loss of life or personal injury. Therefore, under specific terms and conditions, P&I Clubs have waived the "pay to be paid" defence for crew claims related to loss of life and injury.

In this case,[172] Bingham LJ observed that the perspective that a pay-first clause does not bind a third party does not go against the purpose of the 1930 Act. He stated that this is not except by disallowing Clubs a potential defence, thereby subjecting them to liability towards the third party that exceeds what they would have owed to the member. The Club's responsibility to the member was to make payment, specifically and solely to a member who had incurred actual losses (through payment to the third party).[173]

In summary, the legal validity of the "pay to be paid" rule was established in *Fanti and Padre Island*, which was filed while the 1930 Act was in force. The House of Lords held that the "pay to be paid" clause in the Club's rules is applicable, and the Club would not indemnify a member unless they compensated the third party. Additionally, this case blocked a provision in the 1930 Act that allowed third parties to apply directly to the P&I Club in case of a member's insolvency,[174] which was filed while the 1930 Act was in force. The House of Lords held that the "pay to be paid" clause in the Club's rules is applicable, and the Club would not indemnify a member unless they compensated the third party. Additionally, this case blocked a provision in the 1930 Act that allowed third parties to apply directly to the P&I Club in case of a member's insolvency.

Stuart-Smith LJ observed that permitting insurance companies to rely on pay-first clauses as a defence under the draft bill could create a situation entirely contrary to the 1930 Act.[175] According to him, this would allow any liability insurer to establish a scenario violating the law with a simple provision, even if it did not consistently insist on its enforcement. For example, even in cases of death and personal injury claims, P&I Clubs could exploit third parties using this rule, thus preventing the protection of third parties' rights. The common concern among reform supporters was that the "pay to be paid" rule could lead to unjust outcomes by causing delays and economic losses due to third parties' inability to claim compensation from the insurer directly.

On the other hand, IG[176] opposed the reform, arguing that the "pay to be paid" rule is essential for the functioning of P&I Clubs, and any reform may lead to Clubs relocating to other jurisdictions.[177] Moreover, during ongoing discussions

172 *The Fanti and the Padre Island* [1991] 2 AC 1.
173 *The Fanti and the Padre Island* [1991] 2 AC 1.
174 *The Fanti and the Padre Island* [1991] 2 AC 1.
175 Joint Report 2001, para 5.35; *The Fanti and the Padre Island* [1991] 2 AC 1.
176 International Group of P&I Clubs.
177 "Third Parties Rights Against Insurers" (2009) https://publications.parliament.uk/pa/ld200910/ldpublic/third/memos/m12.pdf accessed 2 January 2024.

on maritime liability insurance at the international level, IGP&I argued that such a radical reform of the law could be risky.

Considering all these opinions, the Commission has concluded that the law should be revised based on the views of consultants who opposed the reform rather than radically changing the "pay to be paid" rule. Clubs typically may waive this rule for their active members. However, the club may adopt a stricter stance if a member has become insolvent, and the waiver would solely benefit third parties. The 2010 Act includes provisions for direct action against liability insurers in the event of the insured's insolvency. According to Section 1 of the Act, a third party is permitted to bring a direct action against the insurer if the insured becomes insolvent.

Nevertheless, clubs can still assert the "pay to be paid" defence against third parties. Therefore, under club insurance, P&I Clubs will continue to rely on the "pay to be paid" rule, except in cases of death or personal injury. In cases of death or personal injury, the Club will be unable to rely on this rule and will be required to compensate the third party.[178]

Some jurisdictions do not recognize the "pay to be paid" rule as valid and allow third parties to claim directly against P&I Clubs. However, enforcing this rule within the English Courts prioritizes P&I Clubs' interests over those of third parties. In the reform process, as evidenced by the decisions of the Law Commission, England is aware of the significance and impact of legally protecting the club insurance market in terms of public interest and the national economy. For example, the Commission has recognized the economic concerns raised by the IGP&I and has revised the "pay to be paid" rule not to harm the club insurance industry. The Clubs are also aware of their contribution to the national economy, extending beyond their insurance services. Factors such as the arbitration clause in English Club rules, stipulating that all disputes be dealt with in London arbitration, and the employment opportunities and safe conduct of maritime trade activities facilitated by club insurance contribute directly or indirectly to the national economy. Therefore, England's legal policy provides a highly conducive environment for the club insurance market. The legal validation of the "pay to be paid" rule through court judgements is a concrete example of this approach. All these examples and applications support the book's argument regarding the critical role of legal policies in strengthening club insurance.

### B. THE *PRESTIGE* AND THE "PAY TO BE PAID" RULE

One other notable case in which the "pay to be paid" the English Courts enforced rule is *Prestige*.[179] The *Prestige* concerns a dispute between Spain and the London P&I Club, the insurer of the M/T Prestige oil tanker, which caused

178 Joint Report of July 2001, paras 5.37, 62.

179 *The London Steam Shipowners Mutual Insurance Association Ltd v The Kingdom of Spain (The Prestige (No. 2))* [2013] EWHC 3188 (Comm).

considerable damage when it sank off the coast of Galicia in 2002. The ship sank in November 2002 with a cargo of approximately 77,000 metric tons of heavy fuel oil. Subsequently, the resulting pollution affected much of Spain's northern coast and France's southern Atlantic coast. The *Prestige* was entered into the London P&I Club, which included pollution risks under its insurance coverage. In 2003, the London Club paid the pollution compensation under its rules and the relevant CLC certificate (Blue Card) provisions. However, the damage incurred was much more significant. The Club refused to pay the remaining claim, stating that it was not liable for claims exceeding the CLC limit, and initiated arbitration proceedings in London against Spain and France in January 2012 to confirm this decision. The Club defended itself based on the "pay to be paid" and arbitration clauses. Subsequently, the Club obtained an enforcement order from the English court based on Section 66 of the Arbitration Act 1996 to enforce the arbitration award. Spain and France objected to this enforcement order, citing the State Immunity Act 1978[180] (SIA 1978).[181] However, this objection was not accepted by the Court of Appeal.[182]

On the other hand, France and Spain commenced legal proceedings against shipowners and the London P&I Club. The Spanish Supreme Court determined that Spain had the right of direct action against the London Club under Spanish law and that the Club was liable for up to 1 billion US dollars for claims related to oil pollution. Spain succeeded in registering this judgement of the Spanish Court in English courts. However, the Club objected to this registration order based on Article 34(3) of the Brussels Regulation, arguing that it conflicted with the previously obtained enforcement order. The Court of Appeal referred questions on the interpretation of Regulation 44/2001[183] to the Court of Justice of the European Union (CJEU).

The CJEU ruled that the enforcement order was based on an arbitration award and was therefore excluded from the Brussels Regulation and that the award could not be recognized in Spain.[184] However, it determined that a judgement by a court

180 The State Immunity Act 1978, enacted by the UK Parliament, incorporates the principles outlined in the 1972 European Convention on State Immunity into British legislation. This act altered the doctrine of absolute state immunity to one of limited immunity, allowing foreign states to be subject to lawsuits in British courts for specific activities, typically commercial in nature. For more information, see Stephan Bird, "The State Immunity Act of 1978: An English Update" (1979) 13 *International Law* 619.

181 Spain and France have claimed sovereign immunity under Section 2 of the SIA 1978 and argued that they are not bound by the enforcement order.

182 [2015] EWCA 2792 Civ 333.

183 Council Regulation (EC) No 44/2001 of 22 December 2000 on Jurisdiction and the Recognition and Enforcement of Judgments in Civil and Commercial Matters (OJ 2001 L 12, p. 1).

184 The Court of Justice of the European Union (CJEU) issued a verdict on *Case C-700/20*, which involved a referral for a preliminary ruling from the High Court of Justice (England & Wales), Queen's Bench Division (Commercial Court) in the United Kingdom. This case pertains to the Prestige sinking, and the CJEU determined that arbitration proceedings initiated in the United Kingdom do not have the authority to prevent the acknowledgment of the Spanish Court's decision mandating the insurer to provide compensation for the oil spill's damages.

in one Member State based on an arbitration award could not prevent the recognition of a judgement obtained from another Member State. This is a situation where a court in the first Member State cannot issue a judgement with a similar outcome without violating the provisions and fundamental objectives of Regulation 44/2001. This regulation relates to lis pendens and arbitration conditions.[185] According to Article 27 of Regulation 44/2001, the lis pendens principle refers to situations where any court other than the court first seized must stay its proceedings until a decision is made by the court first seized.

The CJEU ruling ensures that these provisions and objectives cannot be circumvented by arbitration proceedings followed by judicial proceedings seeking to have the terms of the arbitral award entered into a judicial decision.[186] The Court ruled that a judgement entered in terms of an arbitral award cannot enjoy mutual recognition between Member States, as arbitration is excluded from the scope of the regulation.[187] However, such a judgement may be regarded as a judgement within the meaning of Article 34(3) of the regulation[188] alone, capable of preventing the recognition of judgements from other Member States if those judgements are irreconcilable.[189]

This discussion, which was significant when the UK was a member of the EU, has now lost its relevance. The decisions of the CJEU from that time are no longer binding for the UK following Brexit. The Brussels Regulation and the Brussels Recast Regulation are no longer applicable except for pending cases. Therefore, if a case similar to Prestige were to come before an English court today, the court could issue an anti-suit injunction against the party violating the arbitration agreement, independent of the CJEU's decisions and regulations. This ensures that third parties wishing to claim directly against clubs based on foreign laws must comply

185 Court of Justice of the European Union (CJEU), Case C-700/20 *London Steam-Shipowners' Mutual Insurance Association Limited v Kingdom of Spain.*

186 The CJEU also noted that a jurisdiction clause agreed between an insurer and an insured party cannot be invoked against a victim of insured damage who wishes to bring an action directly against the insurer. The Court emphasized that it is the responsibility of the Court seized intending to enter a judgement in the terms of an arbitration award to verify that the provisions and fundamental objectives of Regulation No 44/2001 have been complied with to prevent circumvention of those provisions and objectives. In this case, the CJEU found that the arbitration proceedings in London and the civil action in Spain had the exact cause of action and were between the same parties, and the Court should ensure that the rules on *lis pendens* laid down in that regulation were followed. This case highlights the importance of ensuring compliance with regulations and fundamental objectives to prevent circumvention and ensure adequate compensation for damages suffered.

187 "Press Release No 104/22 - Advocate General's Opinion in Judgment of the Court in Case C-700/20" (20 June 2022) https://curia.europa.eu/jcms/upload/docs/application/pdf/2022-06/cp220104en.pdf accessed 13 May 2023.

188 Article 34(3) of Regulation No 44/2001: "A Judgment shall Not be Recognised: If It is Irreconcilable with a Judgment Given in a Dispute between the Same Parties in the Member State in which Recognition is Sought".

189 Article 34(3) of Regulation No 44/2001: "A Judgment shall Not be Recognised: If It is Irreconcilable with a Judgment Given in a Dispute between the Same Parties in the Member State in which Recognition is Sought".

with the arbitration clause. Since clubs can invoke the "pay to be paid" rule against third parties in arbitration proceedings, English courts' anti-suit injunctions are essential.

In March 2022, the English Court of Appeal ruled there was no need to reference the CJEU, citing the unresolved human rights issue against the Club. Therefore, the Court of Appeal set aside the judgement referring to the CJEU. The Court of Appeal rejected Spain's appeal against this judgement. The Club reinitiated arbitration in January 2023, and Sir Peter Gross was appointed as the sole arbitrator. In summary, in this arbitration, Sir Peter Gross concluded in the first partial award that the CJEU decision did not bind English courts and himself as the arbitrator. In the second partial award in March 2023, he found that Spain violated the Club rules' arbitration clause. Spain claimed that a law error was made based on s. 69 of the 1996 Act and appealed this award, which was dismissed.

Meanwhile, the Club argued that recognizing and enforcing the Spanish court judgement contradicts English public policy, citing Regulation (EC) No. 44/2001, Article 34(1). Butcher J affirmed that the principle of *res judicata* is a fundamental aspect of public policy.[190] Accordingly, *res judicata* serves as a substantive legal rule to prevent the abuse of multiple lawsuits and court processes, ensuring legal finality. These objectives are integral to public policy. Consequently, Butcher J granted the Club's appeal against the Spanish Recognition Order by concluding that the principle of *res judicata* is pertinent to public policy objectives under Article 34(1). He also ruled that Sir Peter Gross could not grant an injunction against Spain in the arbitration proceedings, acknowledging that under s. 13(2)(a) of the SIA 1978,[191] states have a court that could not enforce sovereign immunity, and therefore, such an injunction.

In the other arbitration proceeding, Dame Elizabeth Gloster had ruled in the decisions dated 8 February[192] and 2 May,[193] awarding compensation and issuing anti-suit injunctions against France. France appealed these arbitration awards to the English Commercial Court. By accepting France's appeal, Butcher J determined that an anti-suit injunction could not be granted by a tribunal against a state for failing to comply with an obligation to arbitrate.[194] According to the Senior Courts Act 1981 section 50, if the tribunal lacks jurisdiction to rule on an injunction, it clearly has no authority to grant relief. However, he dismissed the appeal regarding the compensation award.

In summary, this case again underscores the necessity for third parties and parties to the contract to adhere to the "pay to be paid" and arbitration clauses. Additionally, the English court, in an unusual decision, stated that the reference conditions of the CJEU exceeded their limits and that it did not have the authority to make

190 [2021] EWHC 1247 (Comm).
191 SIA 1978, s 13 (2)(a) states that: "relief shall not be given against a State by way of injunction or order for specific performance or for the recovery of land or other property."
192 First Partial Award – 8 February 2023.
193 Second Partial Award – 2 May 2023.
194 [2023] EWHC 2473 (Comm).

judgements in this way, thus refusing to comply with these judgements. The court also questioned the fairness of the CJEU's substantive judgements. Furthermore, these judgements have demonstrated that English courts will not grant injunctions against states in commercial disputes where there is a breach of arbitration agreements and will apply section 13(2)(a) of the SIA 1978 to uphold sovereign immunity.[195] In other words, they are significant as they show that English courts will not permit an anti-suit injunction to be granted against a state by a tribunal for failing to comply with an obligation to arbitrate. Therefore, the *Prestige* has significant implications in many respects.

### *3. Club's Assumption of Member's Rights through Subrogation*

Analyzing how Clubs provide compensation services to their members is essential to understand better how Clubs differ from other types of insurance. Therefore, examining the implementation of the principle of subrogation in Club rules will help elucidate this difference through concrete examples of Club rules. The argument advocated in the book, which emphasizes the unique character of club insurance and, thus, the need to protect Club rules within the framework of legal policies, is substantiated through the analysis of these rules.

The subrogation principle, which is based on the equitable doctrine, is a fundamental principle in contracts of indemnity.[196] The purpose of this principle is to prevent anyone from profiting from damages incurred and to ensure that individuals are not compensated for more than the insured losses incurred under the insurance contract.[197] Under this principle, the insurer who indemnifies the insured becomes the successor to the insured's rights against the third party.[198] The insured, whom the insurer has indemnified, is prevented from receiving compensation from the third party again, and this right passes to the insurer.[199]

195 Robert Merkin, "Protection & Indemnity Clubs and Arbitration Clauses" in Ozlem Gurses (ed), *Research Handbook on Marine Insurance Law* (Edward Elgar Publishing 2024) Ch 9, 202.

196 George W Nowell, "Subrogation" in Matthew A. Marion (ed), *MTHE Special Report* (Document No 761, Marine Protection & Indemnity Policy Annotations Project Subcommittee on Hull and P&I Insurance Committee on Marine Insurance and General Average Maritime Law Association of the United States, San Francisco 2001) 12795; Hazelwood and Semark, 285.

197 For more information about principle of subrogation, see Merkin and Steele, 97; Hodges, 17; Baatz, 443.

198 See *Tyco Fire & Integrated Solutions (UK) Ltd v Rolls-Royce Motor Cars Ltd* [2007] EWHC 3159 (TCC); *Cooperative Retail Services Ltd v Taylor Young Partnership Ltd* [2002] UKHL 17; *Gard Marine & Energy Ltd v China National Chartering Co Ltd (The Ocean Victory)* [2017] UKSC 35; *The Yasin* [1979] 2 Lloyd's Rep 45; *Petrofina (U.K.) Ltd v Magnaload Ltd* [1984] QB 127; *National Oilwell (UK) Ltd v Davy Offshore Ltd* [1993] 2 Lloyd's Rep 582.

199 Lord Blackburn defined the principle of subrogation in *Burnard v Rodocanachi* as follows: "The general rule of law (and it is obvious justice) is that where there is a contract of indemnity (it matters not whether it is a marine policy, or a policy against fire on land, or any other contract of indemnity) and a loss happens, anything which reduces or diminishes that loss reduces or diminishes the amount which the indemnifier is bound to pay; and if the indemnifier has already paid it, then, if anything which diminishes the loss comes into the hands of the person to whom he has

In insurance law, the subrogation principle prevents the insured from receiving compensation twice, and the insurer replaces the insured as the claimant. According to Bennett, the insurer becomes the successor to the insured's rights to the third party to the extent that they compensate the insured under the subrogation principle.[200] The third party is primarily liable for the damage suffered by the insured under insurance law. If the insured chooses to indemnify this damage from the insurer and not from the third party, the principle of subrogation applies, and the insurer's secondary liability comes into play.[201]

The recent judgement[202] by the High Court defines the subrogation principle, stating that when a party is insured against a specific risk and incurs a loss due to the occurrence of that insured event, the insurer compensates the insured for the suffered loss.[203] However, the insurer is also entitled to pursue a subrogated claim in the name of the insured against any other party legally responsible for the event. Insurance does not absolve the wrongdoer or the legally responsible party of any liability they would have had had the insurance policy not existed to compensate for causing the event.[204]

As this definition highlights, if the insured experiences a loss due to a risk covered by insurance, the insurer indemnifies the insured for this loss. It takes over the insured's rights against the third party legally responsible for the loss.[205] This is known as the right of subrogation.

The subrogation right outlined in the Club rules aligns with the subrogation principle.[206] Under this principle, unless explicitly agreed otherwise in writing by the Managers, when the Club settles a claim on behalf of an Owner, it becomes

---

paid it, it becomes an equity that the person who has already paid the full indemnity is entitled to be recouped by having that amount back." See *Burnard v Rodocanachi* (1882) 7 App Cas 333 (HL).

200 Bennett, *Marine Insurance*, 276.

201 Saban Kayihan, "Zarar Sigortalarında Sigortacının Halefiyeti" (2016) 22(3) *Marmara University Faculty of Law Journal of Legal Studies* 1598.

202 *The Rugby Football Union v Clark Smith Partnership Limited and FM Conway Limited* [2022] EWHC 956 (TCC); *Haberdashers' Aske's Federation Trust Ltd v Lakehouse Contracts Ltd* [2018] EWHC 558 (TCC); *Axa Insurance UK plc v Financial Claims Solutions Ltd* [2018] EWCA Civ 1330.

203 The High Court's recent judgment defines the subrogation principle as follows: "The concept of subrogated rights is well known. If a party is insured against an insured risk, and that risk eventuates and causes loss, the insurer will make good to the insured party the loss suffered because of the occurrence of the event, the risk of which was an insured risk. However, the insurer is entitled to bring a subrogated claim, which is a claim in the name of the insured party, against any other party legally responsible for the event. The existence of the insurance does not relieve the wrongdoer (or the other party legally responsible for the event) of any liability it would otherwise have, absent the existence of the insurance policy, to make recompense for having caused that event." See *Haberdashers' Aske's Federation Trust Ltd v Lakehouse Contracts Ltd* [2018] EWHC 558 (TCC).

204 *Haberdashers' Aske's Federation Trust Ltd v Lakehouse Contracts Ltd* [2018] EWHC 558 (TCC).

205 Bennett, *Marine Insurance*, 776; Gurses, 258; Nowell, 73.

206 See Britannia P&I Club, Rule 5(2); West of England P&I Club, Part II, Rule 10; UK P&I Club, Rule 5/P(iii); Steamship P&I Club, Rule 42; Shipowners' P&I Club, Part 6, Rule 43/3; North of England P&I Club, Rule 34(3); The London P&I Club, Rule 3.2.

subrogated to the Owner's rights concerning the claim up to the extent of the payment.[207] This includes the entitlement to any interest accrued on the amount before its recovery and the right to seek reimbursement for any costs incurred in pursuing these rights. Therefore, if a Club member receives compensation from the Club for damages resulting from a covered risk, the Club assumes subrogated rights against any third party in line with the member's entitlements.[208]

However, Merkin argues that the principle of subrogation can lead to conflicts of interest between insurers and policyholders in certain situations.[209] According to the author, subrogation is sometimes accused of providing unexpected gains to insurers due to determining relevant premiums without considering some risks.[210] In other words, insurers may overlook some of the risks they have committed to and, as a result, profit from the losses incurred by policyholders. For example, insurers may prioritize their interests in pursuing subrogated claims over the interests of the insured party. In addition, the subrogation principle may create disincentives for the insured party to pursue claims against third parties as they have already received compensation from their insurer. This could lead to a reduction in the overall compensation paid out to damaged persons for losses. Thus, while the subrogation principle is essential in preventing double recovery, it has drawbacks and should be considered considering these potential conflicts of interest.

### *4. "Overspill Claims" Payments Distinguishing Clubs from Other Marine Insurers*

Overspill claims payment services of Clubs are distinctive features setting Clubs apart from other marine insurers. According to the IGP&I Agreement 2023, overspill claims mean any liabilities covered by the Pool that exceed the current amount reinsured under the General Excess Loss Contract.[211] The issue of overspill claims in maritime insurance is governed by the demand limits established by the Clubs. Overspill claims are claims that exceed a specific limit, and as such, their payment is distributed among the Clubs that are party to the Pool Agreement according to specific rules and rates.

An "overspill claim" occurs when a part of a pool claim exceeds the reinsurance limit set by the International Group, which is currently at US $2.1 billion.[212] In such

207 For example, in Britannia P&I Club rulebook Rule 5(2), the right of subrogation is regulated as follows: "Unless otherwise agreed in writing by the Managers; where the Association has paid a claim to or on behalf of an Owner, the Association shall be subrogated to the rights of the Owner in respect of the claim to the extent of that payment, including the right to any interest accruing on that amount before its recovery and the right to recover any costs incurred in relation to the exercise of such rights."

208 Hazelwood and Semark, 285.

209 Merkin and Steele, 103.

210 Merkin and Steele, 103.

211 See the International Group Agreement 2023.

212 See "Reinsurance Contract GXL Structure for 2024/25" https://www.igpandi.org/article/reinsurance-contract-gxl-structure-for-202425/ accessed 4 May 2024.

cases, the excess amount is shared proportionately among the Clubs. Each Club's share is determined based on the total liability limits of all vessels insured with the Club, calculated according to LLMC 1976.[213] However, each Club's contribution is capped at a maximum of 2.5% of this total liability limit.[214] Also, it is worth noting that claims resulting from oil pollution fall outside the scope of this system, and compensation for such claims is provided under a different framework.

To facilitate the payment of overspill claims, the Clubs have established a fund, replenished through various means such as interest income, contributions from other Clubs, and overspill calls collected from members; however, in the event of a dispute between the Club and the member who made the overspill claim, a special board known as the Panel[215] has been established to resolve the issue.

After hearing arguments from both parties, the Panel decides on disputes related to the Club's inability to pay or underpayment of the overspill claim. However, it is worth noting that the Panel is not obliged to provide any justification for its decisions, and there is no option for appealing the Panel's decisions.[216] Therefore, the Panel holds the ultimate authority to resolve disputes related to overspill claims in the maritime insurance industry.

These factors concretely demonstrate that clubs play a dominant role in the decision-making process. Practices such as the absence of an appeal process for panel decisions and the lack of a requirement for justification highlight this dominant role. Members are obliged to accept Clubs' decisions to refuse overspill claims. The rationale behind Clubs that have discretion over the fulfilment of these claims is their prioritization of the Club's and its members' collective economic interests. Therefore, Clubs have established separate decision-making bodies to carefully handle and evaluate overspill claims. The closure of judicial recourse against these Club decisions and the acceptance of this rule by English law are significant policies that encourage the development of the club insurance industry. Adopting these policies in other countries will accelerate the development of the club insurance industry.

## IV. Analysis of How the Rights and Obligations of Parties in Club Insurance Are Addressed in Turkish P&I Rules

This title will focus on how the Turkish P&I Rules handle the rights and obligations of the parties involved in club insurance. As outlined in the introduction of Chapter 3, the regulations governing the rights and obligations of parties in English and Turkish P&I Club rules are similarly structured. However, despite the similarity in Club rules, significant differences emerge between Turkish and English law in the context of P&I Club insurance. Among the arguments of this

213 International Convention on Limitation of Liability for Maritime Claims 1976, art 6(1)(b).

214 See "Reinsurance Contract GXL Structure for 2024/25" https://www.igpandi.org/article/reinsurance-contract-gxl-structure-for-202425/ accessed 4 May 2024.

215 See The London P&I Club, Rule 33.4.

216 See North of England P&I Club, Rule 36(3)(j).

book is the proposition that Türkiye should model English law and enact legal reforms in its pursuit of developing the club insurance industry. This chapter addresses the need for reform within the framework of Club rules and legal regulations governing the rights and obligations of parties. Under this heading, the rules of the Turkish P&I Club will first be examined to support the book's argument. Subsequently, the approach of legal policies to these rules will be compared through examples from England and Türkiye, and the conclusions reached will be discussed.

The primary obligations of members under Turkish P&I rules include the payment of premiums, providing accurate and complete information to the Club, not disclosing risks under insurance during the membership period, notifying the Club immediately of any risk that occurs, reducing resulting damages, and allowing the Club to investigate and gather information.[217] Members also have the right to claim compensation for damages from the Club and receive legal and technical support. Turkish insurance law regulations govern these rules, and members must comply with their legal obligations.

From the perspective of Turkish P&I, the insurer's obligations[218] include providing members with information about insurance coverage and conditions,[219] issuing an entry certificate to the member, providing coverage covered by the insurance, providing legal and technical support, and insuring losses within the scope of the insurance.[220] Additionally, while not mandatory, the Club may decide to provide security to the member. The Club also has rights, including the right to receive information from both the insured and the damaged party, the right to subrogation, and the right to settlement.[221]

One of the most controversial Turkish P&I rules is the "pay to be paid" rule.[222] This rule states that, unless the insurer decides otherwise, an assured right to recover regarding any liabilities is conditional. The member must first discharge or pay the same out of their funds unconditionally, not through a loan or otherwise. This rule is like those found in English Clubs and prevents the direct action right of the third party, requiring the member to indemnify the third party before claiming compensation from the Club. However, this rule contradicts Article 1478 of the

217 See Turk P&I, Section G, Rule 7–8.

218 See Kübra Yetiş Şamlı, "Considerations on the Art. 1423 of the Commercial Code Regulating the Insurer's Information Duty" (2016) 22(3) *Marmara University Faculty of Law Journal of Legal Studies* 2977 et seq., for a detailed discussion on the insurer's duty of disclosure under Turkish law.

219 See Turk P&I, Section H, Rule 12.

220 Mehmet Mulazimoglu, "Insurer's Debts and Liabilities under the Liability Insurance" (2015) 5(1) *Journal of Akdeniz University Faculty of Law* 229.

221 Ilknur Ulug Cicim, "Obligations, Rights and Authorities of the Insurer in Liability Insurance Regarding the Claim of Compensation Suspended to the Insurer" (2013) 3(2) *Akdeniz University Journal of Law Faculty* 12.

222 The "pay to be paid" rule is regulated in Turk P&I, Section F, Rule 6.9 as follows: "Unless the insurer determines, it is a conditional precedent of an assured's right to recover in respect of any liabilities that he must have first discharged or paid the same out of funds belonging to him unconditionally and not by way of loan or otherwise."

TCC,[223] which mandates that third parties can directly apply to the insurer. While there has not been a dispute regarding this rule in Turkish Courts, it is likely that if such a case arose, the Court would invalidate the Club rule and apply the mandatory provision of the law instead.

Considering the legal framework in Türkiye, the legal validity of contracts hinges on their compliance with mandatory provisions of the law. Hence, should the "pay to be paid" rule in Turkish P&I rules become the subject of litigation, it would not be upheld by Turkish Courts and would be deemed invalid. Therefore, legal reform is necessary, particularly concerning the "pay to be paid" rule. This will entail a review of the relevant provisions of the law to ensure consistency with the rules of the Turkish P&I. Such a measure is essential to provide a solid legal basis for the Turkish P&I and to avoid any potential conflicts between the rules of the Turkish P&I and Turkish law.

In summary, the rules of the Turkish P&I company regulate the rights and obligations of the involved parties. In doing so, the Turkish P&I company has adopted the rules of English Clubs as a guiding template and established a framework resembling the English model. However, while implementing this framework, the Turkish P&I company disregarded the inconsistency of the rules with Turkish legal regulations. There is a considerable risk of these rules being invalidated by Turkish courts.

Two different options can be considered to mitigate this risk. The first is to modify the Club rules to align with Turkish laws, particularly those that recognize the direct action rights of third parties. The second option is for Turkish law to adopt a legal policy that validates Club rules. The first option is compatible with the existing principles of insurance law in Türkiye. However, it undermines the development of the club insurance sector. The second option represents an approach that supports and accelerates this development. However, it contradicts Turkish insurance law, prioritizing the satisfaction of third-party compensation claims.

Nevertheless, this book's argument focuses on prioritizing the development of this sector in Türkiye. The contribution of developing the club insurance industry serves a superior public interest compared to the necessity of promptly satisfying third-party compensation claims. Therefore, legal policies should be reformed to encourage this and prioritize the application of Club rules in Turkish law.

## V. Comparative Analysis and Conclusion

Chapter 3 conducted a comparative analysis of the English and Turkish models regarding the rights and obligations of parties in club insurance, supporting the argument that England provides a more favourable legal environment for the club insurance industry. This analysis did not solely focus on the Clubs' rules but also examined the legal frameworks in both countries. These examinations revealed parallel regulations regarding the rights and obligations in Turkish and English P&I

223 See Article 1478 of Turkish Commercial Code No. 6102.

Club rules. However, significant differences emerged, particularly concerning the obligations of Clubs to compensate members and third parties.

Under Turkish law, club insurance is classified as liability insurance.[224] In liability insurance, these third parties who suffer damage due to the insured's actions are not parties to the insurance contract. Nevertheless, the TCC[225] grants them exceptional right to claim compensation for the damages they have suffered directly from the insurer. This right arises from the law and is not contingent upon the insurance contract.[226] In other words, the third party's right to direct action against the insurer stems from the TCC.

In Article 1478 of the TCC, the direct action right is designed to protect the interests of third parties. It eliminates needing a separate court ruling to determine the insurer's liability. This legal provision establishes the direct action right of third parties to claim insurance coverage, stemming from statutory law rather than mutual consent or contractual relations.[227]

In Turkish law, the exercise of direct action rights by third parties against the insurer does not make them parties to the insurance contract.[228] The insured remains the definite party to the insurance contract. Therefore, the third party does not enter the insured's shoes within this legal framework.

In contrast, under English law, the opposite practice exists due to the principle of subrogation. An essential consequence of this difference between English and Turkish law is that while English law allows Clubs to assert defences protected under Club rules against third-party claims, Turkish law does not.

In English law, the approach towards balancing the rights and obligations between members and third parties in P&I Clubs demonstrates a notable tendency towards favouring the Clubs. While this may appear unfavourable to members, it protects them and the Club. Therefore, these stringent rules are not typically applied against members, and the Club provides insurance coverage due to its broad discretion. However, when a member is liable for damages to a third party, Club rules are strictly applied against the substituted third party. In certain situations where a third party, such as in the event of a member's insolvency, has the direct action right, the Club's obligation to compensate the third party is subject to challenging conditions. Since the third party is considered to have stepped into the member's shoes, the member must fulfil the obligations under the Club rules. The third party often struggles to fulfil these obligations, thereby relieving the Club of the obligation to compensate the third party. By doing so, Clubs indirectly protect their members'

224 Samim Unan, *İsteğe Bağlı Genel Sorumluluk Sigortasında Riziko* (Beta Press, Istanbul 1998); Alganturk Light, 117.

225 Article 1478 of the TCC.

226 See Article 1478 of the TCC; Kerim Atamer, "Yeni Türk Ticaret Kanunu Uyarınca Zarar Sigortalarına Giriş" (2011) 27(1) *Bank and Commercial Law Journa*l 86.

227 Kemal Şenocak, "Karayolları Trafik Kanunu'na Göre Mağdurun Doğrudan Doğruya Sigortacı Karşısındaki Alacak Hakkı" (2009) 25(4) *Journal of Bank and Commercial Law* 279.

228 Elif Beyza Akkanat Ozturk, "Sorumluluk Sigortalarında Zarar Görenin Doğrudan Dava Hakkı" (2020) 42 *TAAD* 472.

interests while safeguarding their economic interests. Therefore, the design of Club rules to favour the Club does not pose problems for members. The Club can use its discretion to soften these rules and provide the necessary coverage to its members.

Given the legal disparities between English and Turkish law, the effectiveness of club insurance in Türkiye becomes the focal point. These differences underscore the need to identify legal measures that could enhance the effectiveness of club insurance in Türkiye.

Examining the legal differences between English and Turkish law highlights the need for strategic measures to strengthen the position of Turkish P&I insurance. Notably, the legal landscape in England provides P&I Clubs with a higher level of protection to safeguard commercial interests. These policies have supported the global leadership position of English P&I Clubs and facilitated the establishment of a robust economic infrastructure. In contrast, Türkiye has not granted any legal privileges or protections specifically for club insurance. Instead, it has applied the legal provisions established for liability insurance to club insurance. While Turkish P&I, established in 2014, aimed to build a vital infrastructure by adopting the rules of English P&I Clubs, achieving this goal entirely is impossible without adopting appropriate legal approaches. While adopted without modification, some of these rules can potentially violate Turkish laws, particularly those that restrict or complicate third parties' direct action rights.

A reform effort should be undertaken to provide legal privileges exclusively applicable to club insurance in Turkish law to strengthen Turkish P&I insurance and enhance its competitiveness on the international stage. Existing legal regulations in Turkish P&I rules will continue to be enforced until the courts review them. However, any Club rules that restrict the right to direct action and are brought before Turkish courts will be deemed legally invalid. The elimination of this risk is necessary to achieve the goal of developing the club insurance sector.

In conclusion, examining the legal framework concerning club insurance in Türkiye is necessary to discern practical strategies for enhancing the effectiveness of the club insurance industry. This effort entails a comprehensive review of existing legal regulations and exploring new measures to provide an appropriate legal environment for P&I Clubs. In this context, the book suggests considering the adoption of legal policies regarding club insurance from English law as a model.

# 4 Direct Action Against P&I Clubs in Turkish and English Law

## I. Introduction

This chapter examines the legal framework governing third-party direct action rights against P&I Clubs, with a particular focus on the contrasting approaches of English and Turkish law. The International Group of P&I Clubs provides liability coverage for over 90% of ocean-going tankers,[1] yet the scope of this insurance is limited to payments made by the insured member to third parties. Consequently, if the member has not made a payment, the Club is not obligated to indemnify the third party. The difficulty third parties face in directly pursuing claims against a P&I Club, particularly under English law, raises the contentious issue of whether direct legal action against Clubs should be permitted.[2]

The discussion begins with an examination of Turkish law, analyzing the legal classification, application, and scope of third-party direct action rights. The impact of these rights on the development of club insurance in Türkiye is assessed, along with an evaluation of whether English legal principles could serve as a model. The chapter then explores English legal reforms and court decisions, highlighting the role of Club rules that limit direct action rights. Provisions such as the "pay to be paid" and arbitration clauses are critically examined in terms of their effects on both insured members and third parties.

A key element of this analysis is the landmark *Yusuf Cepnioglu*,[3] case, which provides a basis for comparing English and Turkish legal approaches. The chapter presents a critical assessment of this judgement and its implications for club insurance disputes. By analyzing these legal perspectives, the chapter offers a comparative framework for understanding how different regulatory approaches influence the balance between the protection of Clubs and the rights of third parties.

1 International Group of P&I Clubs, "About the International Group of P&I Clubs" https://www.igpandi.org/about last accessed 13 May 2022.

2 Rhidian Thomas, "Third-Party Claims Against P&I Clubs in the UK" (2021) 26 *Journal of International Maritime Law* 385.

3 *Shipowners' Mutual Protection and Indemnity Association (Luxembourg) v Containerships Denizcilik Nakliyat ve Ticaret AS (The Yusuf Cepnioglu)* [2016] EWCA Civ 386.

DOI: 10.4324/9781003628897-4

## II. The Legal Relationship between P&I Clubs and their Members that Distinguishes Club Insurance from other Insurance Contracts

In the context of direct action disputes, this title will discuss the legal relationship between P&I Clubs and their members, which sets club insurance apart from traditional insurance contracts. Unlike conventional insurers, P&I Clubs maintain a distinct bond with their members, characterized by mutual obligations, shared interests, and collaborative decision-making processes. This specialized relationship enables P&I Clubs to provide comprehensive insurance coverage and tailored services tailored to the specific needs of their members, including addressing direct action disputes effectively. By examining this legal relationship, the research aims to demonstrate how the structure and dynamics of club insurance differ significantly from those of standard insurance contracts, particularly concerning the resolution of direct action claims.

In direct action conflicts involving P&I Clubs, the legal relationships among the parties involved are intricate and multifaceted. While Hazelwood's concept of a "network of reciprocal guarantees"[4] may have held merit in the past, the present-day reality of P&I Clubs and their membership structures calls into question the applicability of this notion. Specifically, the procedure whereby the Club accepts a member as a partner through selective election among its members weakens the "mutuality" nature of club insurance. In other words, the assumption that all Club members are automatically deemed partners has lost its validity in contemporary times because the Club does not automatically accept every member as a partner.

Consequently, it would be more appropriate to characterize each member as solely an insured party rather than occupying the dual roles of the insurer and insured. Hazelwood further contends that a shift in the general acceptance of the mutual structure within P&I Clubs is underway.[5] He posits that the rise of Clubs where the corporate entity assumes the role of insurer challenges the conventional understanding of members and their dual roles within the contractual framework.[6] It becomes evident that the concurrent roles of insured and insurer ascribed to members no longer align with the contemporary landscape of Club contracts.

The legal relationship between the member and the third party is one of liability. This liability may be based on various legal reasons such as contract, tort, law, or public law. There is no direct legal relationship between the third party and the Club, meaning that the Club is typically not under any obligation to the third party. Instead, the member's liability towards the third party is governed by the insurance contract between the Club and the member. However, this does not imply a legal relationship between the Club and the third party.

4 Hazelwood and Semark, 9.
5 Hazelwood and Semark, 64.
6 Hazelwood and Semark, 64.

Ulfbeck provides several examples of liability relations that may arise between the third party and the member. In cases where direct action is taken against the right to load, the third party can sue the insurance company if the load is damaged during transportation, and the carrier is held responsible.[7] This is because there is a contractual relationship between the third party and the insured member. In other situations, with no contractual relationship between the third party and the insured member, direct action may still be possible in tort situations. For example, in the case of a collision between two ships resulting in damage to one of the ships, the shipowner of the damaged vessel may wish to exercise the right of direct action against the counterpart's liability insurer.[8] Likewise, direct action rights may arise for those damaged by bodily injuries caused by a collision or environmental pollution caused by ships.

In Turkish law, the legal relationship between a third party exercising the direct action right and the Club is not considered a contractual relationship.[9] For instance, when a third party seeks to exercise their direct action right against the Club, they are not considered to stand in the member's shoes. They exercise an independent right derived from the law. Therefore, the obligations that the member should fulfil according to the Club rules are not expected to be fulfilled by the third party. The Club cannot refrain from its compensation liability by claiming that the third party failed to fulfil these obligations.

The approach of English law to this issue is the opposite of Turkish law. When a third party exercises its direct action right, it is considered to stand in the member's shoes.[10] Consequently, they cannot have better rights than the members.[11] Similarly, the third party must fulfil all obligations stipulated in the Club rules. The Club can also assert all defences from club rules against their members to third parties.

Disputes arising from direct action rights typically stem from the different characterizations of the third party's legal status. While Turkish law does not make the third party a party to the contract, English law considers them to be a person standing in the place of the assured. Therefore, exercising this right becomes more difficult and complex for the third party. For example, in *Yusuf Cepnioglu*,[12] the Court of Appeal in England interpreted the direct action right in TCC,[13] claiming that the law makes the third party a party to the contract. However, the TCC intends to grant the third party an independent right only.[14] Exercising this right does not

7 Vibe Ulfbeck, "Direct Actions Against the Insurer in a Maritime Setting: The European Perspective" (2011) 2 *Lloyd's Maritime and Commercial Law Quarterly* 293.

8 Ulfbeck, "Direct Actions Against the Insurer in a Maritime Setting: The European Perspective".

9 Şener Akyol, *Tam Üçüncü Şahıs Yararına Sözleşme* (Istanbul 2018) 85.

10 Adrian Briggs, "Direct Actions and Arbitration: All at Sea" (2016) *Lloyd's Maritime and Commercial Law Quarterly* 328.

11 Merkin, Protection & Indemnity, 189.

12 [2016] EWCA Civ 386; [2016] 1 Lloyd's Rep 641.

13 Article of 1478 the Turkish Commercial Code No. 6102.

14 Ecehan Yeşilova Aras, *Yolcunun Uğradığı Bedensel Zararlardan Dolayı P&I Kulübüne Doğrudan Başvuru Hakkı* (International Congress on Legal Liability for Bodily Injuries, Cyprus 2019) 65.

in any way place the third party in the shoes of the insured. Since the English court did not interpret this from the perspective of Turkish law, it concluded differently from the intended purpose of the TCC.[15]

This section will highlight these differences while evaluating the legal policies of both countries regarding the third party's direct action right. The approach of English law, which prioritizes the application of Club rules in direct action disputes and thus provides a highly favourable legal environment for Clubs, will be discussed within the framework of this right. In contrast, it will be demonstrated that in Turkish law, which is dominated by policies aimed at protecting the victim, this approach is detrimental to the development of the club insurance industry. Consequently, it will be emphasized that Türkiye should address the need for legal reform regarding the direct action rights of third parties in club insurance by modelling the legal policies of England.

## III. Analysis of Turkish Law Prioritizing the Protection of Third Parties in Direct Action Disputes

### *A. Introduction*

This section will discuss how Turkish law safeguards the interests of third parties in direct action disputes. The analysis will explore Turkish law's legal provisions and precedents prioritizing protecting third-party rights and interests when pursuing claims against insurers, including P&I Clubs. By examining this aspect, the research will shed light on how Turkish legal principles and practices differ from English law, contributing to a broader understanding of the legal framework governing direct action disputes in Türkiye.

In a legal system where the right of direct action against P&I Clubs is recognized, a crucial point to be determined is whether the Clubs can assert arbitration and "pay to be paid" defences against third parties.[16] Analyzing this right's nature is necessary to determine whether Clubs can assert these defences. Therefore, the regulation of direct action rights in Turkish law will be discussed first. Subsequently, it will be debated whether this right is contractual or independent. Following this determination, it will be clarified whether the Club can assert the pay to be paid and arbitration rules against third parties within the framework of Turkish law.

In Turkish law, although there is no specific regulation about club insurance, it is accepted that the provisions governing liability insurance also apply to club insurance.[17] The provisions outlined in Articles 1473 to 1485 of the TCC No. 6102 concerning liability insurance are invoked in disputes concerning club insurance. Notably, Article 1478 of the TCC explicitly addresses the right of third parties

15 Briggs criticizes the approach of the Court of Appeal in the *Yusuf Cepnioglu* case for determining that a third party exercised a right under the contract without interpreting it from the perspective of Turkish law. See Briggs, "All at Sea", 330.

16 Merkin, Protection & Indemnity, 189.

17 Alganturk, 81; Acar, *Club Insurance*, 25.

to take direct action against liability insurers. This provision, which introduced the right of direct action for the first time, has effectively established a clear path for third parties to initiate legal proceedings directly against insurers. Before the enforcement of TCC No. 6102, the Supreme Court had rendered judgements of the direct recourse of third parties to insurers.[18] Following the enforcement of TCC No. 6102 on 1 July 2012, the legal ambiguities and disputes about this issue have been effectively resolved within Turkish law. Therefore, within the framework of the direct action right, third parties who have suffered damage can approach the liability insurer of the insured party, even without an insurance contract with the insurer. This right applies equally to disputes arising in the context of club insurance.[19]

Turkish law, including the right of direct action in the legislation, aims to protect third parties by swiftly addressing their losses in the event of the insured's insolvency. While liability insurance primarily serves to indemnify the insured for their liability towards third parties, the law prioritizes safeguarding the interests of the damaged party, considering the potential insolvency of the insured. Simultaneously, it is believed that this provision alleviates the burden on the insured, thereby facilitating the achievement of the underlying purpose of liability insurance. However, it is essential to emphasize that despite this right, liability insurance remains fundamentally a contract benefiting the insured and does not transform into a third-party-oriented contractual arrangement in any manner.[20] Nevertheless, recognizing this right without any limitation by third parties in P&I Club insurance disputes is inconsistent with the nature of club insurance. Although P&I Club insurance is classified within liability insurance, as previously mentioned, it differs from traditional insurance in many aspects. Considering the characteristic features of P&I Club insurance, the law should regulate an exceptional provision regarding this matter.

### *B. Direct Action Against Insurer (P&I Club) under the Abolished Turkish Commercial Code No. 6762*

When examining the concept of direct action in Turkish law, it is noteworthy that this right was initially granted to third parties solely concerning fire insurance under the abolished Commercial Law.[21] However, no comprehensive provision explicitly addressed the right of direct action for liability insurers. Subsequently, the right of direct action against insurers was extended to mandatory insurance in the Traffic and Transport Law.

Although not explicitly codified, the Turkish Supreme Court recognized the third party's right to direct action against insurers concerning all types of liability

18 Turkish Supreme Court, *Judgement No. 5101/2606*, 25 April 1989.

19 Asaf Goktug Akdere, "P&I Kulüp Sigortalarında Doğrudan Dava Hakkı" (Master thesis, Ankara University Law Faculty 2021) 2.

20 See The justification of Article 1478 of the TCC No. 6102.

21 Article 1310, Turkish Commercial Code No. 6762 (abolished).

insurance.[22] For instance, the Supreme Court's 1996-dated judgement[23] addressed the carrier's liability insurance dispute arising from the Convention on The Contract for The International Carriage of Goods by Road (CMR). The Court's analysis encompassed both compulsory and optional financial liability insurance. The CMR convention did not explicitly require carriers to obtain insurance; however, trucks seeking entry into European countries were obliged to hold CMR insurance. As a result, CMR insurance effectively became a de facto mandatory financial liability insurance. Accordingly, the Supreme Court ruled that third parties should have the right to direct action concerning compulsory liability insurance.[24]

Another Supreme Court judgement affirmed recognizing the third party's right to direct action in 1971.[25] The Court's legal basis for this judgement prioritized protecting the rights of the injured third party over considerations of public interest.[26] While some authors in Turkish legal doctrine regarded these Supreme Court judgements as equitable, others criticized them. Kender, for instance, criticized the judgements, arguing that the third party's right to direct action against insurers could only be exercised if recognized in the law or specified in the insurance contract between the insured and the insurer.[27] Without such provisions, the third party could only seek compensation from the insured.

However, Kender's perspective advocating for legal regulation to exercise this right did not align with the principle of protecting the victim, which is predominant in Turkish insurance law.[28] In Turkish law, the judge must fill this gap by employing judicial discretion when a dispute is presented to the Court without an explicit legal provision. In the cases brought before the Court of Appeals, there was no explicit statutory provision addressing the right of third parties to direct action. Therefore, Kender's criticism of the court's authority to fill this gap when the direct action right of third parties was not regulated by law at the time was unjustified.[29] The Court attempted to fill this legal gap by exercising its discretion to protect the victim. Turkish Courts have sought to ensure an equitable resolution for third parties

22 In the case dated 25 April 1989 (Decision No. 5101/2606), the Turkish Supreme Court recognized the right of an injured party in a liability insurance to directly seek compensation from the insurer.

23 The Judgement of the Turkish Supreme Court Law General Assembly *Decision No. K. 1996/18* dated 31.01.1996.

24 The Judgement of the Turkish Supreme Court Law General Assembly *Decision No. K. 1996/18* dated 31.01.1996.

25 The Judgement of the Turkish Supreme Court of Commerce Department *Decision No. E. 1971/1376, K. 1971/5339* dated 13/07/1971.

26 The Judgement of the Turkish Supreme Court of Commerce Department *Decision No. E. 1971/1376, K. 1971/5339* dated 13/07/1971.

27 Rayegan Kender, "Mesuliyet Sigortasının Mahiyeti ve Türleri, Teori ve Uygulama Açısından Mesuliyet Türleri" in *III. Insurance Seminar, Istanbul, 4–7 April 1977* (Sigorta Hukuk Türk Derneği, Ankara 1977) 9.

28 Kender, "The Nature and Types of Liability Insurance, Liability Insurances in Terms of Theory and Practice".

29 Kender, "The Nature and Types of Liability Insurance, Liability Insurances in Terms of Theory and Practice".

in liability insurance disputes by recognizing and implementing the direct action right. The jurisprudential approach has filled the legal gap and acknowledged the protection of the rights of third parties.

According to Tekinay, if a third party's direct action right against the insurer is not regulated by law, it exists just if expressly provided for in the insurance contract between the insured and the insurer.[30] According to the author, in the absence of a provision in the insurance contract, a third party could only claim compensation from the insured. However, this perspective yielded the same results as the notion that the third party does not have a direct action right against the insurer. This was because neither insurance contracts nor Club rules allow third parties to have a direct action right. Therefore, the view advocated by the author was that third parties do not have a direct right to litigation.

Alganturk shares a similar view with Tekinay. She asserts that this right can only be recognized if it is explicitly granted to the third party in a valid contract between the Club and its members.[31] Alganturk maintains that the third party does not possess the right of direct action since it is impossible to bestow such a right upon them in the insurance contract between the Club and its members.[32]

During the TCC No. 6762,[33] when the direct action right against insurers was not regulated in Turkish law, Imre[34] and Ozsunay[35] argued in favour of granting this right to third parties. However, their arguments lacked a solid legal foundation. Despite acknowledging the equitable nature of compensating the third party, they struggled to establish the legal basis for the right of direct action within the framework of liability law. The absence of a mandatory legal provision and the contradiction with the "principle that the contract will only rule between the parties" contributed to this predicament.

In summary, when TCC No. 6762 was in effect, no legal regulation governing the right of direct action existed. However, the Turkish Supreme Court declared that the "pay to be paid" principle specific to club insurance was acknowledged by the Court. As a result, it was determined that a third party could not directly sue the Club. This judgement, relating to an incident under the former code, does not apply to the subsequently enacted TCC No. 6102. After categorizing club insurance as a marine insurance contract where members' liability to third parties is covered through mutual insurance, the Supreme Court rejected the third party's direct action claim, citing the "pay to be paid" rule specific to club insurance. According

30 Selahattin Sulhi Tekinay and others, *Borçlar Hukuku Genel Hükümleri* (7th edn, Istanbul 1993) 222.

31 Alganturk, 141.

32 Alganturk, 141.

33 Turkish Commercial Code No. 6762 (abolished).

34 Zahit Imre, "Motorlu Taşıt Araçlarının Mecburi Mesuliyet Sigortası ve Kapsamı," in *Traffic Insurance v Commercial and Banking Law Week, 25–28 April 1973* (BTHAE Publications, Ankara 1975) 268.

35 Ergun Ozsunay, "Trafik Kazasında Zarar Gören Üçüncü Kişinin Sigortacıya Karşı Doğrudan Doğruya Alacak Hakkı" in *Traffic Insurance v Commercial and Banking Law Week, 25–28 April 1973* (BTHAE Publications, Ankara 1975) 400.

to this rule, a member cannot approach the Club without compensating the third party, and it applies equally to third parties. This case holds particular significance in club insurance, as it demonstrates the Supreme Court's reluctance to recognize direct action claims by individuals who have suffered losses under insurance contracts against the insurer in the context of club insurance. However, it should be noted that this judgement was rendered before the enactment of Article 1478 of the TCC No. 6102, which recognizes the right of direct action by third parties against liability insurers. Since no similar dispute has come before the Supreme Court after the implementation of this law, it remains uncertain how the Court would rule in a comparable case. Nevertheless, in the event of a similar dispute, there is a significant likelihood that the Supreme Court would depart from its previous case law and align its decision with the provisions regarding direct action in TCC No. 6102.

### C. *Direct Action Against the Insurer (P&I Club) under the Turkish Commercial Code No. 6102*

In Türkiye, the direct action rights of third parties against insurers were first recognized with the enactment of Law No. 6102 in 2012. Under the principle of "privity of contracts" in Turkish law, contracts establish rights and obligations exclusively between the parties involved.[36] In other words, individuals not party to a contract cannot assert rights based on that contract.[37] However, Turkish law recognizes certain exceptions to this rule, particularly in liability insurance.[38] One such exception is the "third party's right to direct action against the insurer," regulated by Articles 1473 and 1478 of the TCC.

Part VI of the TCC No. 6102 regulates insurance law. However, there are no provisions in the law regarding marine insurance. The general insurance provisions will also apply to marine insurance. P&I insurance, which is relevant to our topic, is considered liability insurance under Turkish law.[39] Liability insurance is addressed in Articles 1473 to 1485 of the TCC. Therefore, all provisions concerning liability insurance, as stipulated in the law, will also apply to P&I insurance.[40] However, the law will only apply to disputes within the scope of Turkish law. In contrast, if club insurance is obtained from a foreign Club, the law chosen in the Club rules will apply to the dispute instead of Turkish law.

36 Kemal Oğuzman and M. Turgut Öz, *Borçlar Hukuku Genel Hükümler Cilt-1* (12th edn, Vedat, Istanbul 2015) 28; Rona Serozan, *Borçlar Hukuku Genel Bölüm Üçüncü* Cilt (6th edn, Filiz, Istanbul 2014) 31; Gediz Kocabaş, "Üçüncü Kişi Yararına Sözleşmede Yararlananın Edimi Ret Hakkı" (2016) 22 *Marmara University Faculty of Law Journal of Legal Studies* 1798.

37 Şebnem Akipek and Erkan Küçükgüngör, *Sözleşmeler Rehberi* (2nd edn, Yetkin, Ankara 2002) 35.

38 Acar, *Club Insurance*, 510.

39 Yeşilova Aras, *Yolcunun Uğradığı Bedensel Zararlardan Dolayı P&I Kulübüne Doğrudan Başvuru Hakkı*.

40 Yeşilova Aras, *Yolcunun Uğradığı Bedensel Zararlardan Dolayı P&I Kulübüne Doğrudan Başvuru Hakkı*.

The TCC has chosen to regulate all types of insurance within the same systematic framework. However, it would have been more appropriate for the government to regulate marine insurance through a separate law. This is because the provisions applicable to marine insurance must be more flexible, given the nature of this type of insurance. Due to the inclination of Turkish insurance law towards protecting the victim, the law's articles are drafted in a highly interventionist manner. However, a legal framework aimed at protecting the victim in marine insurance would be insufficient to meet the needs of the industry. It would hinder the economic development of maritime trade and insurance activities. This flexibility becomes even more critical, especially in the context of club insurance. The operation of Clubs relies on this flexibility and the priority application of Club rules. Therefore, applying a highly interventionist law to club insurance in Türkiye negatively affects this industry's activities and economic development. Hence, legal reform efforts in Türkiye should focus on creating a more flexible and liberal law that explicitly addresses marine and club insurance.

Taking a closer look at the provisions regarding the right of direct action in the law, Article 1473/1 of the TCC clarifies the subject and scope of liability insurance contracts, which also apply to club insurance. It stipulates that

> 1) Under a liability insurance contract, *the insurer shall pay to the victim* compensation up to the amount stipulated in the insurance contract, for the liability of the insured due to an event that occurred, unless otherwise agreed, during the contract period, even if the loss materialised after that period.[41]

This article clarifies the scope and subject of liability insurance, stating that the insurer must compensate the victim up to the amount specified in the insurance contract. Kender criticizes this regulation, contending that the legal definition of liability insurance fails to align with its legal nature and subject matter.[42] He argues that the accurate definition of liability insurance entails the insurer assuming responsibility for damages suffered by third parties due to the insured's actions.[43] The insurer assumes liability for all claims that third parties may have against the insured. Kender argues that the flaw in the text lies in the phrase "the insurer shall pay to the victim." If the third party chooses not to exercise the "right to direct action against the insurer" and instead approaches the insured, the insured, not the insurer, will compensate for the damages. Only when the third party opts to exercise the "right to direct action against the insurer" does the insurer become responsible for compensating the damages attributable to the insured. Kender asserts that

41 The translation was taken from the *Yusuf Cepnioglu* case. See [2016] EWCA Civ 386 (emphasis in original).

42 Rayegan Kender, "Karayolları Motorlu Araçlar Zorunlu Mali Sorumluluk (Trafik) Sigortası Genel Şartlarındaki Değişikliklerin Değerlendirilmesi" (2017) 13(1) *Journal of Yeditepe University Law Faculty* 9.

43 Kender, "Karayolları Motorlu Araçlar Zorunlu Mali Sorumluluk (Trafik) Sigortası Genel Şartlarındaki Değişikliklerin Değerlendirilmesi".

while the right to direct action is acknowledged as an additional safeguard for the third party, it is mistakenly understood from the text that the third party must utilize the right to direct action.[44] While Kender's criticism on this matter may appear valid, it is evident that the legislator aimed to underscore the mandatory nature of a right that safeguards the interests of the third party rather than defining liability insurance through Article 1473.

Nevertheless, it must be acknowledged that the mandatory nature of the law's text is relative. In other words, if the third party wishes to exercise their right to direct action and claim damages from the insurer, the insurer must provide compensation. However, the third party may also pursue this claim against the insured. The objective of the law is not to compel the third party to exercise their right to direct action. Considering that Article 1473 was formulated to protect the interests of the third party, it becomes challenging to concur with Kender's criticism.

Alganturk made another criticism of the content of the article. Alganturk argued that the phrase "unless otherwise provided in the contract" should not be included in Article 1473 as it could be misinterpreted.[45] Otherwise, insurers could make regulations contrary to the purpose of the law by stating in the insurance contract that they would only indemnify the insured.[46] Atamer opposed this criticism. Atamer, a commission member who prepared the Turkish Commercial Code, stated that the phrase "unless otherwise provided in the contract" in Article 1473 was intended to determine the scope of the contract.[47] With this phrase, the parties were given freedom of choice regarding whether the subject of the liability insurance contract would be based on the occurrence or the compensation claim.[48] In English law, occurrence-based liability insurance, which focuses on the event causing the liability, is the type of contract that provides the most comprehensive protection to the insured.[49] However, parties prefer an insurance contract called claims-made, which is active when the claim is made due to its high cost.[50] The cost is lower when

44 Kender, "Karayolları Motorlu Araçlar Zorunlu Mali Sorumluluk (Trafik) Sigortası Genel Şartlarındaki Değişikliklerin Değerlendirilmesi", 2.

45 Conference Notes, *P&I Insurance and Maritime Insurance Law within the Scope of the New Turkish Commercial Law* (Istanbul 2013) https://docplayer.biz.tr/734155-Yeni-turk-ticaret-hukuku-kapsaminda-p-i-sigortasi-ve-deniz-sigorta-hukuku-29-kasim-2013-deniz-ticaret-odasi-konferans-salonu-toplanti-notlari.html accessed 22 April 2024.

46 Conference Notes, *P&I Insurance and Maritime Insurance Law within the Scope of the New Turkish Commercial Law.*

47 Conference Notes, *P&I Insurance and Maritime Insurance Law within the Scope of the New Turkish Commercial Law.*

48 Conference Notes, *P&I Insurance and Maritime Insurance Law within the Scope of the New Turkish Commercial Law.*

49 For more information about based on occurrence and claims made insurance contracts, see Robert Works, "Excusing Non-occurrence of Insurance Policy Conditions in order to Avoid Disproportionate Forfeiture: Claims-Made Formats as a Test Case" (1998) *College of Law Faculty Publications* 506.

50 Works, "Excusing Non-occurrence of Insurance Policy Conditions in order to Avoid Disproportionate Forfeiture: Claims-Made Formats as a Test Case", 508.

the contract is based on a claims-made type, making liability insurance more widespread.[51] Since it was not intended to completely abandon the occurrence-based contract model in the Commercial Law Commission, it was adopted as a solution that should be understood as "unless otherwise provided in the contract, an occurrence-based insurance contract will be concluded."[52] Therefore, parties can also agree to insurance coverage based on claims made in the insurance contract.[53]

In summary, as Atamer also pointed out, it is impossible to eliminate the third party's direct action right based on this phrase. The phrase "unless otherwise provided in the contract" in Article 1473 is solely and exclusively an expression aimed at determining the scope and content of the contract. Alganturk's criticisms on this matter do not align with the purpose of the law. The law does not desire the establishment of a contract contrary to the direct action right. Therefore, we disagree with the author's criticisms on this matter.

We explained in the previous section that TCC No. 6762 does not regulate the direct action right in liability insurance. In the context of liability insurance, the Court of Appeal has issued various judgements to fill this legal gap, but the need for legislation to address this gap has arisen over time. For this purpose, TCC No. 6012 introduced the direct action right of the third party against the liability insurer through Article 1478.[54] Article 1478 regulates the "direct action right against the insurer" as follows: "The victim may claim its loss up to the insured sum directly from the insurer provided that the claim is brought within the prescription period to the insurance contract."[55] According to this article, although not a party to the

51 Works, "Excusing Non-occurrence of Insurance Policy Conditions in order to Avoid Disproportionate Forfeiture: Claims-Made Formats as a Test Case", 509.

52 Conference Notes, *P&I Insurance and Maritime Insurance Law within the Scope of the New Turkish Commercial Law*.

53 The articles of TCC No. 6102 applicable to insurance contracts are structured to also encompass marine insurance. Therefore, unless otherwise specified in marine insurance policies, it is assumed that they are of the occurrence-based type as stated in Article 1473 of TCC. The Law Commission has explained the rationale for this regulation as follows: "This provision of the bill provides a general definition of liability insurance. The regulation stipulates that the event giving rise to the risk must occur within the contract period. It was considered that if the principle of the insurer being liable for damages arising during their period due to an event that occurred in the past had been adopted, the practicability of such insurance would be significantly reduced. This is because the insurer, when entering a contract, would want to know all the insured's past activities and how they were conducted. Otherwise, the insurer would face the danger of encountering large risks. Moreover, such a regulation would open the door to malicious practices. For instance, individuals who think they may face a compensation claim due to a mistake they made would immediately seek to enter an insurance contract. For these reasons, the insurer's liability has been linked to events that occur within the contract period that require the insured's liability. At this point, it is not important whether the damage occurs or is claimed after the contract period for the insurer's liability to be mentioned. However, since the provision is not mandatory, it is also possible for the parties to determine the risk differently according to the types of liability insurance through the contract" (translated by author). See Rationale of the TCC No. 6102, available at www.ticaretkanunu.net/gerekce accessed on 15 August 2024.

54 Art. 1478 of Turkish Commercial Code No. 6102.

55 The translation was taken from the *Yusuf Cepnioglu* case. See [2016] EWCA Civ 386.

insurance contract, a third party can claim compensation directly from the insurer, limited to the coverage amount specified in the insurance contract.[56]

Direct action rights allow third parties to claim compensation directly from the insurer without suing the insured.[57] Most scholars interpreting this provision argue that the regulation is intended to protect third parties and that its text clearly expresses this purpose, leaving no gaps for alternative interpretations.[58] These views are valid for classical liability insurance, and the direct action right of third parties should be supported. However, advocating the same view for club insurance contracts is challenging. Recognizing this right within the scope of club insurance contracts would be highly detrimental to the industry. It would hinder the application of Club rules and impede the provision of comprehensive insurance services to members. Therefore, expanding the right's application should not encompass club insurance.

Atamer argues that including the right to direct action in the TCC eliminates ambiguity and hesitations in its application, establishing a clear, applicable rule for all liability insurance.[59] He supports this arrangement by highlighting that the "pay to be paid" rule is invalid under Turkish law, and the insurer cannot invoke this defence against the third party. However, one aspect criticized by Atamer is that although this regulation does not transform liability insurance into a contract favouring the third party, it may excessively rigidify the boundary between the two contracts, potentially complicating contract interpretation.[60] Atamer's criticism holds merit in practice, as drawing a clear boundary between the two contracts can be challenging. On the other hand, if a liability insurance contract is intended to confer a benefit on a third party, it must be expressly stipulated in the contract. If the contract does not favour the third party, the right to direct action by a third party would not be included in any insurance contract but would instead arise from the law. Thus, while the practical delineation of boundaries may pose challenges, this situation is unlikely to cause significant problems in the legal interpretation of contracts.

According to Eksi, a jurist who supports the legal regulation of the right to direct action, this right constitutes an equitable arrangement to protect the third party. However, Eksi notes that this right is restricted or even prohibited in some countries, primarily to protect the insurer rather than the third party. Such a situation may lead to difficulties in Turkish Courts when dealing with cases involving foreign elements. Indeed, as Eksi points out, there are uncertainties regarding whether provisions prohibiting "the right to direct action against the insurer" will be considered by the Court in cases with foreign elements brought before Turkish Courts.[61]

56 Eksi, 31.
57 Paul E Gilbert, "Direct Actions against Insurance Companies: Should They Join the Party?" (1971) 59(2) *California Law Review* 543.
58 Eksi, 31; Atamer, 85.
59 Atamer, 85.
60 Atamer, 86.
61 Eksi, 31.

Another issue that would pose a problem is the difficulty in recognizing and enforcing a decision obtained from a Turkish court in disputes where Turkish law is applied, particularly in English courts.[62] For example, if the insurer is one of the English P&I Clubs in a collision incident in the Istanbul Strait, the situation becomes quite challenging. Under Turkish law, the third party can assert their direct action right against the Club. However, in the rules of English P&I Clubs, it is stated that English law will be applied to all disputes, and English law prioritizes the application of Club rules. Therefore, the ability of the third party to exercise their direct action right against the Club within the framework of Club rules and English law is subject to quite strict conditions. The third party cannot apply to the Club without meeting these conditions.

Consequently, even if the third party obtains a favourable judgement from Turkish courts, English courts will not recognize this judgement. When the third party brings proceedings against the Club relying on its rules, it is considered a breach of the implied contract between the third party and the Club. While the TCC aims to protect third parties, it puts them into a more significant predicament. Spending time to obtain a judgement that English courts will not recognize will result in further economic loss for the third party. Therefore, in the global context of club insurance and maritime trade industries where English law predominates, it makes little sense for other states to grant direct action rights to third parties against English P&I Clubs. Third parties who cannot assert this right against English P&I Clubs will be able to do so against Turkish P&I Clubs based on Turkish laws that support direct action rights. In this scenario, the economic pressure on Turkish P&I will increase significantly. Turkish legislators must reconsider this practice, which will create a highly disadvantageous situation for Turkish P&I. While Türkiye aims to develop the club insurance industry globally, it faces the risk of achieving the opposite result. Therefore, as argued in the book, we recommend that Türkiye restrict the direct action rights of third parties in the context of club insurance by regulating it with a separate provision in line with the English model.

### D. The Mandatory Nature of Article 1478 of the Turkish Commercial Code No. 6102 and Its Inability to Be Overridden by Contract

This section will examine Article 1478 of the Turkish Commercial Code No. 6102, emphasizing its mandatory character and the consequent inability to be altered or waived through contractual agreements.

Determining whether Article 1478 of the TCC regulates the mandatory right to direct action is significant in assessing the possibility of eliminating or restricting this right in insurance contracts between the insured and the insurer. If the legal provision is deemed mandatory, the parties to the insurance contract cannot enter into an agreement that violates this article of the law. Any provisions

62 Conference Notes, *P&I Insurance and Maritime Insurance Law within the Scope of the New Turkish Commercial Law*.

in contravention of this mandatory provision would be legally void. Conversely, if this legal provision is considered non-mandatory, the parties in the insurance contract may include clauses that eliminate or limit the third party's right to direct action. For instance, in England, the Contracts (Rights of Third Parties) Act 1999 granted certain rights to third parties in a contract, but these regulations were not mandatory. As a result, liability insurers either omitted or made it challenging for third parties to invoke these clauses in the insurance contracts they entered with the insured, contrary to the Act. Consequently, the rights the Act provided to the third party held little practical significance and enforceability.

Although Article 1478 of the TCC is not explicitly listed in Article 1486, which identifies mandatory provisions, some authors have argued that Article 1478 is not mandatory.[63] However, when determining the mandatory nature of a provision, it is inadequate to rely solely on explicit statements in the law. Numerous articles in the TCC that are considered mandatory are not explicitly stated in the legislation. Determining whether a provision is mandatory may also involve examining the article's purpose, the legal interest it seeks to protect, or interpreting its language.

According to the prevailing opinion in the doctrine, Article 1478, which regulates the right to direct action, is mandatory.[64] Ulas maintains that the article's formulation necessitates an understanding that neither the insured nor the insurer can deviate from its provisions, rendering it mandatory.[65] Acar argues that if Article 1478 of the TCC was not intended to be mandatory, the phrase "if there is no provision contrary to the contract" would have been included.[66] However, the law does not include such wording in the article. Therefore, the parties to the insurance contract, as the insured and the insurer, cannot introduce provisions that restrict or eliminate the third party's right to direct action. Even if they attempt to do so, such provisions do not supersede the mandatory provision of the law.

Eksi contends that Article 1478 of the TCC is inherently mandatory.[67] According to Eksi, if this article were not mandatory, the parties to the insurance contracts would have unrestricted discretion to waive the third party's right to direct action, which would contradict the law's protective purpose for the third party.[68]

It is reasonable to align with the majority opinion in the doctrine regarding the mandatory nature of Article 1478, as it effectively serves the regulation's purpose. Indeed, accepting that this provision is mandatory is crucial for its effective

63 Birgül Sopaci Oztuna, "Türk ve Alman Hukukunda Yeni Düzenlemeler Işığında Sorumluluk Sigortasında Doğrudan Talep Hakkı" (2011) 27(2) *BATIDER* 26.

64 Atamer, 85; Eksi, 10; Isil Ulas, *Uygulamalı Zarar Sigortaları Hukuku* (8th edn, Ankara 2012) 783–784; Serdar Acar, *Sorumluluk Sigortacısının Doğrudan Davada Dayanabileceği Savunmalar* (Vedat, Istanbul 2012) 9–15; Burcu Celikcapa Bilgin, "Right of Direct Action against Liability Insurers under the New Turkish Commercial Code" (2015) 1 *Turk Com L Rev* 265.

65 Ulas, 783–784.

66 Acar, *Direct Action*, 9–15.

67 Eksi, 10.

68 Eksi, 10.

implementation. Otherwise, this arrangement would become a provision that exists solely in the law but lacks enforceability. The right to direct action against the insurer, granted by law to the third party, is not a matter that the insured and the insurer can freely disregard. The law's intent is not to safeguard the insurer's interests as the stronger party.

On the contrary, this regulation aims to protect the interests of the weaker party, i.e., the third party. Provisions safeguarding the weaker party's interests can only serve their purpose effectively when mandatory. Therefore, it is necessary to acknowledge that the third party's right to direct action in TCC is a mandatory provision.

### *E. The Application of Article 1478 of the Turkish Commercial Code in Foreign-Related Disputes Due to Its Procedural Nature*

This title will analyze Article 1478 of the Turkish Commercial Code, focusing on its procedural aspects and how it applies to disputes involving foreign elements. The classification of Article 1478 of the TCC as either procedural or substantive law remains a contentious issue in Turkish legal discourse. This determination holds significant implications for identifying the applicable law in Turkish Courts, particularly those involving foreign elements and the right to direct action.[69]

If Article 1478 pertains to substantive law, the state's law agreed upon by the parties in the insurance contract will govern the case. Conversely, if it relates to procedural law, Turkish law must be applied by the Court in cases involving foreign elements.

According to Yesilova, Article 1478 of the TCC falls within substantive law.[70] Under this interpretation, the existence of the third party's right to direct action against the insurer would be contingent upon the law chosen and agreed upon in the insurance contract. In Turkish law, determining the applicable state law in cases with foreign elements is guided by the provisions outlined in The Turkish Code of Private International Law and International Civil Procedure (CPIL).[71]

According to Article 24(1) of the CPIL, the parties to a contract may opt for a particular state law to govern the substance of their agreement.[72] For instance, in P&I Club insurance contracts, the parties might elect to apply English law. As a result, any disputes would be resolved following English law, which restricts the third party's right to direct action against the insurer to a more limited extent than Turkish law. Due to contractual provisions, the third party's ability to effectively

69 Eksi, 12.

70 Yesilova Aras, *Yolcunun Uğradığı Bedensel Zararlardan Dolayı P&I Kulübüne Doğrudan Başvuru Hakkı*, 146.

71 The Turkish Code of Private International Law and International Civil Procedure (CPIL) enacted on 27 November 2007 was entered into force on 12 December 2007.

72 Article 24(1) of the CPIL is regulated as follows: "The law explicitly designated by the parties shall govern the contractual obligation relations. The designation which can be concluded without hesitation from the provisions of the contract or is understood from the affairs of the case is also valid."

exercise their right to direct action against the insurer may be hindered in many instances.

In scenarios where the parties have chosen a foreign state law, a conflict with Turkish public order would arise if it rendered the exercise of the injured party's right to direct action complex or eliminated. In such cases, Article 5 of the CPIL[73] would come into effect, stipulating that the provisions of the CPIL shall not apply if the foreign state law is contrary to Turkish public order.[74]

However, it is essential to approach the notion of public order with caution, as interpreting it too broadly may lead to excessive interference by the Courts in cases with foreign elements, undermining the parties' freedom to choose their governing law. The notion of public order should not be expansively construed, as it may impede the parties' free will and encroach upon the principles of freedom of contract and international legal norms.

If we considered Article 1478 of the TCC as a provision of procedural law rather than substantive law, distinct outcomes would emerge concerning the applicable law and the direct action right of the injured party. Courts must apply domestic law in procedural matters, even in cases involving a foreign element. Procedural issues are invariably governed by the lex fori, signifying that matters about procedural law are determined according to the law of the jurisdiction in which the case is filed. Neither the parties nor the Court possesses the authority or prerogative to select the governing law in procedural matters. The Turkish Supreme Court has also underscored that, in cases with foreign elements, the lex fori, i.e., Turkish law, shall prevail concerning procedural law.[75]

It would be more appropriate to perceive Article 1478 of the TCC as a regulation of procedural law, irrespective of its inclusion in the TCC rather than procedural laws. This is because procedural provisions in Turkish law are not exclusively confined to procedural legislation. Numerous regulations on procedural law are also found within laws that govern substantive matters. For instance, while Article 1473 of the TCC pertains to the substantive rule governing the direct payment of insurance compensation to the injured party, Article 1478, which addresses the right to legal action, constitutes a procedural regulation. As the right to sue is inherently procedural, it is regulated explicitly as a separate article within the law. As a result, it should be acknowledged that Article 1478 is considered a provision related to procedural law as it emphasizes a procedural right for third parties to initiate legal action.

73 Article 5 of CPIL is regulated as follows: "If the provision of the foreign law to be applied in a certain case is openly contrary to the public order of Türkiye, the said provision shall not be applied. Where it is deemed necessary, Turkish law shall be applied."

74 Ekşi, 12.

75 Turkish Supreme Court, 2nd Law Department, Decision No. E. 2012/616, K. 2012/26084, dated November 5, 2012.

### *F. The Independent Nature of the Direct Action Right in the Turkish Commercial Code Unaffected by Contractual Provisions*

This title will explain the direct action right established as an independent right in the Turkish Commercial Code. Determining whether the right to direct action, as stipulated in Article 1478 of the TCC, is an independent right derived from the law or a contractual one assumes paramount importance, particularly in direct action lawsuits. This determination also influences whether Clubs can invoke contractual defences against third parties. Recognition of the direct action right as a contractual empowers Clubs to assert defences such as "arbitration" or "pay to be paid" against third parties. These defences bolster the position of Clubs in direct action lawsuits and prevent third parties from seeking compensation directly from the Clubs. However, if the direct action right is independent, Clubs cannot rely on contractual defences against third parties based on their contractual agreements with the insured. In such cases, the direct action right would cease to be a contractual entitlement of the third party and assume the character of a legally recognized right that must be enforced. Consequently, asserting contractual defences to impede the exercise of this right becomes challenging when third parties demand compensation directly from the Club. Hence, it is crucial to determine the true nature of the direct action right.

Article 1473(1) of the TCC establishes that the insurer's obligation to provide compensation arises from the insured's liability resulting from an "event stipulated in the insurance contract." However, it is crucial to recognize that while this liability is connected to a contractually specified event, third parties' right to direct action is not a contractual right but an independent right derived directly from the law itself. The legislator has explicitly stated that the triggering event for this liability must be one specified in the insurance contract. Therefore, the reference to the contract in the legislative text does not transform the right to direct action into a contractual right.

Article 1484 of the TCC states that this right is an independent right derived from the law. This article stipulates that even if the insurer is relieved, wholly or partially, from fulfilling their debt towards the insured, the obligation to perform continues until the compulsory insurance amount is satisfied.[76] Notably, Article 1484 of the TCC applies to compulsory liability insurance. In Turkish law, P&I insurance has been included within the scope of compulsory liability insurance in certain situations, as stipulated in specific regulations. The "Regulation on Insurance and Inspection of Ships Related to Maritime Liens,"[77] which came into effect in 2010, encompasses insurance against maritime liens and includes

76 Article 1484 of the TCC states that: "Even if the insurer is completely or partially relieved from the performance of debt against the insured, the performance of the debt continues until the compulsory insurance amount."

77 "Regulation on Insurance and Inspection of Ships Related to Maritime Liens" Official Gazette, 14.11.2010/27759.

the definition of P&I Club insurance in Article 4(e). The regulation applies to all Turkish-flagged vessels with a commercial purpose and a gross tonnage exceeding 300 GT and vessels visiting Turkish ports/facilities regardless of their flag. According to the regulation, vessels flying the Turkish flag shall be insured by their owners with protection and indemnity insurance against maritime claims, and all vessels arriving at port facilities within this regulation's scope must possess valid protection and indemnity insurance against maritime claims.[78] This regulation indicates that P&I Club insurance is deemed mandatory in certain situations under Turkish legislation, and it is subject to all provisions outlined in the TCC concerning compulsory insurance. Therefore, when a third party exercises the right to direct action against the insurer under Article 1478 of the TCC, the insurer's obligation to fulfil the claim against the third party remains, even if the insurer's liability to perform ceases due to non-payment of premiums or termination of the contract.

Another example of why direct action should not be considered as a contractual right is the prohibition of set-off in the law. Article 1480 of the TCC stipulates that the insurer cannot set off the insurance compensation payable to the third party with its receivables arising from the insurance contract.[79] Accordingly, the Club cannot claim that its member has a premium debt and that this will be deducted from the compensation paid to the third party. The Club can only assert this claim against its members. If the direct action right had been regulated as a contractual right, in this case, the law would have allowed the insured to assert all defences arising from the contract against the third party. However, adopting the opposite approach, the law aimed to eliminate factors that could hinder the use of this right. This provision is among the protective provisions outlined in Article 1486 of the TCC. Therefore, it is mandatory, and contracts contrary to this provision are invalid under Turkish law.

The aim of our explanations is not to support the protection of the direct action right against Clubs in Turkish law. On the contrary, the reason for this comprehensive analysis was to show that the legal regulations regarding the direct action right in Turkish law tend to protect third parties against Clubs disproportionately. Turkish law applies general insurance law principles to club insurance as well. However, this approach harms the club insurance industry, especially regarding third parties' direct action rights. Clubs should be allowed to operate within a more flexible and protective legal framework. Therefore, as stated in the book argument, Turkish law should adopt policies that restrict the use of direct action rights by third parties against Clubs and are more favourable to Clubs.

78 Hacı Kara, "Deniz Alacakları İçin Gemilerin Sigortalanması Mecburiyeti (The Obligation of Insuring Ships for Maritime Claims)" http://www.hacikara.com/en/publications/internet-publications/detail/11/the-obligation-of-insuring-ships-for-maritime-claims/ accessed 20 May 2023.

79 Article 1480 of TCC No. 6102 states that "(1) The insurer shall not set-off the insurance compensation it will pay to the victim with the receivables arising from the insurance contract" (translated by the author).

## IV. Analysis of English Law Prioritizing Club Rules in Direct Action Disputes

This title will discuss how English law precedes Club rules in direct action dispute cases. The focus will be on English law's legal framework and principles, prioritizing the application of Club rules over other considerations when resolving such disputes.

When analyzing the direct action rights of third parties within the framework of English law, this chapter will demonstrate how this legal system provides a conducive environment for Clubs. The English legal model clearly shows the importance of the legal regulations applied to club insurance in developing this industry. Recognizing the benefits of developing this industry for the country, England opts for a legal policy that limits third-party direct actions against Clubs. Also, in this legal approach, prioritizing the implementation of Club rules enables Clubs to conduct their activities freely. Through this freedom, Clubs can provide more comprehensive insurance services to their members, ensuring the safe conduct of maritime trade activities. Thus, by maintaining leadership globally in the club insurance and maritime trade industries, English P&I Clubs contribute significantly to the country's economy. The relationship between a country's legal policy and its contribution to the national economy should not be overlooked. The undeniable contribution of English law's policies to the emergence and development of the club insurance industry in England should be acknowledged. This section will examine these policies concretely through court judgements and laws.

### *A. The Evolution of Direct Action Rights of Third-Party in English Insurance Law: Analysis of the 1930 and 2010 Acts*

The position of third parties in English law, particularly in the period preceding the enactment of the Third Parties (Rights against Insurers) Act 1930 (hereinafter referred to as the "1930 Act"), was significantly constrained by the principle of privity of contract.[80] Under this principle, contractual rights and obligations were confined to the contracting parties, effectively barring third parties from making claims against insurers or accessing information regarding the terms of the contract.[81] As a result, third parties seeking indemnification were compelled to pursue claims against the insured party rather than directly against the insurer.[82]

In recognition of the inequities arising from the doctrine of privity, the 1930 Act was introduced to extend legal protections to third parties,[83] particularly in cases

80 See *Thomas v Thomas* (1842) 2 QB 851; *Tweddle v Atkinson* [1861] EWHC J57 (QB); *Dunlop Pneumatic Tyre Co. Ltd. v Selfridge & Co. Ltd.* [1915] A.C. 847.

81 Robert Merkin, *Marine Insurance Legislation* (4th edn, Informa Law 2010) 12. Also, for detailed information see Robert Merkin, *Privity of Contract: The Impact of the Contracts (Rights of Third Parties) Act 1999* (LLP, London 2000) 1 et seq.

82 Ling Zhu and Xiuhua Pan, "Compulsory Insurance and its Implications" (2016) *LMCLQ* 569.

83 Robert Merkin and Séverine Saintier, "Privity of Contract: Statutory Developments" in Robert Merkin and James Devenny (eds), *Essays in Memory of Professor Jill Poole: Coherence, Modernisation*

where the insured party was insolvent.[84] The Act permitted third parties to initiate direct action against insurers by transferring the insured's rights to the third party under such circumstances. However, despite its objectives, the 1930 Act faced criticism for its procedural complexities and limitations. The Act imposed onerous requirements on third parties, such as the necessity to prove both the insured's insolvency and establish a liability relationship with the insured before they could pursue direct action against the insurer.[85]

The 1930 Act operated on the principle of subrogation,[86] whereby the third party assumed the insured's rights vis-à-vis the insurer upon the insured's insolvency.[87] Nevertheless, the effectiveness of the Act was curtailed by the burdensome procedural steps required for subrogation to occur.[88] Third parties were required to initiate insolvency proceedings against the insured and establish liability relationships[89] through court orders, arbitration awards, or contractual provisions,[90] often resulting in protracted and costly litigation.[91] This complexity was further exacerbated in cross-border disputes, particularly those involving P&I Clubs, where the insured and the third party might be situated in different legal jurisdictions.[92]

Critics of the 1930 Act,[93] such as Padovan, highlighted the substantial difficulties third parties faced in meeting these requirements, especially when dealing with

---

*and Integration in Contract, Commercial and Corporate Laws* (Informa Law from Routledge 2018) Ch 7, 137.

84 Johanna Hjalmarsson, "Direct Claims against Marine Insurers in the English Legal System" (2010) 18 *Asia Pac L Rev* 259; Adriana Vincenca Padovan, "Direct Action of a Third-party Against the Insurer in Maritime Insurance with a Special Focus on the Developments in Croatian Law" (2003) 42(157) *Poredbeno Pomorsko Pravo* 35–83.

85 According to the 1930 Act, s 1 (1), in the event of the insured's insolvency, the rights against the insurer are transferred to the third party after a liability relationship has been established between the insured and the third party.

86 Hazelwood and Semark, 292.

87 Jerome C Scowcroft, "Protection and Indemnity Insurance – Pay to Be Paid Clauses Third-party Claims – (British) Third Parties (Rights against Insurers) Act 1930" (1989) 20 *J Mar L & Com* 205.

88 Rhidian Thomas, "Third-Party Direct Rights of Action against Insurers under UK Law and International Maritime Liability Conventions" in *Regulation of Risk* (Brill/Nijhoff 2022) 689 https://doi.org/10.1163/9789004518681_024 accessed 20 May 2023.

89 Paul Myburgh, "Taxonomizing Third-Party Rights of Direct Action Against Marine Liability Insurers" in Ozlem Gurses (ed), *Research Handbook on Marine Insurance Law* (Edward Elgar Publishing 2024) Ch 10, 207.

90 The Court of Appeal, in *Post Office*, rejected the third party's application, asserting that it was necessary for the third party to establish a liability relationship with the insured before initiating legal action against the insurer. This establishment of liability could be accomplished through a court, arbitral order, or by means of a contractual agreement. See *Post Office v Norwich Union Fire Insurance Society Ltd* [1967] 2 QB 363. See also, for similar judgements, *Bradley v Eagle Star Insurance Co Ltd* [1989] AC 957 (*Bradley v Eagle Star* case); *Thornton Springer v NEM Insurance Co Ltd and others* [2000] 2 All ER 489.

91 Mark Tilley, "Protection and Indemnity Club Rules and Direct Actions by Third Parties" (1986) 17 *J Mar L & Com* 427, 436.

92 *The Vainqueur Jose* [1979] 1 Lloyd's Rep 557; *The Allobrogia* [1979] 1 Lloyd's Rep 190.

93 Tilley, 36; Hazelwood and Semark, 294.

insolvent companies.[94] The lengthy process of re-registering insolvent companies, establishing liability relationships,[95] and navigating cross-border legal frameworks made it nearly impossible for third parties to secure timely compensation.[96] Furthermore, the Act's provisions[97] concerning the third party's right to information were vague and inadequate, further complicating the compensation process.[98] Third parties often had to initiate legal proceedings without knowing whether the insured's policy would cover their claims, leading to unnecessary legal costs and delays.[99] Efforts were undertaken to enhance the provisions of the 1930 Act[100] concerning the right to information and to address these challenges more effectively.[101] Subsequently, the English Court of Appeal issued judgements concerning the right to information before establishing a liability relationship between the third party and the insured.[102] Notably, in cases such as *First National Tricity Finance*[103] *and Simon Freakley,*[104] the Court recognized the third party's right to receive information independently of the liability requirement. These judgements aimed to facilitate third parties' access to information.

Responding to these criticisms, the Law Commission initiated reform efforts,[105] culminating in the Third Parties (Rights against Insurers) Act 2010, which superseded the 1930 Act.[106] The 2010 Act sought to rectify the shortcomings of its predecessor by streamlining the procedural requirements for third parties seeking compensation from insurers.[107] A fundamental reform introduced by the 2010 Act was establishing a single lawsuit procedure,[108] allowing third parties to determine both the insured's and insurer's liability within one action, thereby eliminating the need for multiple proceedings.[109]

94 Padovan, 63.

95 *Post Office v Norwich Union Fire Insurance Society Ltd* [1967] 2 QB 363.

96 *Post Office v Norwich Union Fire Insurance Society Ltd* [1967] 2 QB 363.

97 1930 Act, s 2.

98 For example, in *Bradley v Eagle Star*, the Court held that the third party's right to information arises upon the establishment of a liability relationship with the insured and the occurrence of subrogation. See *Bradley v Eagle Star Insurance Co Ltd* [1989] AC 957.

99 Thomas, "Direct Rights", 705.

100 See 1930 Act, s 2(1).

101 Hazelwood and Semark, 293.

102 *First National Tricity Finance Ltd. v OT Computers Ltd (In Administration*) [2004] EWCA Civ 653; *Centre Reinsurance International Co v Freakley* [2005] EWCA Civ 115.

103 *First National Tricity Finance Ltd. v OT Computers Ltd (In Administration)* [2004] EWCA Civ 653.

104 *Centre Reinsurance International Co v Freakley* [2005] EWCA Civ 115.

105 The Law Commission and The Scottish Law Commission, Third Parties Rights Against Insurer, Joint Report of July 2001, Law Com No 272 (Scot Law Com No 184) https://www.scotlawcom.gov.uk/files/9512/7989/6682/rep184.pdf accessed 22 May 2022.

106 See Art. 3.13 of the Joint Report of 2001.

107 Michelle George and Rebecca Huggins, "Third-Party Risks" in Lord Mance, Iain Goldrein, and Robert Merkin (eds), *Insurance Disputes* (3rd edn, Informa 2011) 486.

108 This is stated in Act 2010 s 1 (3) as follows: "The third party may bring proceedings to enforce the rights against the insurer without having established the relevant person's liability; but the third party may not enforce those rights without having established that liability."

109 Thomas, "Direct Rights", 701.

The 2010 Act also significantly improved the third party's right to information.[110] Unlike the 1930 Act, which restricted access to information until after the liability relationship was established, the 2010 Act[111] enables third parties to obtain information about the insurance contract without first proving liability.[112] This reform[113] has been reinforced by judgements, such as in *Harcourt v FEF Griffin & Ors*,[114] where the Court underscored the importance of providing all relevant information to ensure a fair and effective resolution of disputes.[115]

Despite these advancements, the 2010 Act retains some aspects of the subrogation principle from the 1930 Act. Consequently, while third parties can now more easily initiate claims against insurers, they still inherit the rights and obligations of the insured, including defences the insurer might have had against the insured. In the context of P&I insurance, for example, the "pay to be paid" rule remains a valid defence against third-party claims, except in cases involving death or personal injury in marine insurance.[116]

The decision to maintain the subrogation-based framework rather than adopting a new liability framework was significantly influenced by industry stakeholders, particularly P&I Clubs. The Law Commission's reports indicate that these Clubs played a substantial role in shaping the final provisions of the 2010 Act, particularly in preserving their ability to assert defences like the "pay to be paid" rule.[117] This has led to criticism that, although the 2010 Act represents an improvement over the 1930 Act, it does not fully protect third parties in all circumstances, particularly in the complex landscape of marine insurance.[118]

However, while these doctrinal views advocate for the protection of third parties, they often overlook the disadvantageous position this would create for the Clubs. It is imperative to support the legal policy that regulations concerning the direct action rights of third parties should not apply to marine and Club insurance. Evaluating Club insurance under the same legal framework as other conventional liability insurance types contradicts the unique nature of this form of insurance. Clubs operate on the principle of mutuality, aiming primarily to provide their members with fast and affordable insurance coverage. The continuity of this comprehensive insurance coverage depends on the Club's ability to operate flexibly and maintain economic stability. Therefore, granting extensive direct action rights to third parties risks increasing economic pressure on Clubs, complicating their

110 For detailed information on the Commission's views, see Joint Report of July 2001, paragraph 4.29, and subsequent paragraphs.

111 See the 2010 Act, s 11, Sch 1.

112 Merkin, Goldrein, and Mance, *Insurance Disputes*, 489.

113 The Law Commission Report No. 272, para 1.8.

114 *Harcourt v FEF Griffin* [2007] EWHC 1500 (QB).

115 For the decision of the court to accept the request of the third party to obtain information about the scope of the insurance contract, see *Harcourt v FEF Griffin* [2007] EWHC 1500 (QB).

116 Thomas, "Direct Rights", 698.

117 See Joint Report of July 2001, 25.

118 Johanna Hjalmarsson, "Direct Action against P & I Clubs" (2008) 139 *Insurance & Reinsurance Law Briefing* 7.

operations. Hence, shaping legal policies to meet the industry's needs is essential. The policy adopted by English law in this regard is particularly appropriate for the Club insurance industry.

In summary, while the 2010 Act represents a significant improvement over the 1930 Act, particularly in simplifying procedures and enhancing third-party rights to information, its retention of the subrogation principle and certain defences for insurers continues to impose limitations on third parties' ability to secure compensation. While the 2010 Act addresses many criticisms of the 1930 Act, particularly in reducing procedural complexity and clarifying the right to information, its reliance on subrogation means that third parties still face challenges in fully exercising their rights, particularly in specialized areas such as P&I insurance.

### *B. The "Arbitration Clause" and "Pay to Be Paid" Defences in Direct Action Disputes under English Law*

#### *1. Arbitration Clauses and the Anti-Suit Injunctions*

Through a critical examination of practical implementation, legal regulations, and the implications for arbitration provisions within Club rules, the following analysis highlights the intricate dynamics and far-reaching ramifications inherent in arbitration practices within the English legal framework. Additionally, this examination sheds light on the judicial validation of arbitration clauses, exemplified by the influential *Scott v Avery*[119] decision, aiming to provide valuable insights into the complexities surrounding the practice of arbitration.

The 1996 Arbitration Act is significant in English law as the primary legislative framework governing arbitration. Beyond its overarching authority over arbitration proceedings, this Act significantly influences the formulation of arbitration provisions within Club rules. The legal validity bestowed upon arbitration clauses embedded in Club rules is particularly significant, a pivotal milestone established through the landmark *Scott v Avery*.[120] The *Scott v Avery* clause in Club rules encompasses two crucial elements: Firstly, it imposes an arbitration obligation on both Club members and third parties involved in disputes, and secondly, it establishes a precedent whereby the claimant's right to initiate legal proceedings is contingent upon prior exhaustion of the arbitration process to resolve the dispute. In cases where a Club member or third party seeks legal action outside of arbitration, the Club can seek a stay of legal proceedings[121] injunction from the English Courts, leading to the suspension of legal proceedings initiated by the non-compliant party concerning the arbitration clause.[122]

119 *Scott v Avery* (1843–1860) All E.R. Rep 1 (HL).
120 *Scott v Avery* (1843–1860) All E.R. Rep 1 (HL).
121 See Arbitration Act 1996, s 9.
122 For more information, see Andrew Tweeddale and Keren Tweeddale, *Scott v Avery Clauses: O'er Judges' Fingers, Who Straight Dream on Fees* (Sweet & Maxwell 2011) 423–427.

Anti-suit injunctions are also employed against parties who fail to adhere to the arbitration clause within P&I Club rules. English Courts possess the authority to issue anti-suit injunctions,[123] restraining parties from commencing legal proceedings in foreign jurisdictions when such disputes fall within their jurisdictional purview.[124]

The English courts' authority to grant anti-suit injunctions is based on Section 37 of the Senior Courts Act 1981.[125] Section 44(2)(e) of the Arbitration Act 1996 provides interim arbitration measures but does not cover permanent injunctions and imposes certain restrictions[126] not found in Section 37 of the 1981 Act. Anti-suit injunctions target the parties improperly initiating proceedings rather than the foreign courts themselves.[127]

For the English court to grant an anti-suit injunction, it must have jurisdiction over the claimant in the foreign proceedings.[128] Such permission may be granted under Civil Procedure Rules (CPR) 62.5(1)(c) or CPR Practice Direction 6B.[129] P&I Club Rules are typically governed by English law, and it is not expected that any other jurisdiction would govern an arbitration clause.[130]

To obtain an injunction, the applicant must demonstrate, with a high degree of probability, the existence of a valid arbitration clause.[131] The court may refuse the injunction if there are exceptional circumstances, such as delay by the applicant.[132] An injunction cannot be refused on the grounds of *forum non conveniens*. Finally, claims that the arbitration clause is invalid under the law of the jurisdiction where the proceedings are initiated are not considered in the English courts' decisions regarding anti-suit injunctions.

The principles developed by the English Courts regarding the issuance of anti-suit injunctions have been summarized by Cresswell J in *American International Specialty Lines Insurance Co v Abbott Laboratories*.[133] In this case, the stay

123 *Times Trading Corporation v National Bank of Fujairah (Dubai Branch) (The Archagelos Gabriel)* [2020] EWHC 1983 (Comm); *Aggeliki Charis Compania Maritima SA v Pagnan SpA (The Angelic Grace)* [1995] 1 Lloyd's Rep 87, 92; *Enka Insaat ve Sanayi AS v OOO "Insurance Company Chubb"* [2020] EWCA Civ 574; *OT Africa Line Ltd v Magic Sportswear Corporation* [2005] EWCA Civ 710; *AES Ust-Kamenogorsk Hydropower Plant LLP v Ust-Kamenogorsk Hydropower Plant JSC* [2013] UKSC 35.

124 Jonatan Echebarria Fernández, *Jurisdiction and Arbitration Agreements in Contracts for the Carriage of Goods by Sea: Limitations on Party Autonomy* (Informa 2021) 98.

125 Senior Courts Act 1981, s 37.

126 Arbitration Act 1996, 44(2)(e).

127 Robert Merkin, *Arbitration Law* (Maritime Insights & Intelligence, London 2024) para 8.82.

128 *AES Ust-Kamenogorsk Hydropower Plant LLP v Ust-Kamenogorsk Hydropower Plant JSC* [2013] UKSC 35.

129 Civil Procedure Rules (CPR) 62.5(1)(c); CPR Practice Direction 6B.

130 Merkin, *Arbitration Law*, para. 8.82.

131 *Ulusoy Denizcilik AS v COFCO Global Harvest (Zhangjiagang) Trading Co Ltd* [2020] EWHC 3645 (Comm).

132 *Africa Finance Corporation & Others v Aiteo Eastern E & P Company Limited* [2022] EWHC 768 (Comm).

133 *American International Specialty Lines Insurance Co v Abbott Laboratories* [2004] 1 Lloyd's Rep 815.

application was dismissed because the claim that the contract contained an arbitration clause incorporated from a separate agreement was rejected.[134]

The principles are as follows: Jurisdiction should be exercised only when justice requires it, and injunctions should be directed at the party pursuing or threatening to pursue proceedings, not at the foreign court itself. An injunction should be granted only when it will be effective against a party subject to the court's jurisdiction and will provide a meaningful remedy, indirectly affecting the foreign court.

The court will restrain a party from commencing or continuing proceedings in a foreign court only if those proceedings are vexatious or oppressive; this requirement is generally met when foreign proceedings are initiated in breach of an arbitration clause or an exclusive jurisdiction agreement. Suppose parties to a contract agree to confer exclusive jurisdiction on a particular court or arbitration tribunal, and a claim falling within the scope of that agreement is brought in a different forum. In that case, the court will use its discretion to enforce the contractual bargain, requiring the party commencing proceedings in the non-contractual forum to show solid reasons for doing so.

This discretion must be flexible; a party may lose its right to equitable relief due to delay or other unconscionable conduct. The principles governing the granting of injunctions and stays are not the same; comity is considered for injunctions but not for stays. If a dispute is between two contracting parties and one sues the other in a non-contractual forum for claims falling within an exclusive jurisdiction or arbitration clause, the clause will likely be enforced, but not invariably.

The court may refuse to grant an injunction or stay if the interests of non-contracting parties are involved or if claims outside the clause are part of the dispute, creating the risk of parallel proceedings and inconsistent decisions. There is no principled distinction between injunctions restraining proceedings in breach of an arbitration clause and those in breach of an exclusive jurisdiction clause; both are justified when damages would be an inadequate remedy without the injunction.

When it is arguable whether foreign proceedings were brought in breach of contract, an injunction should not be granted because such proceedings cannot be said to be vexatious or oppressive. In cases alleging a breach of an arbitration agreement governed by English law, the applicant must show a strong likelihood that its claim is well-founded and entitled to restrain the foreign proceedings; the possibility of the respondent ignoring the court's order does not dismiss the application.

A successful applicant for relief against a clear breach of an arbitration clause is generally awarded costs on an indemnity basis.[135]

In the *AES Ust-Kamenogorsk Hydropower Plant LLP v Ust-Kamenogorsk Hydropower Plant JSC*,[136] the court ruled that even if arbitration proceedings had not been initiated, in the presence of an arbitration agreement, the other party could

134 For detailed information, see Merkin, *Arbitration Law*, para 8.82.

135 Merkin, *Arbitration Law*.

136 *AES Ust-Kamenogorsk Hydropower Plant LLP v Ust-Kamenogorsk Hydropower Plant JSC* [2013] UKSC 35.

not initiate legal proceedings in another court and granted an anti-suit injunction. This authority has sparked extensive debate in international private law, particularly regarding whether it represents an encroachment upon the jurisdiction of foreign states.[137] However, proponents of the English Courts' authority argue that its purpose is to restrain parties acting in contravention of the arbitration clause rather than to restrict the authority of foreign states.[138]

*The Front Comor*[139] was a prominent example of using anti-suit injunctions. In this instance, insurers initiated litigation in Italy, violating the arbitration agreement, prompting West Tankers to seek an anti-suit injunction from the English Court. The House of Lords ruled in favour of granting the injunction against the insurers, intending to prevent parties from breaching the agreed-upon arbitration agreement. Noussia argues that judgements involving anti-suit injunctions should not be viewed as undermining the harmonization and consolidation of private international law, emphasizing their role in safeguarding the distinctive characteristics of English law.[140]

Similarly, Clift supports the use of anti-suit injunctions by English Courts, asserting that this authority should not be perceived as interference with the jurisdiction of foreign Courts but rather as a response to the non-compliant party's failure to respect the jurisdiction of the English Courts.[141] Baatz lends further support to the Court's authority by suggesting that parties failing to comply with the arbitration clause could face imprisonment or fines for violating the anti-suit injunction issued by the Court.[142]

Conversely, Lord Mance highlights the need for caution when exercising this authority, particularly in cases where the dispute also falls within the jurisdiction of the foreign state where legal proceedings have been initiated, as it may indirectly infringe upon the jurisdiction of foreign states.[143] Likewise, it is essential to note that the CJEU considers anti-suit injunction judgements made by English Courts as interventions in the jurisdiction of member states,[144] asserting that such judgements

137 Fernández, 99; Gabrielle Kaufmann-Kohler, "How to Handle Parallel Proceedings: A Practical Approach to Issues such as Competence-Competence and Anti-Suit Injunctions" (2008) 2 *Dispute Resolution International* 112.

138 *West Tankers Inc and another v Ras Riunione Adriatica Di Sicurta SpA and another (The Front Comor)* [2005] EWHC 454; [2005] 2 Lloyd's Rep 257 (*The Front Comor* case).

139 *West Tankers Inc and another v Ras Riunione Adriatica Di Sicurta SpA and another (The Front Comor)* [2005] EWHC 454; [2005] 2 Lloyd's Rep 257 (*The Front Comor* case).

140 Kyriaki Noussia, "Anti-Suit Injunctions and Arbitration Proceedings: What Does the Future Hold?" (2009) 26 *Journal of International Arbitration* 311–336, 335.

141 Rhys Clift, *Forum Shopping, Anti-Suit Injunctions and EU Law: A Brief Overview (and Update)* (Hill Dickinson LLP, February 2007) 6.

142 Baatz and others, *Maritime Law*, 9.

143 Sir Jonathan Mance, "Civil Jurisdiction in Europe: Choice of Court Clauses, Competing Litigation and Anti-Suit Injunctions" (Speech delivered at the Second Conference of European Commercial Judges, Paris, 14 October 2004) 4.

144 *Allianz SpA (formerly Riunione Adriatica di Sicurtà SpA) v West Tankers Inc (The Front Comor)* (2009) CJEU Case C-185/07, [2009] ECR I–00673.

contravene the principle of mutual trust.[145] For instance, in the *Front Comor* brought before the English Court, the Court ruled that the arbitration fell outside the scope of the Brussels Convention and issued an anti-suit injunction against the party breaching the arbitration clause. However, this decision was subsequently reviewed by the CJEU, which deemed the ruling on the anti-suit injunction to be inappropriate.[146]

However, in the recent case *QBE Europe SA/NV v Generali Espana de Seguros Y Reaseguros*,[147] the English High Court issued an anti-suit injunction to curtail legal proceedings initiated by insurer Generali España ("Generali") in Spain to enforce compliance with a London arbitration agreement in an insurance policy. In summary, on 3 July 2016, the motor yacht Angara allegedly caused damage to an underwater electrical cable connecting the islands of Mallorca and Menorca, resulting in hydrocarbon pollution in the local area. The insurer, Generali, settled the cable owner's claim for legal liability and property damage under the insurance

145 Kaufmann-Kohler, 112.

146 Discussing the *West Tankers* case, which is from the pre-Brexit era and has lost its relevance today, is essential to understand how the UK's EU membership affected anti-suit injunction judgements. The case involved significant damage resulting from a collision between a ship chartered by West Tankers and a jetty owned by Erg Petroli SpA (Erg) in Italy. Allianz, the insurer covering the damage, initiated legal proceedings against West Tankers in Italian courts based on subrogation principles. Meanwhile, Erg commenced arbitration proceedings in London against West Tankers for additional damages not covered by the insurance policy, pursuant to their contractual agreement. In response to the insurer's lawsuit in Italy, West Tankers sought an anti-suit injunction from the English Supreme Court, arguing that the insurer, as Erg's successor, should comply with the arbitration clause in the contract. The court granted the injunction, halting the proceedings initiated by the insurer in Italy. The case eventually reached the House of Lords, which referred it to the CJEU for clarification. The CJEU examined whether a party bringing a lawsuit in the competent court of an EU member state violated the arbitration agreement under the Brussels Regulation (EC Regulation 44/2001). The CJEU concluded that while the case before the English courts fell outside the scope of the Brussels Regulation, it could still obstruct the system's objectives. The Brussels system aimed to harmonize jurisdictional rules in civil and commercial matters and ensure the free circulation of judgements within the EU. The CJEU also found that the insurer's claim for damages for torts in Italy fell within the scope of the Brussels Regulation, implying that the Italian court should decide on the arbitration claim. The CJEU determined that member states' courts could not issue anti-suit injunctions against each other concerning ongoing cases. It emphasized that such injunctions, even in cases involving the breach of an arbitration agreement, would contradict the Brussels Regulation. This ruling was particularly significant as it marked the first instance where courts of member states were prohibited from issuing anti-suit injunctions in potential conflict with the Brussels system, irrespective of the existence of an arbitration agreement. Subsequently, the implementation regulation of the Brussels I Regulation (Regulation No. 1215/2012) revised the rules concerning the recognition and enforcement of civil and commercial judgements and updated the regulations on judicial disputes between EU member state courts. (Regulation (EU) No 1215/2012 of the European Parliament and of the Council of 12 December 2012 on Jurisdiction and the Recognition and Enforcement of Judgments in Civil and Commercial Matters (Recast)). However, post-Brexit, the Brussels Regulation and CJEU decisions are no longer binding on the UK. Consequently, the impact of the West Tankers decision has ceased for current cases. For a similar decision, see *Case C-159/02 Turner v Grovit and Others* [2004] ECR I–03565.

147 *QBE Europe SA/NV and QBE (UK) Ltd v Generali Espana de Seguros y Reaseguros* [2022] EWHC 2062 (Comm), para 65.

policy. Subsequently, Generali was subrogated regarding the possible rights the insured yacht owners might have.

On 23 February 2022, Generali exercised its right of direct action in Spanish courts against QBE UK, the P&I insurer for the yacht, seeking compensation for the loss and damage arising from the incident. Generali grounded this on the 2014 Spanish Maritime Navigation Law (MNA). In response, QBE Europe and QBE UK (collectively QBE), the Yacht's P&I insurer, urgently applied to the English Court for an anti-suit injunction to prevent Generali from pursuing proceedings in Spain. QBE argued that any dispute regarding the P&I policy's liabilities is subject to English law and London arbitration, as stipulated in the policy. In this context, QBE sought a court order against Generali, emphasizing the governing law clause in the P&I policy and requesting an anti-suit injunction to prohibit Generali from continuing legal proceedings in Spain.

The anti-suit injunction was deemed "quasi-contractual" due to Generali not being a party to the underlying policy containing the arbitration agreement.[148] Despite relying on the direct action right in Spanish insurance legislation to bring a claim in Spain, Generali's compensation claim was based on the policy. Therefore, the English High Court emphasized that Generali must adhere to the obligations and arbitration clause outlined in the policy to pursue compensation based on the policy.[149]

The Court was not persuaded by Generali's arguments, which were presented as solid reasons to reject the anti-suit injunction. Generali contended that the London arbitration agreement applied strictly between the insurer and the insured, excluding third parties; however, the Court dismissed this argument. Similarly, the Court rejected Generali's assertions that the policy excluded third-party rights under the TPA 1999. Consequently, Generali failed to convince the Court that granting the anti-suit injunction would be inappropriate. In this case, the Court followed *Yusuf Cepnioglu*, upholding the enforcement of the arbitration clause within the contract and issuing the anti-suit injunction against Generali.

This judgement underscores the robust approach of English courts post-Brexit, demonstrating their commitment to holding third parties accountable to arbitration agreements, even when such parties are not signatories to the agreement. Despite not being parties to the underlying agreement, third parties will face anti-suit measures if they fail to comply with the arbitration clause. In other words, this case is quite significant as it highlights the determination of English courts to issue anti-suit injunctions concerning proceedings in the courts of EU member states post-Brexit. Furthermore, the judgement indicates that English courts will continue to uphold compliance with arbitration agreements in insurance contracts as part of English public policy.[150]

148 *QBE Europe SA/NV and QBE (UK) Ltd v Generali Espana de Seguros y Reaseguros* [2022] EWHC 2062 (Comm), para 65.

149 *QBE Europe SA/NV and QBE (UK) Ltd v Generali Espana de Seguros y Reaseguros* [2022] EWHC 2062 (Comm), para 65.

150 *QBE Europe SA/NV and QBE (UK) Ltd v Generali Espana de Seguros y Reaseguros* [2022] EWHC 2062 (Comm), para 69.

Consequently, the English courts aim to achieve practical justice between parties through anti-suit injunctions. If the Court determines that the defendant's initiation of proceedings in a foreign court, contrary to the forum specified in the contract, is clearly unjust, it employs the anti-suit injunction as an immediate and effective remedy. Allowing the foreign proceedings to continue can result in unnecessary litigation costs and time wastage, potentially leading to a different outcome in the dispute. Forcing a party to participate in a lawsuit in an unfamiliar jurisdiction may result in inadequate defence, even if they have strong claims.

Anti-suit injunctions prevent disputes from being adjudicated outside the natural forum, thus avoiding multiple lawsuits in different courts or arbitration tribunals. This measure is crucial for clubs that provide insurance services in many jurisdictions. Resolving disputes in unfamiliar jurisdictions can be costly and disadvantageous. To mitigate this risk, clubs invoke the arbitration clause in their rules against both members and third parties. By issuing anti-suit injunctions, the English courts aim to minimize this risk.

### 2. *Asserting the Arbitration Clause against Third Parties Under the Club Rules and English Law*

The jurisdiction and choice of law clauses in contracts between P&I Clubs and their members are binding in English law. A significant debate is whether this binding effect extends to third parties seeking to enforce the direct action right against Clubs. Essentially, third parties are strangers to the insurance policy and have not consented to any choice of forum or applicable law.[151] However, English courts have ruled that third parties seeking to sue Clubs directly must comply with the contractual obligations outlined in the insurance policy between the Club and the member.[152] The underlying principle behind these judgements is that third parties cannot have better rights than the insured.[153]

The issue of whether arbitration clauses in Club rules bind third parties has been addressed by English law, which affirms the principle of subrogation.[154] For instance, in *Freshwater v Western Australia*,[155] the English Court held that the arbitration clause binds the third party, emphasizing that the third party, relying on the insurance policy, is also bound by other provisions within the policy. Consequently, compliance with insurance contract provisions between the Club and the insured is required if the third party seeks to exercise the right to direct action. Thus, the Club can invoke the arbitration clause against

151 Paul Myburgh, "Non-Parties, Forum Agreements and Expanding Anti-Suit Injunctions" (2020) *LMCLQ* 345, 351.

152 Myburgh, "Non-Parties".

153 Merkin, "Protection & Indemnity", 189.

154 *Freshwater v Western Australia Insurance Co. Ltd.* [1933] 1 KB 515 (*Freshwater v Western Australia* case); *Dennehy v Bellamy* [1938] 2 All ER. 262.

155 *Freshwater v Western Australia* case.

the third party. Clark argues that these judgements by English Courts were intended to ensure justice and resolve disputes in the most appropriate forum for the parties involved.[156]

Having established that the Club can assert an arbitration defence against a third party, another significant issue is whether the English courts can issue an anti-suit injunction against the third party if they violate the arbitration clause and initiate legal proceedings in a foreign jurisdiction.[157] In such instances, the Court can issue an anti-suit injunction against the third party, preventing them from commencing legal proceedings in the foreign jurisdiction.[158] For example, the English Court ordered an anti-suit injunction in *Yusuf Cepnioglu*,[159] where a third party filed a lawsuit against the Club in a competent Turkish Court.[160]

English Courts have stated that they do not intend to impede the jurisdiction of foreign states through anti-suit injunctions. English Courts issue anti-suit injunctions against third parties, citing the principle of subrogation. To achieve this, English courts have grouped cases where the direct action right is exercised under "quasi-contractual" anti-suit injunctions to ensure compliance with the jurisdiction and choice of law clauses in Club rules.[161] "Quasi-contractual" is a term developed in English law to allow anti-suit injunctions against third parties.[162] According to this term, although the third party is not a party to the contract and, therefore, not bound by the contractual forum clause under contract law, they are nonetheless required to adhere to these provisions because they base their claim for damages on the contract.

Consequently, English courts have gained the authority to issue injunctions against third parties who do not adhere to the arbitration clause in the insurance policy, even if they are not parties to the contract.[163] The authority of English Courts in this regard appears to be extensive. These injunctions ensure

156 Anthony Clarke, *The Differing Approach to Commercial Litigation in the European Court of Justice and the Courts of England and Wales I. Amicus Curiae* (Institute of Advanced Legal Studies, London 2006) 2–8 https://sas-space.sas.ac.uk/135/1/ClarkeSirAnthonyIssue065.pdf accessed 26 May 2023.

157 *Aggeliki Charis Compania Maritima SA v Pagnan SpA ("Angelic Grace")* [1995] 1 Lloyd's Rep 87; *Schiffahrtsgesellschaft Detlef Von Appen GmbH v Wiener Allianz Versichrungs AG & Voest Alpine Intertrading GmbH* [1997] EWCA Civ 1420; *The London Steamshipowners' Mutual Insurance Association Ltd v The Kingdom of Spain & anr* [2015] EWCA Civ 333; *The Yusuf Cepnioglu* case.

158 However, in *Hari Bhum*, the Court arrived at a contrasting conclusion, determining that it was unnecessary to issue an anti-suit injunction against the party that failed to adhere to the arbitration clause. See *Through Transport Mutual Insurance Association (Eurasia) Ltd v New India Insurance Co (The Hari Bhum)* [2005] EWHC 455 (Comm).

159 The *Yusuf Cepnioglu* case.

160 Similarly, *The London Steamshipowners' Mutual Insurance Association Ltd v The Kingdom of Spain & anr* [2015] EWCA Civ 333.

161 Myburgh, "Non-Parties", 351.

162 Thomas Raphael, *The Anti-Suit Injunction* (2nd edn, OUP, Oxford 2019) Ch 10 ("Quasi-Contractual Anti-Suit Injunctions") 10.01.

163 Myburgh, "Non-Parties", 351.

that legal proceedings are conducted within the framework of a single legal system, which is why London arbitration and English law are often chosen in club rules. Otherwise, each insured member might be subject to their country's laws, disadvantaging the clubs. Recognizing this risk, English courts issue these injunctions, especially in club insurance disputes, to ensure adherence to arbitration clauses and choice of law provisions. Therefore, applying anti-suit injunctions is necessary to support legal certainty for clubs and safeguard the club insurance industry.

### *C. The "Pay to Be Paid" Rule, which is Highly Significant for Clubs in Direct Action Disputes*

Due to the principle of "mutuality" in P&I Clubs, each member acts as an insurer towards each other. When one member incurs liability to a third party, that member assumes the insured's position while the other members act as insurers.[164] Therefore, the member must first indemnify the third party from their funds.[165] The member cannot transfer this liability to others without compensating the third party. After indemnifying the third party, the member can seek reimbursement from the Club to cover their losses. The foundation of the "pay to be paid" rule[166] stems from this mutuality relationship, and it is a significant rule that distinguishes club insurance from other conventional insurance. Additionally, this rule is an effective defence commonly relied upon by P&I Clubs in disputes related to direct actions brought by third parties against the Clubs.[167]

The validity of the "pay to be paid" rule in Club rules was initially addressed in the judgement of the *Allobrogia*[168] and subsequently affirmed in the judgements of the *Fanti and the Padre Island*.[169] These judgements concluded that the member possesses a contingent right, that the "pay to be paid" rule does not contravene Article 1(3) of the Third Parties Act, that the purpose of the Act is not to place the third party in a more favourable position than the insured, and that the Club has the right to defend against the insured in the same manner as against the third party.[170] Merkin criticized this judgement by stating that if the shipowner were not willing to indemnify the third party, the Club would not have any amount to pay. Therefore, the third party cannot direct action against the Club.[171] According to Thomas, the House of Lords, with this judgement, while the 1930 Act was in force, opened

164 Thomas, "Protection and Indemnity", 33–34.
165 Myburgh, "Direct Action", 207.
166 For detailed explanations of this rule, see Chapter 3.
167 Justice Belinda Ang, "Anti-Suit Injunctions in Maritime Disputes: A Trend that Threatens to Be Out of Control" (2021) *National University of Singapore Centre for Shipping Law Working Paper* 15.
168 The Court has not arrived at a conclusive determination on this matter, acknowledging it as a secondary concern. See *The Allobrogia* case.
169 *The Fanti and the Padre Island* [1991] 2 AC 1.
170 *The Fanti and the Padre Island* [1991] 2 AC 1.
171 Merkin, "Protection & Indemnity", 184.

the way for Clubs to render third-party direct action claims ineffective based on the "pay to be paid" rule.[172]

While the 2010 Act stipulates that the transfer of rights in an insurance contract to a third party cannot be subject to a condition requiring the insured to perform against the third party, subsection six excludes marine insurance from this provision. However, it should be noted that in cases involving personal injury or death, Clubs cannot invoke the "pay to be paid" rule. As a result, Clubs can still rely on the "pay to be paid" defence against third parties, as established in *Fanti and the Padre Island*.[173] This conclusion is further supported by one of the recent judgements in *Yusuf Cepnioglu*, where the English Court upheld the Club's arbitration and "pay to be paid" defences.[174]

According to Hjalmarsson, English law prioritizes protecting the shipping and insurance industries over public policy.[175] However, Hjalmarsson critiques this approach, asserting that the provisions governing direct actions should be uniformly applied to all insurers without granting special privileges to P&I Clubs.[176] However, English Courts adopt a distinct perspective on equity, deeming it inappropriate for the Court to interfere with contractually agreed provisions between the parties.[177] Therefore, the resolution must be based on the explicit terms of the contract.

In conclusion, English law has adopted a legal policy that allows Clubs to rely on the "pay to be paid" rule in direct action disputes, and they have demonstrated their determination to continue this policy through court judgements. These judgements are criticized for making it difficult to compensate third parties. However, preserving the "pay to be paid" is a crucial rule in club insurance, and it contributes to the safe conduct of maritime trade activities by providing insurance coverage to Club members. Clubs maintain their bargaining power by asserting their Club rules against third-party compensation claims. Supporting the approach adopted by English law in favour of Clubs is essential to prevent the increase in economic pressure on Clubs and ensure the development of this sector.

In the contrary scenario, there is a risk that shipowners may not be provided with comprehensive insurance coverage. The extensive coverage of club insurance is based on applying Club rules within the framework of contractual freedom. Although asserting these rules against third parties may make it difficult to compensate them, Clubs often choose to address these claims through negotiation, seeking to balance their interests. Therefore, the argument in favour of allowing this flexibility in legal policies in club insurance is also advocated in the book.

172 Thomas, "Protection and Indemnity", 39.
173 Hazelwood and Semark, 302.
174 Zhu and Pan, 571; Briggs, "All at Sea", 327.
175 Hjalmarsson, "Direct Action", 7.
176 Hjalmarsson, "Direct Action", 7.
177 Keith Michel and Simon Congdon, "Third Parties Rights Against Insurers" (1989) *LMCLQ* 495.

### D. *Analysis of Direct Action Right in Foreign Law through Yusuf Cepnioglu Case*

In jurisdictions where the direct action right is recognized,[178] lawsuits against P&I Clubs continue to be filed based on this right. In these lawsuits against P&I Clubs, jurisdiction and choice of law clauses in insurance contracts can be overcome, and more importantly, defences arising from the "pay to be paid" rule can be rendered inapplicable by foreign courts. These judgements undoubtedly increase the number of lawsuits against P&I Clubs and frequently subject them to third-party compensation claims.

In cases where third-party direct action claims are based on foreign law, complications may arise if the underlying contract is subject to English law. The solution is straightforward if the foreign law grants a direct action right to the third party contingent upon the contract. In that case, the third party's direct action right is valid only if stipulated in the contract, and the contract terms bind the third party invoking this right.[179] However, the solution is not as simple if the foreign law recognizes a direct action independent of the contract. In this scenario, the issue arises of which law governs the characterization of the third party's claim against the insurer.[180] The court must determine whether this claim derived from foreign law should be assessed under that country's or English law applicable to the contract. This determination also answers whether the third party is bound by the Club rules when exercising the right to bring a direct action. The court's careful consideration of these findings is crucial for determining whether the third party's claim has been made under the insurance policy's terms.

The English court addressed these questions in the *Yusuf Cepnioglu*,[181] which is significant as the first case to discuss and compare the differences between Turkish and English law regarding third-party direct action against P&I Clubs. According to the conclusions drawn from this case, since the contract underlying the third party's claim is subject to English law, the characterization of this claim and the scope and conditions of the insurer's liability should be considered under English law.[182] Therefore, this case has provided significant gains for the Clubs in terms of its outcomes.

The *Yusuf Cepnioglu* is related to whether the Club rules would bind a third party and whether Clubs can rely on the defences, jurisdiction, and choice of law rules outlined in their Club rules against direct action claims of third parties. The Court of Appeal clarified these issues. Additionally, the Court clarified whether an anti-suit injunction preventing the prosecution of direct action disputes abroad could be ordered.

178 For example, direct rights exist in Denmark, most American States, Tunisia, many Scandinavian countries, Spain, and Türkiye.

179 Raphael, *Quasi-Contractual*, 10.22.

180 Raphael, *Quasi-Contractual*, 10.22.

181 *Shipowner's Mutual Protection & Indemnity Association (Luxembourg) v Containerships Denizcilik Nakliyat ve Ticaret AS (The Yusuf Cepnioglu)* [2016] EWCA Civ 386.

182 Raphael, *Quasi-Contractual*, 10.29.

The case involves grounding the ship *Yusuf Cepnioglu* on the island of Mykonos, Greece, on 8 March 2014. Although the necessary rescue services were provided, the ship could not be saved. As a result, the cargo continued, and the ship was lost, according to the consignments organized by the charterers. Subsequently, the charterers informed the shipowners and other lessors about the damages they suffered. The charterers initiated arbitration proceedings in London against the shipowners to demand compensation for the cargo losses. However, their attempts were unsuccessful, and they could not obtain the necessary security directly from the shipowners. Therefore, the charterers sued the P&I Club, which the ship was a member of in the UK. While asserting this claim, they relied on Article 1478 of the TCC,[183] which regulates the right of direct action. The case was initiated in Turkish Courts. However, there were some obstacles to the charterers' pursuit of this case in Turkish Courts. These obstacles were jurisdiction, choice of law, and "pay to be paid" rules specified in the Club rules. According to these rules, English law would apply to compensation claims against the Clubs, and London arbitration would have jurisdiction. The Club argued that the charterers violated the Club rules by bringing a lawsuit in Türkiye and that the dispute should be resolved according to English law and in London arbitration. Therefore, the Club obtained an anti-suit injunction against the charterers from the English High Court. Upon the Club's obtaining the anti-suit injunction, the charterers appealed to the Court of Appeal in England.

In this case, the court first determined whether the third party's claim was based on the insurance policy and subsequently examined whether the claim was made following this policy.[184] This assessment involved evaluating the foreign law within the English conflict of laws rules.[185] Under this framework, a third party's direct action right, recognized under foreign law, is not considered an independent right but a claim to enforce obligations under English law.[186] These obligations can only be enforced following the relevant P&I Club policy terms – specifically through English arbitration, governed by English law, and subject to the "pay to be paid" rule.[187] Consequently, the insured's insolvency risk is transferred from the Club to the third party.[188]

The parties to the Club insurance contract are free to agree on the "pay to be paid" rule or to stipulate that any disputes arising under the contract will be resolved through arbitration. These contractual provisions are binding on the

183 Article 1478, TCC No 6102: "The victim may claim his loss up to the insured sum directly from the insurer provided that the claim is brought within the prescription period applicable to the insurance contract."

184 In this case, the court applied the characterization test established by the *London Steam Ship Owners' Mutual Insurance Association Ltd v Kingdom of Spain, The Prestige (No 2)* [2015] EWCA Civ 333.

185 Myburgh, "Direct Action", 211–212.

186 *The Yusuf Cepnioglu* [2016] EWCA Civ 386.

187 Myburgh, "Direct Action", 206.

188 Merkin, *Arbitration Law*, para 8.98.2.

parties. Additionally, by agreeing to the arbitration clause, the parties effectively waive their right to bring claims before the courts of any country. Therefore, if foreign law grants a third party the right to bring a direct action against the insured's liability insurer, the third party is also bound by the contractual obligations, including the "pay to be paid" rule and the requirement to pursue any claims through arbitration. The primary purpose of binding the third party to this contract is to preserve the essence of the contractual obligations.

In the *Yusuf Cepnioglu*, the Court of Appeal concluded that the TCC necessitated that the claimant rely on the policy terms to establish a cause of action.[189] Accordingly, the court classified the direct action right under Article 1478 of the TCC as a derivative right under English law.[190] The court subjected the third party to the contract terms between the Club and its members, having determined that the claim was based on the policy.[191] In this way, the court characterized the claims of third parties relying on the direct action right under foreign law as rights derived from or connected to the P&I policy.[192] This classification is crucial for determining the validity of the arbitration clause within the policy and whether the third party is bound by it.

Thus, when the Club faces a direct action from a third party, it can also assert the arbitration clause within the policy against the third party. If the third party's claim is based on a contract containing an arbitration clause and the third party breaches this clause by bringing the claim to a foreign jurisdiction, there is a risk that the third party may obtain significantly better rights than could be achieved through arbitration. For example, under the TCC,[193] in direct action cases, the insurer's ability to rely on the "pay to be paid" clause may be nullified, potentially placing the third party in a more advantageous position than they would be in arbitration. The approach of English courts in such cases is critical to preventing these risks.

After characterizing charterers' claims as contractual, the Court of Appeal discussed whether a stay of proceedings should be ordered. The Court, characterizing the charterers' claims as contractual, recognized the Club's right to refer a dispute against it to arbitration under the insurance contract. Therefore, the Court ordered the suspension of the lawsuit filed against the charterers in Turkish Courts and issued an anti-suit injunction.

The charterers appealed the judgement, claiming that it undermined Türkiye's public policy and violated principles of courtesy. However, the Court of Appeal

189 [2016] EWCA Civ 386.

190 Merkin, "Protection & Indemnity", 191.

191 [2016] EWCA Civ 386.

192 According to Dickinson, who holds a contrary view, referring to the insurance contract to draw the limits of the right to apply directly to the insurer does not make this right a contractual right or place it in close relation to the contract. See Andrew Dickinson, "The Right to Rome? The Law Applicable to Direct Claims Against Insurers, and Anti-Suit Injunction" (2016) 132 *Law Quarterly Review* 536.

193 Article 1478 of TCC No. 6102.

rejected their claims, stating that the charterers must exercise their contractual claims and obligations and comply with the arbitration rule in the contract. As a result of the judgement, it was decided that the charterers' claim is based on the contract, and therefore, the contract provisions bind them and must resort to arbitration, and the anti-suit injunction should continue.

When the enforceability of anti-suit injunction decisions is evaluated from the perspective of Turkish law, it appears that both the issuance of such decisions by Turkish courts and the recognition and enforcement of anti-suit injunctions issued by foreign courts in Türkiye are legally unfeasible.[194] In the Turkish legal system, the right to seek legal remedies is enshrined as a constitutional right, guaranteeing individuals the freedom to apply to judicial authorities and initiate legal proceedings.[195] Accordingly, anti-suit injunctions, which prevent a party from pursuing litigation in another jurisdiction, constitute a direct interference with the right to seek legal remedies and are, therefore, difficult to accept within Turkish law.

Furthermore, considering the fundamental principles adopted by Türkiye within the framework of its harmonization process with the EU legal system, the applicability of anti-suit injunctions becomes even more controversial. The case law of the CJEU demonstrates a tendency to protect individuals' access to courts in matters concerning jurisdictional regulations among member states. In this context, Türkiye, which continues to pursue full membership in the EU, is unlikely to incorporate such decisions into its domestic legal system in the foreseeable future.[196]

In conclusion, given both constitutional protections and international legal norms, the issuance of anti-suit injunctions by Turkish courts and the enforcement of such decisions rendered by foreign courts in Türkiye is legally impossible and inapplicable.

The *Yusuf Cepnioglu* is a significant ruling that favours Clubs. It also clarifies many uncertainties and inconsistencies regarding the right of third parties to direct action in foreign laws, particularly in English law. With this ruling, English P&I Clubs can more easily assert their contractual defences against the direct action right granted to third parties in foreign laws. It has been made clear that the provisions regarding applying English law and arbitration in the insurance contract will also be valid against third parties. Furthermore, because of classifying the third party's claim as contractual under English law, it was determined that the contractual obligations equally bind both the insured and the third party. Consequently, no distinction was made between a contracting party seeking to enforce a contractual right and a third party attempting to do the same.

194 See Hakan Tüfekçi, "A General Overview of Anti-Suit Injunctions in the Context of English Law, the Brussels Convention Regime, and Turkish Law" (2011) 1 *Galatasaray University Faculty of Law Review* 743, discussing the evaluation of the Court of Appeal 11th Civil Chamber decision dated 1 November 2004, case number E 2004/1141, decision number K 2004/10544.

195 Tüfekçi, "A General Overview of Anti-Suit Injunctions in the Context of English Law, the Brussels Convention Regime, and Turkish Law", 743.

196 Tüfekçi, "A General Overview of Anti-Suit Injunctions in the Context of English Law, the Brussels Convention Regime, and Turkish Law", 744.

## V. Comparative Analysis and Conclusion

Chapter 4 compared the legal framework regarding the right of direct action in English and Turkish law. This comparison revealed results that support the book's argument. For instance, while English law pursues a legal policy that protects Clubs in direct action disputes, Turkish law tends to protect third parties. The impact of these different legal policies is evident from the position the club insurance industry has reached in both countries. England, which prioritizes the application of Club rules and adopts a policy of limited use of the right of direct action, maintains its global leadership position in this industry. On the other hand, in Türkiye, where the opposite legal policy is adopted, it took quite some time for this industry to emerge, and its development has not been as rapid.

Therefore, the book argues that countries aiming to develop the club insurance industry should adopt a more flexible legal policy. This assertion aligns with the argument that legal frameworks supporting a more flexible use of the right of direct action can foster the growth of the club insurance industry, as seen in the case of England's leadership in the global market.

Establishing the first and only Turkish P&I Club in Türkiye underscores its brief history compared to its English counterparts. Under the Regulation on the Establishment and Operation Principles of Insurance and Reinsurance Companies, the Turkish P&I Club diligently pursued a license from the Turkish Prime Ministry Undersecretariat of the Treasury General Directorate of Insurance. Subsequently, on 18 February 2014, the Club acquired its operating license, signifying its alignment with the regulatory prerequisites.

However, this nascent presence has contributed to a dearth of judicial rulings, statutory enactments, and scholarly investigations specifically addressing club insurance within Turkish law. Notably, the provisions within the TCC relating to direct action cater to liability insurance rather than club insurance, given that the TCC was in force before establishing the Turkish P&I Club. As a result, these provisions, designed initially for liability insurance, have been retroactively applied to club insurance, a practice incongruent with their intended scope. Despite the analogous aim of providing liability coverage to their members, Clubs diverge from traditional liability insurers through provisions such as the "pay to be paid" rule, which primarily serves to forestall direct action claims from third parties.

While the right of third parties to initiate direct action against insurers in liability insurance is acknowledged across various countries' laws, the scope of this right remains constrained under English law. Conversely, in Turkish law, the consensus leans toward third parties having the prerogative to assert this right against Clubs. However, it is noteworthy that no litigation has been undertaken in Turkish Courts to date to address this issue, resulting in the absence of judicial precedents concerning the entitlement of third parties to direct action against P&I Clubs within Turkish law. Additionally, the "pay to be paid" rule, a prominent feature in the regulations of English Clubs, is similarly integrated into the rules of the Turkish P&I Club.

The legal frameworks of Turkish and English law about the "right to direct action against the insurer (specifically P&I Clubs)" exhibit notable disparities. In

Turkish law, the right to direct action against the insurer, including P&I Clubs, emerges independently through statutory provisions, devoid of any prerequisites. Unlike English law, this right is not contingent upon contractual obligations. Consequently, neither the insurer nor the P&I Club can assert defences, such as the "pay to be paid" or "arbitration" clauses derived from the insurance contract, against the third-party claimant. Conversely, English law follows a contrasting approach. Specific requirements must be fulfilled for a third party to exercise their right to direct action against a P&I Club. The third party must substantiate their liability relationship with the insured and initiate insolvency proceedings against the insured. Only upon meeting these conditions can the third party assume the right of direct action against the P&I Club by replacing the insured through the principle of subrogation. Subsequently, the third party becomes subject to the P&I Club's defences, originating from the insurance contract. English law ensures that the third party does not attain a better position than the insured, as the latter is replaced under the principle of subrogation.[197] The P&I Club retains the prerogative to assert defences such as the "pay to be paid" and "arbitration" under English law.

The notable disparities between English and Turkish law concerning the right to direct action can be attributed, in part, to the prominence bestowed upon the marine insurance and shipping industries within the framework of English legal principles. This deliberate safeguarding of these industries under English law indirectly protects the national economy. The Maritime Annual Report 2018/19 provides compelling evidence of the substantial economic contribution made by the maritime industry to the UK, with a direct impact of £14.5 billion and an indirect impact reaching an impressive £37 billion.[198] Within this broader context, the report aptly underscores the significant role of P&I Clubs in bolstering the UK economy, thereby underscoring their noteworthy economic significance in sustaining the strength and vitality of the maritime industry within the country.

Notably, including an arbitration clause in the Club rules, mandating that disputes between parties be resolved through London arbitration, exemplifies the undeniable impact on the nation's economy.[199] The Maritime Annual Report 2018/19 reinforces this point by emphasizing the substantial role of P&I Clubs in contributing to the UK economy.[200] Moreover, a comprehensive report published

197 *The Fanti and the Padre Island* [1991] 2 AC 1; Merkin and Steele, 360.

198 Full Report: *Maritime Annual Report 2018 to 2019* (UK Government 2019) https://assets.publishing.service.gov.uk/government/uploads/system/uploads/attachment_data/file/817250/Maritime_Annual_Report_2018_to_2019.pdf accessed 26 May 2023.

199 London not only stands out as a global arbitration hub but also as a significant jurisdiction for the resolution of most commercial disputes. For more information, see Mihail Danov, "Cross-Border Litigation – New Data, Initial Brexit Implications in England and Wales and Long-Term Policy Choices" in Andrea Bonomi and Gian Paolo Romano (eds), *Yearbook of Private International Law: Volume 21* (Verlag Dr Otto Schmidt 2021) 57–100.

200 Report on the Contribution of P&I Clubs to the UK Economy, https://assets.publishing.service.gov.uk/government/uploads/system/uploads/attachment_data/file/948299/OFSI_Guidance_-_Maritime_.pdf accessed 26 May 2023.

by TheCityUK in 2021 explicitly highlights that the mere presence of maritime trade disputes managed by the London Maritime Arbitrators Association has contributed a significant £41 billion to the country's economy.[201] This substantial figure unequivocally underscores arbitration proceedings' economic significance and influence in the maritime industry.[202] Therefore, the legal approach in English law regarding third-party compensation claims against P&I Clubs aligns with public interest driven by preserving the nation's economic well-being.

While Turkish law aims to protect third parties in liability insurance, it is essential to undertake legal reforms, particularly regarding the right to direct action against Clubs, to enable the club insurance industry to attain its envisioned status within the Turkish and international marine insurance industries. Modelling English law's approach to direct action cases, focusing on the "pay to be paid" rule and the implementation of customized reforms for club insurance, will significantly enhance the club insurance industry in Türkiye.

The quandary arises concerning reconciling the public policy goal of protecting third-party interests in direct action disputes to enhance club insurance within the Turkish context. Turkish law, predicated on public policy, envisages liability insurance as a safeguard for third parties, as articulated in Article 1478 of the TCC No. 6102, which accords third parties with the right to direct action. Club insurance, categorized as liability insurance, primarily underwrites the members' obligations toward third parties. Nonetheless, it operates under its distinct set of rules, which are consistently adhered to by most Clubs engaged in maritime trade.

Notably, the Turkish P&I Club rules align with the rules of other industry Clubs. With TCC No. 6102 not specifically addressing club insurance, the conjecture is that the provisions pertinent to liability insurance extend to club insurance. In a dispute preceding the implementation of TCC No. 6102, the Turkish Supreme Court acknowledged the validity of the "pay to be paid" rule, thereby repudiating a third party's direct action claim. This recognition reinforced the distinction between club insurance and other categories of liability insurance. However, it remains uncertain how the Supreme Court will interpret club insurance under the aegis of the new code. If the Court maintains its previous jurisprudence, it will corroborate that club insurance constitutes a unique domain within marine insurance and assert that the direct action regulation of the law does not encompass club insurance. Conversely,

201 Full Report: Legal Excellence: Internationally Renowned UK Legal Services (TheCityUK 2022) https://www.thecityuk.com/media/5url4ni1/legal-excellence-internationally-renowned-uk-legal-services-2022.pdf accessed 26 May 2023.

202 According to Tettenborn, who explains the impact of Brexit on shipping law and the UK, this situation will create more advantages than disadvantages. Particularly, not being bound by the EU's jurisdiction and insolvency rules can be considered among the advantages. Additionally, he mentions that efforts to recognize court judgements of non-member states in the EU will also have a positive contribution. See Andrew Tettenborn, "Shipping Law, Brexit and the City of London" (2022) *LMCLQ* 124, 133. However, Danov indicates that London arbitration is perceived as a suitable option for minimizing litigation risks arising from Brexit. However, on the other hand, he notes that this may raise issues related to the recognition and enforcement of parallel judgements and arbitral awards. See Danov, 71.

should the Court perceive club insurance as falling within the purview of liability insurance and deem the "pay to be paid" rule in Club regulations incompatible with the direct action statute, it would open the gateway for third parties to assert their claims against the Club directly.

Examining Turkish and English legal approaches in direct action against insurers reveals notable disparities and their consequential implications. These differences underscore the contrasting treatment of third-party claimants and the different stances adopted towards P&I Clubs in each jurisdiction. The divergent interpretations of statutory provisions and the prioritization of national interests in English law have shaped the legal landscape.

In Turkish law, the absence of dedicated provisions for club insurance and its categorization as a subset of liability insurance engenders incongruities between the rules of the Turkish P&I Club and the legal framework. This disjunction may precipitate future challenges. Enacting a more comprehensive legal framework tailored to club insurance within Turkish law is imperative to mitigate these contradictions and pre-empt potential complications.

Given Türkiye's overarching objective of augmenting the contributions of P&I Club insurance and maritime trade to the national economy,[203] it becomes incumbent to confer specific legal and economic prerogatives upon the Turkish P&I Club within the existing legal framework. A prospective efficacious solution could involve legal reform that either restricts the right of third parties to initiate direct action or subjects the exercise of this right to explicit conditions tailored to club insurance. Such measures will yield effective results in increasing the activities of the P&I Club insurance sector in Türkiye.

Instituting equilibrium between the rights of third parties to direct action and the fiscal stability and legal assurance of Clubs is imperative, particularly for fortifying club insurance in Türkiye. Achieving this equilibrium entails formulating a distinct regulatory framework for club insurance within the commercial code. Accordingly, the legal validity of Club rules such as "pay to be paid" and arbitration clauses, which limit third parties' direct action against Clubs, must be recognized within the legal framework. However, this framework should unequivocally stipulate the unconditional right of third parties to direct action in cases of personal injury and death within club insurance.

Lastly, it is imperative to acknowledge that a robust legal infrastructure is an indispensable catalyst for enhancing any industry within a country. Industries strengthened by flexible legal frameworks invariably experience accelerated economic growth. As argued in the book, a legal reform that emulates the flexible and liberal approach of English law regarding the direct action rights of third parties should be undertaken to enhance the club insurance industry in Türkiye.

203 Transport Operational Programme 2007–2009, "Republic of Türkiye" https://neighbourhood-enlargement.ec.europa.eu/system/files/2016–12/tk3_transport_op-final_2007_en.pdf 43 accessed 28 May 2023.

# 5 Conclusion

## I. Introduction

Chapter 5 will synthesize the arguments and key findings presented in previous chapters to propose legal reform recommendations and provide conclusions for the book. The main research question guiding this book has been: Should the English law approach serve as a model for the Turkish legal framework governing P&I Clubs, particularly in direct action against P&I Clubs in Türkiye? If affirmative, what legal framework should Türkiye establish regarding the rights and obligations of third parties, Club members, and P&I Clubs?

This book has focused on the impact of the legal approach that prioritizes protecting third-party direct action rights and restricts the P&I Clubs' rules in the marine insurance industry. The existing legal frameworks and judgements about P&I Club insurance in Türkiye and England have been examined to elucidate these impacts. One of the most significant findings of the book is that the legal approach prioritizing the protection of third-party direct action rights hinders the economic growth of the P&I insurance industry. Similarly, the legislative model invalidating Club rules hindering direct action rights' use also yields this effect. From the perspective of P&I Clubs, the increase in direct compensation claims against Clubs directly affects their economic power and resilience.

For example, The International Group of P&I Associations has presented reports criticizing the tendency towards compulsory insurance and the expansion of third-party direct action rights in drafting international agreements or national laws.[1] They have stated that this will increase the number of direct claims against Clubs, thereby increasing economic pressure on the Clubs.[2] Therefore, Clubs frequently express concerns about the potential damage to the P&I insurance

1 International Group Position Statement on the Proposed Civil Liability Directive following the EP TRAN Committee Vote on 27 February 2007 https://static.igpandi.org/igpi_website/media/article_attachments/Post%20TRAN%20IG%20Statement.pdf accessed 3 April 2024.

2 International Group Position Statement on the Proposed Civil Liability Directive following the EP TRAN Committee Vote on 27 February 2007.

DOI: 10.4324/9781003628897-5

industry arising from the underlying aim of compulsory insurance practices, which is promptly compensating damaged persons.[3]

Considering these findings, Türkiye should enact legal reforms in line with the English model to establish a modern and industry-compatible legal framework for P&I insurance. Such reforms will enhance the competitiveness of the P&I Club insurance industry, attract more investment and talent, and facilitate the growth and expansion of businesses and organizations operating in this field.

In summary, this book has provided a critical analysis of two different legal perspectives governing P&I insurance and proposed reform recommendations to assist in the growth and development of the industry. It emphasizes the need for reform to establish a more suitable, efficient, and practical law in countries like Türkiye that aims to develop the P&I Club insurance industry in economic and international activity contexts.

## II. Key Findings and Assessments

This book is a comparative study of the direct action rights of third parties against P&I Clubs under Turkish and English law. The regulations on this right differ significantly between Turkish and English law. One of the most significant differences is that, under English law, third parties must follow a rigorous procedure to claim their damages directly from Clubs. Clubs can invoke provisions such as "pay to be paid" to protect themselves against third-party claims. In contrast, Turkish law allows third parties to directly claim their damages from Clubs without the obligation to first apply to the insured/member.[4] In other words, Clubs cannot use defences such as "pay to be paid" against third-party claims under Turkish law. This difference stems from the fact that, under Turkish law, the principle of protecting the damaged person in liability insurance is prioritized. In contrast, under English law, the principle of freedom of contract is prioritized.

The principle of protecting the damaged person in Turkish insurance law is stated in the rationale of Article 1478 of the TCC.[5] According to this, when the insured compensates third parties for the damage caused, there is a decrease in their assets. Liability insurance aims to compensate for this decrease in the insured's assets. Another purpose and consequence of liability insurance is to ensure that third parties are compensated as soon as possible, thus protecting them against the insured's insolvency. Therefore, Turkish law has ensured third parties' right to take direct action through a legal provision. In Turkish law, this right can be exercised against Clubs without restriction. Clauses restricting this right, such as the "pay to be paid" rule in Club rules, are considered invalid. This stringent application against Clubs hampers the development of the P&I insurance industry in Türkiye.

3 International Group Position Statement on the Proposed Civil Liability Directive following the EP TRAN Committee Vote on 27 February 2007.

4 TCC No 6102.

5 TCC No 6102 Rationale of Article 1478.

Therefore, among the main arguments in this book is the need for legal reform in Türkiye, especially concerning the direct action rights of third parties. Another argument is that this reform should be carried out by taking the protective approach of English law as a model for P&I insurance.

### *A. The Need for Legal Reform Regarding Club Insurance in Türkiye*

Among the primary research questions examined in this book is assessing the need for legal reform to enhance P&I Club insurance in Türkiye. One of the key findings is the existence of this need.

Global trade heavily relies on maritime transport, encompassing over 90% of the world's import-export activities.[6] Considering that the cumulative carrying capacity of the global merchant marine fleets surpassed 2.3 billion deadweight tons by the conclusion of 2022[7] and that the Turkish merchant marine fleet, comprising Turkish-flagged and Turkish-owned vessels, contributes over 6 million DWT to this tonnage,[8] it becomes inexorable to enhance the efficacy of the Turkish P&I Club, both within Türkiye and on a global scale. The structure and essence of P&I insurance have rendered it indispensable for maritime commerce in the contemporary context. The significance of P&I insurance has transcended being a mere necessity; it has metamorphosed into an imperative. Notably, commencing 1 July 2011, Türkiye mandated possessing valid P&I insurance for vessels of 300 GT and above that would enter Turkish ports, as stipulated by regulation.[9] In this regard, the state has prioritized furnishing the Turkish P&I Club with a robust economic and legal infrastructure as soon as possible.

It is underscored in the PricewaterhouseCoopers (PwC) report[10] that a pivotal underpinning of the global pre-eminence of English Clubs is the prevalence of the rule of law and the legal safeguards extended to these Clubs. This report distinctly delineates that the advancement of the Turkish P&I Club hinges significantly on implementing legal reforms in this domain. The culmination of the research and comprehensive discussions presented in this book has unveiled the glaring insufficiency of the prevailing legal framework governing club insurance within Turkish law to facilitate its envisioned development.

As a corollary, we posit that the legal reforms delineated in this book of the substance of club insurance contracts, the validity of Club regulations, and the legal

6 Review of Maritime Transport 2023 (United Nations, United Nations Conference on Trade and Development, Geneva 2023) https://unctad.org/publication/review-maritime-transport-2023 accessed 27 September 2023.

7 Review of Maritime Transport 2023, 27.

8 Review of Maritime Transport 2023, 33.

9 The Regulation on Insurance and Inspection of Ships Related to Maritime Liens, RG 14.11.2010/27759.

10 The report authored by PricewaterhouseCoopers (PwC) underscores the influence of the rule of law and legal factors as one of the key reasons behind the United Kingdom's status as a preeminent maritime hub. See PwC Report on the "UK's Global Maritime Professional Services: Contribution and Trends" (London, April 2016).

character of the Turkish P&I Club must be enacted to surmount the constraints obstructing the growth and progression of this industry. This book's salient finding is the dissonance between the existing regulations and the evolving requisites and demands of the club insurance industry in Türkiye.

Consequently, Türkiye must systematically and comprehensively reform the legal framework of insurance law. This reform should be approached methodically, focusing on club insurance from a distinct perspective. It should address the primary areas of concern, providing the industry with contemporary regulations aligned with prevailing club insurance industry standards. Such a revision will strengthen the club insurance industry in Türkiye, enabling it to develop and fully realize its potential.

### *B. The Suitability of the English Legal Approach as a Model for P&I Club Insurance Reform in Türkiye*

Based on the comprehensive analysis and findings presented in this study, a similar approach to English law regarding the direct action rights of third parties should be adopted in Turkish law. Regulations and judgements concerning the protection of P&I Clubs and their activities in English law (especially the limited direct action rights of third parties against P&I Clubs) are more favourable and supportive to Clubs' legal and economic infrastructure than Turkish legal regulations. The concern that intervention in Club rules would harm contractual freedom in England contributes to the preference for this favourable legal approach. The protective approach of English law towards the contractual freedom of P&I Clubs and the legal framework it provides are significant components that enhance Clubs' economic and international effectiveness.

In Türkiye, however, club insurance is classified among other liability insurance. Therefore, the principles of "protection of the weaker party" and "public interest policy" recognized in insurance law also apply to P&I Club insurance. This approach increases the risk for P&I Club insurers to face direct compensation claims from third parties in Türkiye.

Turkish law has not adopted a protective approach towards Clubs and club insurance contracts, as seen in English law. In other words, the protection of third parties against Clubs outweighs the protection of Clubs against third-party compensation claims. This approach should be abandoned in Türkiye.

One key conclusion is the need for significant changes to Turkish law, particularly concerning direct action disputes, by adopting the English legal model. In direct action cases in England, the Courts take a significantly different approach than the system in Türkiye. In English law, the third party's right to direct action arises from the contract between the member and the Club, and therefore, judgements emphasize that this right is not independent.[11] As a result, provisions and

11 *The London Steam Shipowners Mutual Insurance Association Ltd v The Kingdom of Spain (The Prestige (No. 2))* [2013] EWHC 3188 (Comm); *Shipowners' Mutual Protection and Indemnity*

practices that nullify this right in the contract are accepted and applied effectively. However, if this right had been recognized as an independent right from the law, as in Turkish law, it would not have been possible to nullify the third party's right to direct action through contracts concluded between the member and the Club.

Similarly, the "pay to be paid" rule and "arbitration provisions," which significantly impede the exercise of the direct action right, could not be asserted against third parties. Nevertheless, the importance of the contract in English law has led to the neglect of third parties' rights claims. If Turkish law adopts the importance and priority given to freedom of contract in English law as a principle in the legal regulation to be created for P&I Club insurance, significant changes must be made. Turkish law does not have any special legal regulations for P&I insurance. Therefore, there is a significant gap in this area. It is challenging to apply the law provisions established for other insurance contracts to a specialized and distinct type of insurance, such as P&I Club insurance, and contribute to developing the club insurance policy nationally and globally. Therefore, it is necessary to establish special law provisions that can be applied to P&I Club insurance in Turkish law. In summary, one of the conclusions and recommendations reached in this book is that Turkish law should adopt the approach of English law concerning third-party compensation claims and contractual freedom in club insurance.

### *C. Implementing the English Legal Model in Turkish Law: Key Considerations and Factors*

In formulating legal arrangements in this context, it is imperative to consider an alternative approach distinct from the current paradigm. For instance, it may be beneficial to revisit the principle of safeguarding the weaker party enshrined in Turkish insurance law, relaxing it in favour of club insurance. The boundaries of these principles can be demarcated by adopting English law as a reference model. An illustrative instance of this approach could involve formally recognizing the "pay to be paid" rule, a hallmark of club insurance, within Turkish legal jurisprudence. Under such a construct, a third party would be obliged to pursue damages from the member before initiating proceedings against the Club. While admittedly challenging for third parties exercising their direct action rights, this rule finds acceptance in English Courts, which acknowledge its validity for third parties involved in direct action suits. These instances underscore the more favourable stance of English law towards Clubs in the realms of club insurance and direct action disputes. This pro-club disposition is rooted, in part, in the economic benefits accrued to the public by nurturing this industry.

---

*Association (Luxembourg) v Containerships Denizcilik Nakliyat Ve Ticaret AS* [2015] EWHC 258 (Comm).

England undeniably occupies a paramount position in the global maritime trade and insurance industries.[12] The Maritime Business Industry encompasses numerous high-value activities, and the United Kingdom is widely recognized as a pioneer in this field.[13] This spectrum includes shipbroking, legal services, insurance, consultancy, accountancy, and financial services.

The United Kingdom commands a substantial presence within maritime insurance, commanding a 35% share of the global maritime insurance premiums market.[14] Furthermore, it asserts a dominant foothold in the P&I insurance industry, boasting an impressive 60% market share.[15] A report by PricewaterhouseCoopers (PwC)[16] underscores several key strengths buttressing the United Kingdom's eminence as a premier maritime hub.

The UK's resounding global market share in several pivotal industries is among these strengths. This encompasses a commanding 35% share of the global marine insurance premiums market, a significant presence in shipbroking, contributing 26% of global revenue, a prominent position in maritime law with 25% of maritime legal partners based in the UK, and a robust educational infrastructure.[17]

A noteworthy aspect is the UK's role as the epicentre for many preeminent maritime law and shipbroking firms.[18] These firms contribute significantly to the industry's global prominence, including numerous that have ventured into international expansions by establishing offices worldwide.[19] The United Kingdom is also recognized as the preferred destination for complex risk insurance, benefiting from the profound expertise of institutions such as Lloyd's of London, the International Underwriting Association, and the UK's insurance broking community.

Significantly, the indispensable role of the rule of law and its legal certainty to these industries should not be underestimated in perpetuating this leadership.[20] Therefore, it can be contended that adopting the approach of the English law, which lends preferential treatment to Clubs in direct action litigation, as a model and adapting it to Turkish law could offer a viable mechanism to fortify club insurance in Türkiye.

Furthermore, a comprehensive study should be undertaken to contemplate the acceptance of the "pay to be paid" rule, which is embedded in the regulations of Turkish P&I Clubs but lacks legal standing under Turkish law. Such an initiative

12 The Economic Contribution of the UK Maritime Business Services Industry (Centre for Economics and Business Research report for Maritime UK and Maritime London, May 2022) 7; PwC Report on the "UK's Global Maritime Professional Services: Contribution and Trends" (London, April 2016) 7.

13 The Economic Contribution Report, 7.

14 The Economic Contribution Report, 7.

15 Maritime UK (2019) https://www.maritimeuk.org/about/our-sector/maritime-business-services/ accessed 27 September 2023.

16 Maritime UK.

17 PwC Report, 7.

18 The Economic Contribution Report, 12.

19 TheCityUK Report on "Legal Excellence, Internationally Renowned UK Legal Services 2021" (December 2021) https://www.thecityuk.com/ accessed 27 September 2023.

20 TheCityUK Report, 18.

should be exclusively applicable to direct action lawsuits against Clubs while exempting other forms of liability insurance. This targeted legal framework would ensure that the public policy objectives aimed at protecting third parties and expeditiously compensating their damages, particularly in other categories of liability insurance, remain intact. When making legal provisions, it is also crucial not to foreclose entirely on the avenue for third parties to seek redress from the Club should they be unable to remedy their losses through recourse to the member.

### *D. The Challenges of Implementing English Law Principles in Turkish Law*

In Article 1478 of the TCC,[21] we mentioned that the direct action right of third parties, which is valid for all liability insurance, protects third parties within the framework of the public interest principle. Since club insurance is considered within the scope of liability insurance in Turkish law and a separate law article has not been regulated, it has made it easier for the direct action right to be used against Clubs. Before a law article was regulated for club insurance, a system that distinguishes club insurance from other liability insurance in terms of legal nature should be accepted in Turkish law.

The purpose of club insurance that emerged in England was not to create a classic type of liability insurance.[22] Other liability insurance had already met this need. Therefore, the Club does not aim to remedy the losses of third parties. It is the insurance of members' liability against third parties. In other words, Clubs have only emerged to compensate for the losses of their members. In this context, the decrease in the members' assets due to their compensation for third parties is covered within the scope of club insurance.

Unlike classic liability insurance, the priority in club insurance is not to compensate third parties. The priority of this insurance is to compensate the damage caused by the member's liability to third parties. This distinction should be considered in the legal regulation.

Although there is no separate law article for club insurance in English law, the Courts consider Club rules and contracts concluded between the Club and the member. Hence, clauses in Club rules that make it difficult to use the direct action right are accepted as valid by judgements. Therefore, we can say that club insurance is indirectly distinguished from classic liability insurance in English law.

The Act 2010 in England regulates the rights of third parties against insurers. It introduces some procedural and substantive changes while still showing parallels with previous laws concerning the rights of third parties. This law is designed analytically and rationally, without any concerns related to public policy.[23] According to

21 TCC No 6102.

22 For the detailed information, see Chapter 1, Historical Development.

23 Thomas, "Direct Rights", 714.

the Act 2010, as the third party steps into the insured's shoes, they cannot have more comprehensive rights than those held by the insured. Therefore, the third party is in the same position as the insured regarding rights and obligations. When compensating the third party, the insurer operates within the same obligations as if the claim came from the insured. Similarly, if the insurance contract includes any obligations the insured must fulfil to claim compensation from the insurer, the third party is also bound by these obligations. Thus, the insurer can raise the same defences against third parties as they would against the insured under the contract terms.

Although the 2010 Act is considered to have facilitated third parties' right to make a direct claim against the insurer, this right is not supported by public policy in the same way as in Turkish law. Therefore, to be entitled to compensation, the third party must fulfil the conditions and obligations in the insurance contract, just like the insured.

Concerning club insurance policies, the same situation applies as the 2010 Act is valid in England. The Club rules the same way as the member binds the third party. In practice, it is often not possible for a third party who has made a direct claim to the Club to receive compensation due to the rules and obligations required to fulfil. However, considering that Clubs are established solely to provide cover against their members, who are liable for any harm caused to third parties, it is reasonable to accept that the conscious legal policy of English law is to minimize direct claims by third parties against Clubs. Therefore, English law does not take steps to facilitate direct claims by third parties against Clubs while keeping in mind the purpose of establishing Clubs.

The contrasting stances of the English and Turkish laws on the direct action rights of third parties undoubtedly present significant obstacles to implementing legal reforms in Turkish law. Nevertheless, these challenges can be surmounted by adhering to the stated legal policies and devising innovative solutions for both systems' unique legal and regulatory contexts. Therefore, by supporting the argument that English law creates a favourable legal environment for the development of club insurance, this book underscores the need for legal reform in Türkiye within the framework of the English model.

## III. Legal Reform Recommendations for Türkiye Regarding Club Insurance

Based on the findings presented in this book, a similar approach to English law regarding direct action rights of third parties should be adopted in Turkish law. However, it is crucial to be cautious and address specific fundamental issues while formulating such regulations. An explicit provision should be added to Article 1478 of the TCC No. 6102, which defines and limits the scope of direct action rights exclusively applicable to club insurance. Within these parameters, it should be emphasized that third parties should face no obstacles in asserting their rights directly against the Club in cases of personal injury or death. Conversely, in cases of other claims, an explicit provision should be established requiring third parties first to seek compensation from the Club member. A legal framework should be established for the "pay to be paid" rule.

Article 1478 of the TCC regulates the direct action rights of third parties: "The victim may claim his loss up to the insured sum directly from the insurer provided that the claim is brought within the prescription period applicable to the insurance contract." The proposed amendment to this law is to add a statement explicitly indicating that this provision will not apply to club insurance. Following the proposed amendment, the law article will follow:

> The victim may claim his loss up to the insured sum directly from the insurer provided that the claim is brought within the prescription period applicable to the insurance contract. This article shall not apply to club insurance and mutual insurance.
>
> (emphasis added by author)

Despite its brevity, this addition will have significant implications. With this regulation, Clubs will be able to assert the "pay to be paid" clause against third parties. Preserving the "pay to be paid" rule, one of the most important clauses that distinguish club insurance from other maritime insurances, will be a crucial step in this regard. This rule obliges third parties to approach the Club member before making compensation claims against the Club. Legally recognizing this rule is necessary for the protection and development of the club insurance industry.

A separate law article should specify the definition of club insurance, emphasizing that direct action right exception will apply exclusively to club insurance. Subsequently, another law article should outline another exceptional provision regarding claims for death and injury with the following sentence: "Third parties may exercise direct action rights against Clubs in claims for death and injury." This regulation will promptly address compensation claims for death and injury by third parties. Regulating these two cases as exceptions will prevent suffering more loss.

The arbitration clause in Club rules binds third parties due to the principle of subrogation under English law. English courts impose strict sanctions by granting anti-suit injunctions against third parties who violate the arbitration clause and initiate proceedings in other jurisdictions. However, these injunctions by English courts have been heavily criticized in the context of international law. For instance, the CJEU has deemed such judgements disrespectful to the jurisdiction of other countries. Evaluating this in the context of Türkiye, there is no legal provision mandating third parties to arbitrate disputes as stipulated in Club rules. Conversely, clauses that complicate the compensation of third parties like these are deemed legally invalid. If Türkiye adopts England's legal policy regarding club insurance, mandating arbitration for third parties should be excluded from this legal reform's scope.

Although arbitration is widely used as a dispute resolution method in Türkiye, no specialized arbitration institution is dedicated to maritime trade and insurance disputes. Initiating efforts to establish such an institution in Türkiye would represent a significant step forward. However, arbitration should not be imposed as a mandatory solution for third parties. Considering that arbitration can be a costly mechanism for parties seeking compensation, clauses mandating arbitration in Club rules should not be enforced against third parties within the framework of Turkish law. Instead, third parties should retain the option to resolve their claims and disputes through courts without being bound by arbitration clauses.

In summary, based on the comprehensive findings presented in this book, it is evident that the current legal framework applied to club insurance in Türkiye hinders the growth and development of the industry. The existing regulations are inadequate in meeting the evolving needs and demands of the industry, leading to inefficiencies and constraints that hinder the industry's potential for progress.

It is widely accepted that a sector supported by a protective legal framework is more likely to experience accelerated economic growth and development. Therefore, updating and modernizing the legal regulations governing club insurance is necessary to establish a robust economic and legal infrastructure aligned with contemporary industry practices. Considering these factors, the legal framework of club insurance in Türkiye should be systematically and comprehensively reformed.

In Türkiye, Clubs, members, and third parties can benefit from increased transparency and predictability within the legal framework regulating club insurance by adopting the English model. This will facilitate more efficient claims processing and dispute resolution. Furthermore, reforming the legal framework of club insurance in Türkiye will enhance the competitiveness of the P&I Club insurance market, attract significant investments and talents to the industry, and facilitate the growth and expansion of businesses and organizations operating in this field.

## IV. Conclusion

In conclusion, this book has presented a set of recommendations and arguments from a distinct legal perspective aimed at amplifying the contributions of the club insurance and maritime trade industries to Türkiye's economy. The central argument advocated for a legal framework that restricts the direct action rights of third parties against Clubs. With this distinctive feature, the book emerges as a pioneering research endeavour in the literature, advocating for adopting the English legal model in Türkiye. It accomplished this by comparing the direct action rights of third parties and the "pay to be paid" rule within the legal frameworks of Turkish and English law.

The prevailing tendency in Turkish and international law leans towards recognizing and safeguarding the direct action rights of third parties against Clubs. However, implementing this approach in countries aspiring to cultivate the club insurance and maritime trade industries on the global stage has hindered economic growth objectives. Consequently, such countries must establish a legal framework that acknowledges Club rules and confines the direct action rights of third parties in specific circumstances, safeguarding the distinctive characteristics of P&I Clubs and club insurance.

Türkiye took a significant step towards this goal by establishing the Turkish P&I Club with state support in 2014 and pursuing policies to foster club insurance in the country. Nonetheless, Türkiye's limited historical background and knowledge base in club insurance have influenced the formulation of the legal framework. Unlike Turkish law, which has not underscored the distinctive nature of club insurance and has instead continued to apply legal regulations to all liability insurance types, countries should delineate a specific legal framework tailored to club insurance.

For instance, while Turkish Commercial Code No. 6102 grants third parties the right of direct action in liability insurance, it fails to make an exception for club insurance. Similarly, uncertainties persist regarding the validity of clauses such as "pay to be paid," which are pivotal for Club rules. These clauses risk being deemed invalid by the courts as contractual provisions restricting third parties' direct action rights. This uncertainty deepens further with the involvement of English law, which is frequently preferred in club insurance contracts. According to Turkish law, contractual provisions contradicting the law's mandatory provisions are invalid. Therefore, without granting legal validity to these clauses in Club rules in Türkiye, the anticipated economic growth of the club insurance industry remains unattainable.

The book addressed various questions, each contributing to distinct discussions and conclusions within their chapters. Chapter 1 compared the differences between the Turkish and English legal frameworks concerning club insurance within the framework of Clubs' structure, legal character, and entry procedures and evaluated the harmonization of these differences. Evaluating these points was crucial for understanding the logic and functioning of club insurance. The first chapter concluded that, structurally and procedurally, club insurance in Türkiye and England exhibits quite similar operations. The similarities in the organizational structures of Clubs, the functions of these bodies, entry requirements for members, registration procedures, and other structural aspects of the Clubs operating in these countries are significant factors facilitating the adoption of the English model by Türkiye. However, the approach in Turkish law and literature that classifies club insurance among liability insurance undermines the characteristic features of this type of insurance. Therefore, one of the conclusions reached in the first chapter was the need for club insurance in Türkiye to be reclassified within the law and for a specific legal framework to be established.

Chapter 2 presented findings supporting the argument that the Turkish P&I Club provides similar coverage and approaches to contract termination as the English P&I Clubs. Rules of P&I Clubs operating in England and Türkiye were compared concerning the risks covered by insurance and the reasons for contract termination to support this argument. This comparison, conducted within the framework of a sub-research question aimed at modelling the scope and termination rules of English P&I Clubs to facilitate the development and strengthening of club insurance in Türkiye, yielded results indicating a remarkably similar practice in the scope of club insurance and contract termination between the two models. This result served as a facilitating factor for Türkiye to emulate the English model and supported the book's argument.

A defining distinction between club insurance and other insurance contracts lies in the rules governing the rights and obligations of the parties involved. Furthermore, the impact of these rights and obligations on third parties has been a significant issue in numerous disputes. Therefore, a comprehensive exploration of the rights and obligations of the parties in club insurance and their implications for third parties was necessary to better understand the foundations of many disputes. Chapter 3 demonstrated that Clubs in England enjoy privileged and superior rights and obligations vis-à-vis their members and third parties. This superiority is a crucial factor that has propelled England to a leading position in the global club insurance industry. The research question addressing the distribution of rights and obligations among members and third parties in Club rules supported this argument.

Another result from this chapter was that by granting legal validity to Club rules, England adopted a liberal approach to the club insurance industry. In contrast, Türkiye's more interventionist legal approach means that, in the event of non-compliance with Club rules and the mandatory provisions of the law, they lack legal validity according to Turkish law. These two different approaches have directly impacted the club insurance industry. The conclusions in this chapter were drawn by comparing the rights and obligations of parties in Club rules between Turkish and English P&I Clubs within the legal framework. Primary reference sources included rulebooks and standard contracts of Clubs operating in England and Türkiye. Additionally, some judgements discussing the validity of Club rules were examined to shed light on the approach of English courts to this issue. Although there were no recently dated judgements discussing the validity of these rules in Türkiye, the topic was addressed through practices in Turkish law that legally deem contractual provisions contradicting the mandatory provisions of the law as invalid.

The main argument in Chapter 4 advocated for a legal approach where the direct action right of third parties against P&I Clubs is restricted to strengthening P&I Clubs in a country. Türkiye emerges as a country aiming to expand its club insurance industry to international standards as part of its state policy. However, Turkish law does not provide a protective legal framework conducive to developing the club insurance industry. To support the arguments presented in the fourth chapter, an examination of the driving forces behind the demand for legal reform concerning the resolution of direct action disputes involving P&I Clubs in Türkiye was conducted. Additionally, the legal rights and positions of third parties who suffer losses due to maritime activities were compared between England and Türkiye.

One of the conclusions reached was that under English law, the doctrine of subrogation allows third parties to assume the rights and obligations of the insured in club insurance contracts. In contrast, Türkiye prioritizes the public interest principle that mandates the immediate compensation of third-party damages due to public order considerations. These two approaches are crucial in defining the boundaries of third parties' direct action rights. Following this observation, Chapter 4 analyzed how adopting the English legal model for addressing direct action disputes could enhance Türkiye's club insurance industry and highlighted potential challenges in aligning the English model with the Türkiye context. This analysis was conducted within the framework of a sub-research question aimed at revealing the contradictory approaches of the two states regarding direct action. The chapter supported the argument for legal reform within the club insurance framework in Türkiye to identify and eliminate differences arising from this divergence.

Chapter 5 presented a comprehensive summary of the key findings, recommendations for the necessity of legal reform in Türkiye, and the conclusions of the book. Given the increasing frequency of maritime accidents in the Turkish Straits, the potential advantages and disadvantages of adopting the English legal model were among the key findings of this chapter. It was concluded that the English model provides significant legal safeguards for P&I Clubs. In conclusion, the analyses and evaluations in the book led to the following conclusions regarding the necessity of legal reform in the areas of club insurance and direct action disputes in Türkiye:

1. Legal reform is required in Türkiye to foster the development of the club insurance industry.
2. This legal reform should be based on the legal approach that protects P&I Clubs, as demonstrated by England.
3. Contradictory regulations between Club rules and Turkish law existing within Clubs operating in Türkiye must be addressed.
4. The proposed legal reform should focus on restricting the direct action rights of third parties against Clubs, with clear boundaries defined.
5. Club insurance should be distinguished from other marine and liability insurance within the law.
6. A legal framework must be established to protect the "pay to be paid" clause, which is crucial for Clubs.
7. While arbitration clauses in Club rules can be enforced against members, they should not be compulsory for third parties and should adopt a different approach from English law. In this context, the ability of third parties to initiate lawsuits in national courts should not be impeded.
8. Legal reform efforts should be conducted meticulously, carefully interpreting English law.
9. This book has addressed club insurance from a substantive legal perspective within maritime and insurance law, thus excluding issues about procedural and private international laws.
10. Economic goal analyses concerning the club insurance industry, legislative technique, examination from a private international law perspective, and international arbitration rules require expertise in different fields; hence, detailed studies should be carried out in these areas.

# Bibliography

## Books

Alastair Owen, *The Law of Insurance Warranties: Flawed Reform and a New Perspective* (Informa Law/Routledge, London, 2021).
Andrew Tweeddale and Keren Tweeddale, *Scott v Avery Clauses: O'er Judges' Fingers, Who Straight Dream on Fees* (Sweet & Maxwell, 2011).
Anthony Clarke, *The Differing Approach to Commercial Litigation in the European Court of Justice and the Courts of England and Wales I. Amicus Curiae* (Institute of Advanced Legal Studies, London, 2006).
Ayca Ucar, *Perils of the Seas and Inherent Vice in Marine Insurance Law* (1st ed, Routledge, London, 2023).
Baris Soyer, *Warranties in Marine Insurance* (Cavendish Publishing, London 2006).
Baris Soyer and Andrew Tettenborn (eds), *Maritime Liabilities in a Global and Regional Context* (1st ed, Informa Law from Routledge, 2019).
Bulent Sozer, *Unmanned Ships and the Law* (Informa Law from Routledge, 2023).
Christopher Hill, *Maritime Law (Lloyd's Practical Shipping Guides)* (6th ed, Routledge, London, 2014).
Colin de la Rue, Charles Anderson, and Jonathan Hare, *Shipping and the Environment* (3rd ed, Informa Law from Routledge, London, 2023).
David Kendall and Harry Wright, *A Practical Guide to the Insurance Act 2015* (Informa Law from Routledge, London, 2017).
Didem Alganturk Light, *Club insurance in Marine Insurance Law* (Arikan Press, Istanbul, 2006).
Ecehan Yesilova Aras, *Sorumluluk Sigortalarında Zarar Görenin Doğrudan Dava Hakkı (TTK m. 1478)* (Yetkin Press, Ankara, 2013).
George W. Nowell, *Marine Protection & Indemnity Policy Annotations Project: Assignments* (MLA Special Report, Maritime Law Association of the United States, San Francisco, Summer 2001).
Howard Bennett, *The Law of Marine Insurance* (Clarendon, 1996).
Hugh Evans, Roger Stewart KC, and Kieran Lee Marshall (eds), *Jackson & Powell on Professional Liability* (9th ed, Sweet & Maxwell, 2023).
Ilian Djadjev, *The Obligations of the Carrier Regarding the Cargo: The Hague-Visby Rules* (Springer, 2017).
Isil Ulas, *Uygulamalı Zarar Sigortaları Hukuku (Insurance Law of Liability Insurance: An Applied Approach)* (8th ed, Turhan Kitabevi, Ankara, 2012).
John Birds, Ben Lynch, and Simon Paul, *MacGillivray on Insurance Law* (15th ed, Sweet & Maxwell, 2023).
Jonatan Echebarria Fernández, *Jurisdiction and Arbitration Agreements in Contracts for the Carriage of Goods by Sea: Limitations on Party Autonomy* (1st ed, Informa from Routledge, 2021).

Jonathan Gilman, Claire Blanchard, Mark Templeman, Philippa Hopkins, and Neil Hart, *Arnould: Law of Marine Insurance and Average* (20th ed, Sweet & Maxwell, 2023).
Kemal Oğuzman and M. Turgut Öz, *Borçlar Hukuku Genel Hükümler Cilt-1 (General Provisions of Law of Obligations Volume-1)* (12th ed, Vedat, Istanbul, 2015).
Kenneth S. Abraham, *The Liability Century: Insurance and Tort Law from the Progressive Era To 9/11* (Harvard University Press, 2009).
Kristoffer Svendsen, Endre Stavang, and Greg Gordon, *Knock-for-Knock Indemnities and the Law: Contractual Limitation and Delictual Liability* (Informa Law from Routledge, 2023).
Kyriaki Noussia, *The Principle of Indemnity in Marine Insurance Contracts: A Comparative Approach* (Springer, 2007).
Lord Mance, Iain Goldrein, and Robert Merkin (eds), *Insurance Disputes* (3rd ed, Informa, 2011).
Malcolm Clarke, *The Law of Insurance Contracts* (6th ed, Informa Law from Routledge, 2019).
Malcolm Clarke and Baris Soyer (eds), *The Insurance Act 2015* (Informa Law from Routledge, 2017).
Michael Bundock, *Shipping Law Handbook* (5th ed, Informa, London, 2011).
Ozlem Gurses, *Marine Insurance Law* (Routledge, London, 2023).
Ozlem Gurses (ed), *Research Handbook on Marine Insurance Law* (Edward Elgar Publishing, 2024).
Paul Reed, *Construction All Risks Insurance* (3rd ed, Sweet & Maxwell, 2021).
Paul Richards, *Law of Contract* (11th ed, Pearson, 2013).
Peter MacDonald Eggers and Sir Simon Picken, *Good Faith and Insurance Contracts* (4th ed, Informa Law, 2017).
Peter Young, *Mutuality, The Story of UK Club* (Granta Editions, 1995).
Philip Anderson, *The Mariner's Guide to Marine Insurance* (The Nautical Institute, 1999).
Rayegan Kender, *Türkiye'de Hususi Sigorta Hukuku* (On İki Levha Press, Istanbul, 2016).
Reginald Godfrey Marsden, *International Marine Conference Washington, a Treatise on the Law of Collisions at Sea, With an Appendix Containing the International Regulations for Preventing Collisions at Sea, and Local Rules for the Same Purpose in Force in the Thames, Mersey, and Elsewhere, also the Regulations Approved at the Washington International Maritime Conference* (3rd ed, Stevens and Sons Limited, London, 1891).
Rhidian Thomas, *Marine Insurance: The Law in Transition* (Informa Law from Routledge, 2006).
Rhidian Thomas (ed), *The Modern Law of Marine Insurance: Volume Four* (Informa Law, 2015).
Rhidian Thomas (ed), *The Modern Law of Marine Insurance: Volume Five* (Informa Law, 2023).
Rhys Clift, *Forum Shopping, Anti-Suit Injunctions and EU Law: A Brief Overview (and Update)* (Hill Dickinson LLP, February 2007).
Robert Merkin, *Arbitration Law* (Maritime Insights & Intelligence, London, 2024).
Robert Merkin, *Colinvaux's Law of Insurance* (11th ed, Sweet & Maxwell, 2017).
Robert Merkin, *Marine Insurance: A Legal History: Volumes I & II* (Edward Elgar Publishing, Cheltenham & Northampton, 2021).
Robert Merkin, *Marine Insurance Legislation* (4th ed, Informa Law, 2010).
Robert Merkin, *Privity of Contract: The Impact of the Contracts (Rights of Third Parties) Act 1999* (LLP, London, 2000).
Robert Merkin, Iain Goldrein, and Jonathan Mance, *Insurance Disputes* (3rd ed, Informa, 2011).
Robert Merkin and James Devenny (eds), *Essays in Memory of Professor Jill Poole - Coherence, Modernisation and Integration in Contract, Commercial and Corporate Laws* (Informa Law from Routledge, 2018).

Robert Merkin and Jenny Steele, *Insurance and the Law of Obligations* (Oxford University Press, Oxford, 2013).
Rona Serozan, *Borçlar Hukuku Genel Bölüm Üçüncü Cilt* (6th ed, Filiz Press, Istanbul, 2014).
Samim Unan, *İsteğe Bağlı Genel Sorumluluk Sigortasında Riziko* (Beta Press, Istanbul, 1998).
Şebnem Akipek and Erkan Küçükgüngör, *Sözleşme Rehberi* (2nd ed, Yetkin, Ankara, 2002).
Selahattin Sulhi Tekinay and others, *Borçlar Hukuku Genel Hükümleri* (7th ed, Filiz Yayınevi, Istanbul, 1993).
Şener Akyol, *Tam Üçüncü Şahıs Yararına Sözleşme* (Vedat Kitapçılık, Istanbul, 2018).
Serdar Acar, *Kulüp Sigortası* (Vedat, Istanbul, 2008).
Serdar Acar, *Sorumluluk Sigortacısının Doğrudan Davada Dayanabileceği Savunmalar* (Vedat Press, Istanbul, 2012).
Shengnan Jia and Lijun Liz Zhao (eds), *Commercial and Maritime Law in China and Europe* (Informa from Routledge, 2023).
Simon Baughen, *Shipping Law* (6th ed, Routledge, London, 2015).
Sjur Brækhus and Alex Rein, *Handbook of P&I Insurance* (2nd ed, Assuranceforeningen Gard, Arendal, 1979).
Steven J. Hazelwood and David Semark, *P&I Clubs: Law and Practice* (4th ed, LLP, London, 2010).
Susan Hodges, *Cases and Materials on Marine Insurance Law* (Cavendish, London, 1999).
Terry O'Neill and Jan Woloniecki, *The Law of Reinsurance* (5th ed, Sweet & Maxwell, 2021).
Thomas Raphael, *The Anti-Suit Injunction* (2nd ed, OUP, Oxford, 2019).
Willard Phillips, *Treatise on the Law of Insurance* (New York, 1823).
Y. Nejat Incediken, *Gemi İşletme (II) Kulüp Sigortaları, Olayları ve Uygulamaları* (Eko Matbaacılık, Istanbul, 1994).
Yvonne Baatz, *Maritime Law* (4th ed, Informa, 2017).
Zehra Seker, *Insurance Coverage in the Transport of Cargo by Sea* (Beta Basım Yayın, Istanbul, 2001).

## Articles

A. V. Padovan, "Direct Action of a Third-Party Against the Insurer in Maritime Insurance with a Special Focus on the Developments in Croatian Law" (2003) 42 *PPP God* 35.
Adrian Briggs, "Direct Actions and Arbitration: All at Sea" (2016) *LMCLQ* 327–331.
Andrew Dickinson, "The Right to Rome? The Law Applicable to Direct Claims Against Insurers, and Anti-Suit Injunction" (2016) 132 *Law Quarterly Review* 536.
Andrew Tettenborn, "Shipping Law, Brexit and the City of London" (2022) *LMCLQ* 124.
Aslıhan Sevinc Kuyucu, "Insurance Contracts in CIF Sales and Evaluation of Non-Payment of the Sales Price in Terms of the Insured Interest" (2020) 11(2) *Inonu University Law Review* 724.
Aysegul Bugra, "Compulsory Insurance of Shipowners for Maritime Claims" (2012) 12(9) *Shipping & Trade Law*.
Aysegul Bugra, "Room for Compulsory Product Liability Insurance in the European Union for Smart Robots? Reflections on the Compelling Challenges" in P. Marano, K. Noussia (eds), *InsurTech: A Legal and Regulatory View, AIDA Europe Research Series on Insurance Law and Regulation: Volume 1* (Springer, Cham, 2020).
Baris Soyer, "Sundry Considerations on the Draft Protocol to the Athens Convention Relating to the Carriage of Passengers and Their Luggage by Sea 1974" (2002) 33 *Journal of Maritime Law and Commerce* 519.
Baris Soyer, "Türk ve Alman Hukukunda Yeni Düzenlemeler Işığında Sorumluluk Sigortasında Doğrudan Talep" (2011) 27(2) *BATIDER* 26.

Burcu Celikcapa Bilgin, "Right of Direct Action against Liability Insurers under the New Turkish Commercial Code" (2015) 1 *Turk Com L Rev* 265.
Charles B. Anderson and Colin de la Rue, "The Role of the P&I Clubs in Marine Pollution Incidents" (2011) 85 *Tul L Rev* 1257.
Christopher Parsons, "Moral Hazard in Liability Insurance" (2003) 28(3) *The Geneva Papers on Risk and Insurance: Issues and Practice* 448.
Deniz Servantie, "Comparative Analysis of EU and Türkiye's Maritime Transport Policy" (IKV-European Union and Economic Relations Research Centre, July 2015) https://www.ikv.org.tr/icerik/get/4263/215/ accessed 19 September 2022.
Ecehan Yeşilova Aras, *Yolcunun Uğradığı Bedensel Zararlardan Dolayı P&I Kulübüne Doğrudan Başvuru Hakkı* (International Congress on Legal Liability for Bodily Injuries, Cyprus, 2019).
Elif Beyza Akkanat Ozturk, "Sorumluluk Sigortalarında Zarar Görenin Doğrudan Dava Hakkı" (2020) 42 *TAAD* 472.
Elizabeth Germano, "A Law and Economics Analysis of the Duty of Utmost Good Faith (Uberrimae Fidei) in Marine Insurance Law for Protection and Indemnity Clubs" (2016) 47 *St Mary's LJ* 758.
Emerson H. Tiller and Frank B. Cross, "What is the Legal Doctrine?" (2006) 100 *Northwestern University Law Review* 517.
Ergun Ozsunay, "Trafik Kazasında Zarar Gören Üçüncü Kişinin Sigortacıya Karşı Doğrudan Doğruya Alacak Hakkı" in *Traffic Insurance V. Commercial and Banking Law Week, 25–28 April 1973* (BTHAE Publications, Ankara, 1975) 400.
Franziska Arnold-Dwyer, "Taking an Interest in Insurable Interest" (2015) *Lloyd's Maritime and Commercial Law Quarterly* 271.
Gabrielle Kaufmann-Kohler, "How to Handle Parallel Proceedings: A Practical Approach to Issues such as Competence-Competence and Anti-Suit Injunctions" (2008) 2 *Dispute Resolution International* 112.
Gediz Kocabaş, "Üçüncü Kişi Yararına Sözleşmede Yararlananın Edimi Ret Hakkı" (2016) 22 *Marmara University Faculty of Law Journal of Legal Studies* 1798.
Geoffrey Samuel, "Comparative Law and its Methodology" in Dawn Watkins and Mandy Burton (eds), *Research Methods in Law* (Routledge, 2013).
George B. Freehill, "Mutually Excepted Perils" (1974–1975) 49 *Tul L Rev* 899.
Giulia Argano, "Pirates: A Charterers' Peril of the Sea" (2011) 1 *Southampton Student L Rev* 169.
Hacı Kara, *Deniz Alacakları İçin Gemilerin Sigortalanması Mecburiyeti* (Hacı Kara Publications) http://www.hacikara.com/en/publications/internet-publications/detail/11/the-obligation-of-insuring-ships-for-maritime-claims/ accessed 20 May 2023.
Hakan Tüfekçi, "A General Overview of Anti-Suit Injunctions in the Context of English Law, the Brussels Convention Regime, and Turkish Law" (2011) 1 *Galatasaray University Faculty of Law Review*.
Howard Bennett, "The Marine Insurance Act 1906: Reflections on a Century" (2006) 18 *SAcLJ* 669.
Hugh S. Meredith, "Fines, Penalties, and Other Miscellaneous Liabilities; Expenses of Defense; General Conditions and Exclusions; Grounds for Cancellation; Second Seaman's Policy; Club Letters of Guarantee or Undertaking" (1968–1969) 43 *Tul L Rev* 602.
Hyeon Kim, "Warranty and the Pay-to-Be-Paid Rule in Korea" (2012) 43 *Journal of Maritime Law and Commerce* 566.
Ilknur Ulug Cicim, "Obligations, Rights and Authorities of the Insurer in Liability Insurance Regarding the Claim of Compensation Suspended to the Insurer" (2013) 3(2) *Akdeniz University Journal of Law Faculty* 12.
Jerome C. Scowcroft, "Protection and Indemnity Insurance – Pay to Be Paid Clauses Third-Party Claims – [British] Third Parties (Rights against Insurers) Act 1930" (1989) 20 *J Mar L & Com* 205.

Jody M Schisel-Meslin, "Out of the Club: Out of Luck: Complexities Facing Injured Third Parties Seeking Recovery from P&I Clubs" (2019) 43 *Tul Mar LJ* 328.
Johanna Hjalmarsson, "Direct Action against P&l Clubs" (2008) 139 *Insurance & Reinsurance Law Briefing* 7.
Johanna Hjalmarsson, "Direct Claims against Marine Insurers in the English Legal System" (2010) 18 *Asia Pac L Rev* 259.
John Birds, "Motor Insurers and the Knock for Knock Agreements" (1978) 41 *The Modern Law Review* 201.
John D. Kimball, "The Central Role of P&I Insurance in Maritime Law" (2013) 87 *Tul L Rev* 1147.
John Davies, "A Guide to Directors' Responsibilities under the Companies Act 2006" (2007) *Certified Accountants Educational Trust* 69.
Jürgen Basedow, "Comparative Law and Its Clients" (2014) 62(4) *American Journal of Comparative Law* 821.
Justice Belinda Ang, "Anti-Suit Injunctions in Maritime Disputes: A Trend that Threatens to be Out of Control" (2021) *National University of Singapore Centre for Shipping Law Working Paper* 15.
K. X. Li, "Acceptability of P&I Club Letter as Security" (2000) *International Journal of Shipping Law Part 2*, 78.
Keith Michel and Simon Congdon, "Third Parties Rights Against Insurers" (1989) *LMCLQ* 495.
Kemal Şenocak, "Karayolları Trafik Kanunu'na Göre Mağdurun Doğrudan Doğruya Sigortacı Karşısındaki Alacak Hakkı" (2009) 25(4) *Journal of Bank and Commercial Law* 279.
Kerim Atamer, "Yeni Türk Ticaret Kanunu Uyarınca Zarar Sigortalarına Giriş" (2011) 27(1) *Bank and Commercial Law Journal* 86.
Kübra Yetiş Şamlı, "Considerations on the Art. 1423 of the Commercial Code Regulating the Insurer's Information Duty" (2016) 22(3) *Marmara University Faculty of Law Journal of Legal Studies* 2977.
Kyriaki Noussia, "Anti-Suit Injunctions and Arbitration Proceedings: What Does the Future Hold?" (2009) 26 *Journal of International Arbitration* 311.
Kyriaki Noussia, "Insurable Interest in Marine Insurance Contracts: Modern Commercial Needs versus Tradition" (2008) 39 *Journal of Maritime Law and Commerce* 81.
Leon S. Felde, "General Average and the York-Antwerp Rules" (1952–1953) 27 *Tul L Rev* 406.
Ling Zhu and Xiuhua Pan, "Compulsory Insurance and its Implications" (2016) *LMCLQ* 569.
Malcolm Clarke, "Insurable Interest in Property in England – a Redundant Rule?" (2010) 2(4) *European Journal of Commercial Contract Law*.
Mark Tilley, "Protection and Indemnity Club Rules and Direct Actions by Third Parties" (1986) 17 *J Mar L & Com* 427.
Mehmet Mulazimoglu, "Insurer's Debts and Liabilities under the Liability Insurance" (2015) 5(1) *Journal of Akdeniz University Faculty of Law*.
Meixian Song, "Insurable Interest in the Law of Marine Insurance" (2011) 1 *Southampton Student L Rev* 75.
Michelle George and Rebecca Huggins, "Third-Party Risks" in Lord Mance, Iain Goldrein, and Robert Merkin (eds), *Insurance Disputes* (3rd ed, Informa, 2011).
Mihail Danov, "Cross-Border Litigation – New Data, Initial Brexit Implications in England and Wales and Long-Term Policy Choices" in Andrea Bonomi and Gian Paolo Romano (eds), *Yearbook of Private International Law: Volume 21* (Verlag Dr Otto Schmidt, 2021).
N. A. Martinez and R. van Anrooy, "Compulsory Insurance (Third Party Liability) Requirements for Fishing Vessels: A Case for the Introduction of Compulsory Fishing Vessel Insurance in the Caribbean" in *FAO Fisheries and Aquaculture Circular No. 1199* (FAO, Rome, 2000) 6.

Nuray Eksi, "Milletlerarası Özel Hukuk Açısından Sigortacıya Doğrudan Başvuru Hakkını Kısıtlayan veya Ortadan Kaldıran Yabancı Yasaların Türk Mahkemelerince Dikkate Alınıp Alınmayacağı Sorunu" (2015) 4(2) *International Journal of Commercial and Arbitration Law* 31.

Paul E. Gilbert, "Direct Actions against Insurance Companies: Should They Join the Party?" (1971) 59(2) *California Law Review*.

Paul Myburgh, "Non-Parties, Forum Agreements and Expanding Anti-Suit Injunctions" (2020) *LMCLQ* 345.

Paul Myburgh, "P&I Club Letters of Undertaking and Admiralty Arrests" (2018) 18(4) *CML Working Paper Series* 3.

Paul Myburgh, "Taxonomizing Third-Party Rights of Direct Action Against Marine Liability Insurers" in Ozlem Gurses (ed), *Research Handbook on Marine Insurance Law* (Edward Elgar Publishing, 2024).

Peter MacDonald Eggers, "Direct Action Against Insurers and P&I Clubs" in Baris Soyer and Andrew Tettenborn (eds), *Maritime Liabilities in a Global and Regional Context* (Informa Law from Routledge, 2019).

R. Bhanu Krishna Kiran, "Liability and Compensation for Oil Pollution Damage: An Examination of IMO Conventions" (2010) 3 *NUJS L Rev* 399.

Ralf Michaels, "The Functional Method of Comparative Law" in Mathias Reimann and Reinhard Zimmermann (eds), *The Oxford Handbook of Comparative Law* (Oxford University Press, 2006).

Rayegan Kender, "Karayolları Motorlu Araçlar Zorunlu Mali Sorumluluk (Trafik) Sigortası Genel Şartlarındaki Değişikliklerin Değerlendirilmesi" (2017) 13(1) *Journal of Yeditepe University Law Faculty* 9.

Rayegan Kender, "Mesuliyet Sigortasının Mahiyeti ve Türleri, Teori ve Uygulama Açısından Mesuliyet Türleri" in *III. Insurance Seminar* (Sigorta Hukuk Derneği, Ankara, 1977).

Rhidian Thomas, "Protection and Indemnity Insurance: Is It Truly Insurance?" in Ozlem Gurses (ed), *Research Handbook on Marine Insurance Law* (Edward Elgar Publishing, 2024).

Rhidian Thomas, "Third-Party Claims Against P&I Clubs in the UK" (2021) 26(6) *JIML* 385.

Rhidian Thomas, "Third-Party Direct Rights of Action against Insurers under UK Law and International Maritime Liability Conventions" in *Regulation of Risk* (Brill/Nijhoff, 2022) 689.

Richard Aikens, "Has the Principle of 'Utmost Good Faith' in Marine Insurance Law become Like the Cheshire Cat – Now You See It, and Now You Don't?" in Ozlem Gurses (ed), *Research Handbook on Marine Insurance Law* (Edward Elgar Publishing, 2024).

Richard Kidner, "A History of the Fatal Accident Acts" (1999) 50 *Northern Ireland Legal Quarterly* 322.

Richard Lewis, "Insurer's Agreements Not to Enforce Strict Legal Rights: Bargaining with Government and in the Shadow of the Law" (1985) 48 *Modern Law Review* 275.

Robert Merkin, "Protection & Indemnity Clubs and Arbitration Clauses" in Ozlem Gurses (ed), *Research Handbook on Marine Insurance Law* (Edward Elgar Publishing, 2024).

Robert Merkin, *Reforming Insurance Law: Is There a Case for Reverse Transportation? A Report for the English and Scottish Law Commissions on the Australian Experience of Insurance Law Reform* (Law Commission & Scottish Law Commission, 21 March 2006) http://www.lawcom.gov.uk/docs/merkin_report.pdf accessed 15 May 2023.

Robert Merkin and Séverine Saintier, "Privity of Contract: Statutory Developments" in Robert Merkin and James Devenny (eds), *Essays in Memory of Professor Jill Poole - Coherence, Modernisation and Integration in Contract, Commercial and Corporate Laws* (Informa Law from Routledge, 2018).

Robert Works, "Excusing Non-Occurrence of Insurance Policy Conditions in Order to Avoid Disproportionate Forfeiture: Claims-Made Formats as a Test Case" (1998) *College of Law Faculty Publications* 177.

Robin Pearson, "Carter v Boehm: Facts and Context" (2016) 20(1) *Insurance Law Journal* 19.

Ron Harris, "The Bubble Act: Its Passage and Its Effects on Business Organization" (1994) 54(3) *The Journal of Economic History* 610.
Rui Zheng, "Marine Insurance Law Reform in China: Experiences from the UK" in Shengnan Jia and Lijun Liz Zhao (eds), *Commercial and Maritime Law in China and Europe* (Informa from Routledge, 2023).
Saban Kayihan, "Zarar Sigortalarında Sigortacının Halefiyeti" (2016) 22(3) *Marmara University Faculty of Law Journal of Legal Studies* 1598.
Scott Salisbury, "The Principle of Freedom of Contract: Are the Courts Too Interventionist?" (2016) 5 *Manchester Review of Law, Crime and Ethics* 58.
Sir Jonathan Mance, "Civil Jurisdiction in Europe: Choice of Court Clauses, Competing Litigation and Anti-Suit Injunctions" (Speech delivered at the Second Conference of European Commercial Judges, Paris, 14 October 2004).
Stephan Bird, "The State Immunity Act of 1978: An English Update" (1979) 13 *Int'l Law* 619.
T. G. Coghlin, "Protection & Indemnity Clubs" (1984) *Lloyds Maritime and Commercial Law Court* 403.
Terry Hutchinson, "Doctrinal Research: Researching the Jury" (2008) 12(1) *Legal Research Quarterly* 13.
Terry Hutchinson and Nigel Duncan, "Defining and Describing What We Do: Doctrinal Legal Research" (2012) 17(1) *Deakin Law Review* 83.
Vibe Ulfbeck, "Direct Actions Against the Insurer in a Maritime Setting: The European Perspective" (2011) 2 *Lloyd's Maritime and Commercial Law Quarterly* 293.
W. R. A. Birch Reynardson, "History and Development of P&I Insurance: The British Scene" (1968–1969) 43 *Tul L Rev* 457.
Yueyun Chen and Dongmei Chen, "The Review and Analysis of Compulsory Insurance" (2013) 4(1) *Insurance Markets and Companies: Analyses and Actuarial Computations* 11.
Zahit Imre, "Motorlu Taşıt Araçlarının Mecburi Mesuliyet Sigortası ve Kapsamı" in *Traffic Insurance V. Commercial and Banking Law Week, 25–28 April 1973* (BTHAE Publications, Ankara, 1975) 268.

## Thesis

Dina Esmaeil M. Abuzaid, "Reform of the Doctrine of Utmost Good Faith: A Comparative Study between the UK and Saudi Arabia" (PhD thesis, University of Stirling, 2018).
Eleni Melekou, "The P&I Club Letters of Undertaking as a Modern Form of Security for the Release of Arrested Ships" (Master thesis, QMUL, 2016).
Jianxun Guo, "The Study of Marine Insurable Interest: A Comparison of Laws in China and the United Kingdom" (PhD thesis, University of Exeter, 2017).
Lin MT, "A Selective Appraisal of the P&I Insurance System with Special Reference to Claims for Personal Injury, Illness and Loss of Life" (World Maritime University Dissertations, 2009).
Melisa Konfidan, "Deniz Araçları Sorumluluk Sigortası Sözleşmesi (Marine Vehicles Liability Insurance Agreement)" (PhD thesis, Istanbul University Law Faculty, Istanbul, 2020).
Muhammet Alper Keceli, "Establishing a New Protection and Indemnity (P&I) Insurance Institution in Türkiye" (World Maritime University Dissertations, Malmö, 2012).
Murat Yorulmaz, "Deniz Tasimaciligi ve Deniz Sigortalari (Maritime Transportation and Marine Insurance)" (PhD thesis, Marmara University, Istanbul, 2009).
Nurullah Hakan Peksen, "Türk P&I Kulübünün Kurulmasının Avantaj ve Dezavantajlarının Analizi (Analysis of the Advantages and Disadvantages of the Establishment of the Turkish P&I Club)" (Master thesis, Istanbul University, Istanbul, 2012).
Semin Park, "Analysis on the Current Interpretations of the Duty of Disclosure in English Insurance and Marine Insurance Contracts" (PhD thesis, University of Bristol, March 1996).
Yiqing Yang, "The Past and Future of Utmost Good Faith: A Comparative Study Between English and Chinese Insurance Law" (PhD thesis, University of Exeter, 2017).

## Legislations

Arbitration Act 1996. (England)
Companies Act 2006. (England)
Fatal Accident Act 1846. (England)
Harbour, Docks and Piers Clauses Act 1846. (England)
Insurance Act 2015. (England)
Insurance Law No. 5684. (Türkiye)
Marine Insurance Act 1906. (England)
Merchant Shipping Act 1854. (England)
The Principles of Intervention in Emergency Situations and Compensation for Damages in the Pollution of the Marine Environment with Oil and Other Harmful Substances Law No. 5312. (Türkiye)
The State Immunity Act 1978. (England)
Third Parties (Rights against Insurers) Act 1930. (England)
Third Parties (Rights against Insurers) Act 2010. (England)
Turkish Commercial Code No. 6102. (Türkiye)
Turkish Commercial Code No. 6762. (abolished) (Türkiye)
Turkish Private International Law and International Civil Procedure Code No. 5718 (Türkiye)

## International Conventions, Agreements and Other Regulations

Athens Convention relating to the Carriage of Passengers and their Luggage by Sea (PAL) 1974.
Council Regulation (EC) No 44/2001 of 22 December 2000 on Jurisdiction and the Recognition and Enforcement of Judgments in Civil and Commercial Matters (OJ 2001 L 12, p. 1).
Council Regulation (EU) No 1215/2012 of the European Parliament and of the Council of 12 December 2012 on Jurisdiction and the Recognition and Enforcement of Judgments in Civil and Commercial Matters (Recast).
Directive 2009/20/EC of the European Parliament and of the Council of 23 April 2009 on the Insurance of Shipowners for Maritime Claims.
International Convention for the Unification of Certain Rules of Law Relating to Bills of Lading ("Hague-Visby Rules") (signed 25 August 1924; revised Brussels, 1968).
International Convention on Civil Liability for Bunker Oil Pollution Damage 2001 (Bunkers Convention).
International Convention on Civil Liability for Oil Pollution Damage 1969.
International Convention on Civil Liability for Oil Pollution Damage (1992 CLC).
International Convention on Liability and Compensation for Damage in Connection with the Carriage of Hazardous and Noxious Substances by Sea (HNS) 1996.
International Group Agreement 2023.
International Hull Clauses (IHC) 2003.
International Ocean Towage Agreement Daily Hire (TOWHIRE).
International Ocean Towage Agreement Lump Sum (TOWCON).
Nairobi International Convention on the Removal of Wrecks 2007 (Wreck Removal Convention).
Protocol of 2002 to the Athens Convention Relating to the Carriage of Passengers and their Luggage by Sea 1974 (Athens Convention 2002).
Regulation on the Establishment and Operation Principles of Insurance and Reinsurance Companies published in Official Gazette No. 26623, dated 24 August 2007. (Türkiye)
The Regulation on the Implementation of the Law on the Development of the Maritime Trade Fleet and the Promotion of Shipbuilding Facilities, Official Gazette No. 29454, dated 23 August 2015. (Türkiye)
The Regulation on Insurance and Inspection of Ships Related to Maritime Liens, Official Gazette No. 27759, dated 14 November 2010. (Türkiye)
Regulation on Insurance and Inspection of Ships Related to Maritime Liens, RG 14.11.2010/27759. (Türkiye)
Small Tanker Oil Pollution Assurance Agreement 2006 (as amended 2017).

Small Tanker Oil Pollution Assurance Agreement 2006 (STOPIA).
Tanker Oil Pollution Assurance Agreement 2006 (TOPIA).
United Nations Convention on the Carriage of Goods by Sea ("Hamburg Rules").
York-Antwerp Rules 2016. (Comity Maritime International)

## Reports

The Economic Contribution of the UK Maritime Business Services Industry (Centre for Economics and Business Research Report for Maritime UK and Maritime London, May 2022).

George W. Nowell, "Subrogation" in Matthew A. Marion (ed), *MTHE Special Report, (Document No 761)* (Marine Protection & Indemnity Policy Annotations Project Subcommittee on Hull and P&I Insurance Committee on Marine Insurance and General Average Maritime Law Association of the United States, 2001).

Law Commission and Scottish Law Commission, Draft Bill: Insurable Interest (2018).

Law Commission and Scottish Law Commission, Insurance Contract Law: Business Disclosure; Warranties; Insurers' Remedies for Fraudulent Claims; and Late Payment, LCCP No. 353, SLCDP No. 238 (July 2014).

Law Commission and Scottish Law Commission, Insurance Contract Law: Misrepresentation, Non-Disclosure and Breach of Warranty by the Insured (Law Com No 292, Scot Law Com No 194, 2007).

Law Commission and Scottish Law Commission, Insurance Contract Law: Misrepresentation, Non-Disclosure and Breach of Warranty by the Insured, LCCP No. 182, SLCDP No. 134 (2007).

Law Commission and Scottish Law Commission, Insurance Contract Law: Summary of Responses to Issues Paper 10: Insurable Interest.

Law Commission and The Scottish Law Commission (Law Com No 272, Scot Law Com No 184, Third Parties Rights Against Insurer, Joint Report of July 2001).

PwC Report on the "UK's Global Maritime Professional Services: Contribution and Trends" (London, April 2016).

TheCityUK Report on "Legal Excellence, Internationally Renowned UK Legal Services 2021" (December 2021).

## Club Rules

The Britannia Steam Ship Insurance Association Limited Rules.
The London Steam-Shipowners' Mutual Insurance Association Ltd Rules.
Nordic Marine Insurance Plan 2013 Version 2023 – Commentary (2023).
The North of England Protecting & Indemnity Association Ltd Rules.
The Shipowners' Mutual Protection & Indemnity Association (Luxembourg) Rules.
The Standard Club UK Ltd Rules.
Turkish P&I Club Rules.
The West of England Shipowners Mutual Insurance Association Rules.

## Websites

Athens Protocol 2002 in a Nutshell, "Gard" (20 October 2020) http://www.gard.no/web/updates/content/20740184/athens-protocol-2002-in-a-nutshell accessed 30 April 2023.

BIMCO, "TOWCON 2021" https://www.bimco.org/contracts-and-clauses/bimco-contracts/towcon-2021# accessed 14 December 2023.

Britannica, "Oil Spill" https://www.britannica.com/science/oil-spill#ref1085819 accessed 29 November 2020.

Competition and Consumer Protection Commission, "Public Liability Insurance Market Study" (2020) https://www.ccpc.ie/business/wp-content/uploads/sites/3/2020/12/2020.12.22-CCPC-Public-Liability-Insurance-Market-Study accessed 3 December 2023.

Conference Notes, *P&I Insurance and Maritime Insurance Law within the Scope of the New Turkish Commercial Law* (Istanbul, 2013) https://docplayer.biz.tr/734155-Yeni-turk-ticaret-hukuku-kapsaminda-p-i-sigortasi-ve-deniz-sigorta-hukuku-29-kasim-2013-deniz-ticaret-odasi-konferans-salonu-toplanti-notlari.html accessed 22 April 2024.

Full Report: *Legal Excellence: Internationally Renowned UK Legal Services* (The City UK, 2022) https://www.thecityuk.com/media/5url4ni1/legal-excellence-internationally-renowned-uk-legal-services–2022.pdf accessed 26 May 2023.

Full Report: *Maritime Annual Report 2018 to 2019* (UK Government, 2019) https://assets.publishing.service.gov.uk/government/uploads/system/uploads/attachment_data/file/817250/Maritime_Annual_Report_2018_to_2019.pdf accessed 26 May 2023.

G. Musgrave and D. Heaselden, "Understanding P&I Club" (Presentation, gia.org.sg, 20 December 2022) https://www.gia.org.sg/files/8th_19_12_2014_Understanding_P_I_Club.pdf accessed 20 December 2022.

Gideon Parchomovsky & Endre Stavang, "Contracting Around Tort Defaults: The Knock for Knock Principle and Accident Costs" (The CREE Centre, Working Paper 14/2013) https://www.jus.uio.no/ifp/english/research/news-and events/events/knock_for_knock_stavang_cree_wp_14_2013.pdf accessed 14 December 2023.

Guidelines for Correspondents, "International Group of P&I Clubs" (2015) https://static.mycoracle.com/igpi_website/media/article_attachments/Guidelines-for-Correspondents–2015.pdf last accessed 29 April 2023.

https://publications.parliament.uk accessed 1 January 2024.

https://www.igpandi.org accessed 4 May 2024.

International Conference on the Revision of the Athens Convention Relating to the Carriage of Passengers and Their Luggage by Sea, 1974, LEG/CONF.13/11 (30 August 2002) http://rosaeg.no/erikro/WWW/corrgr/dipcon/11.pdf last accessed 30 April 2023.

International Group of P&I Clubs, "About the International Group of P&I Clubs" https://www.igpandi.org/about last accessed 13 May 2022.

"The International Group of P&I Clubs" igpandi.org accessed 28 April 2023.

Maritime Law Association of the United States, "Journal of Maritime Law & Commerce" https://mla.hofstra.edu/publications/journal-jmlc/index.html last accessed 31 May 2023.

Maritime UK (2019) https://www.maritimeuk.org/about/our-industry/maritime-business-services/ accessed 27 September 2023.

"Press Release No 104/22 – Advocate General's Opinion in Judgment of the Court in Case C-700/20" (20 June 2022) https://curia.europa.eu/jcms/upload/docs/application/pdf/2022-06/cp220104en.pdf accessed 13 May 2023.

Report on the Contribution of P&I Clubs to the UK Economy https://assets.publishing.service.gov.uk/government/uploads/system/uploads/attachment_data/file/948299/OFSI_Guidance_-_Maritime_.pdf accessed 26 May 2023.

Republic of Türkiye, "Transport Operational Programme 2007–2009" https://neighbourhood-enlargement.ec.europa.eu/system/files/2016–12/tk3_transport_op-final_2007_en.pdf accessed 28 May 2023.

Review of Maritime Transport 2023 (United Nations, United Nations Conference on Trade and Development, Geneva, 2023) https://unctad.org/publication/review-maritime-transport-2023 (accessed on 27 September 2023).

Turkish P&I, "About Turk P&I" https://www.turkpandi.com/en/about-turk-p-i/about-turk-p-i accessed 1 May 2023.

UK P&I Club, "POST-CASUALTY TOWAGE: The Risks and the Process Required to Maintain P&I Coverage" https://www.ukpandi.com/media/files/imports/13108/briefings/23321-towage_guidance_note.pdf accessed 14 December 2023.

World Maritime University, "Guidelines for Correspondents, International Group of P&I Clubs" (2015) https://static.mycoracle.com/igpi_website/media/article_attachments/Guidelines-for-Correspondents–2015.pdf last accessed 29 April 2023.

# Index

MIX
Papier | Fördert gute Waldnutzung
FSC® C083411

Kolibri 360 GmbH
Ferdinand-Jühlke-Straße 7
99095 Erfurt, Deutschland
produktsicherheit@kolibri360.de